STYL

Lessons in Clarity and Grace

STYLE

Lessons in Clarity and Grace

TENTH EDITION

Joseph M. Williams
The University of Chicago

Revised by

Gregory G. Colomb
The University of Virginia

Longman

Boston   Columbus   Indianapolis   New York   San Francisco   Upper Saddle River
Amsterdam   Cape Town   Dubai   London   Madrid   Milan   Munich   Paris   Montreal   Toronto
Delhi   Mexico City   Sao Paulo   Sydney   Hong Kong   Seoul   Singapore   Taipei   Tokyo

Senior Sponsoring Editor: Virginia L. Blanford
Senior Marketing Manager: Sandra McGuire
Senior Supplements Editor: Donna Campion
Production Manager: Fran Russello
Project Coordination, Text Design,
   and Electronic Page Makeup: GGS Higher Education Resources,
  A Division of PreMedia Global, Inc.
Cover Designer Manager: Jayne Conte
Cover Designer: Bruce Kenselaar
Printer and Binder: Courier Companies, Inc.
Cover Printer: Lehigh Phoenix

For permission to use copyrighted material, grateful acknowledgment is made to the copyright holders on p. 259, which are hereby made part of this copyright page.

Library of Congress Cataloging-in-Publication Data
Williams, Joseph M.
  Style : lessons in clarity and grace / Joseph M. Williams. — 10th ed.
    p. cm.
  Includes bibliographical references and index.
  ISBN 0-321-47935-1
  1. English language—Style. 2. English language—Technical English.
3. English language—Business English. 4. English language—Rhetoric.
5. Technical Writing. 6. Business writing. I. Title.
  PE1421.W545 2007
  808.042—dc22

                                       2006026432

1 2 3 4 5 6 7 8 9 10—13 12 11 10

Longman
is an imprint of

ISBN-13: 978-0-205-74746-7
ISBN-10:   0-205-74746-9

PEARSON

www.pearsonhighered.com

To my mother and father
. . . English style, familiar but not coarse,
elegant, but not ostentatious . . .
—SAMUEL JOHNSON

CONTENTS

PREFACE

Most people won't realize that writing is a craft.
You have to take your apprenticeship in it like anything else.
—KATHERINE ANNE PORTER

THE TENTH EDITION

The tenth edition of any book is worthy of notice, of a book as influential as this one, of celebration. Though it should be Joe Williams writing these words and revising this edition, I am honored to do it in his place. One of my first acts as a professional was to read and comment on the first typescript of this book, and I have watched and sometimes participated in its refinement and growth through nine editions. Since that first act of kindness (I gained more than he from the exchange), Joe shared with me every major professional project, from creating the Little Red Schoolhouse (at first open lectures, then a class, then a writing program at the University of Chicago, and now a multi-university enterprise) to writing a few more books.

For this edition, I have acted as a proxy, not a caretaker. Joe improved this book with every revision, and I have tried to do the same. The book has grown steadily since that typescript, somewhat in length and vastly in substance. In the first edition Joe covered only a portion of its current topics, and a small core of its current lessons. Over the years, as new material was developed and then proofed in the crucible of the Little Red Schoolhouse, Joe brought it into *Style* when he deemed it ready. I too have made improvements where I could, and additions where I thought them ready. Some changes Joe had already planned, some we worked on together, and some he had not yet thought to do. I hope that no one will be able to tell which is which.

What's New

The changes for this edition are not as dramatic as those for the last. The ninth edition brought a new subtitle, new Quick Tips, new lessons where epilogues used to be, and Jefferson where Lincoln used to be. For the tenth, I have sought to consolidate and improve that new structure and to fill in a few gaps.

Here's what I have changed:

To Lesson 1, I've added a brief discussion of how the principles in this book can help readers understand difficult texts. Throughout the rest, I have added short bits of practical advice on how specific principles can do that.

In Lesson 2, I've slightly reduced the attention to grammar mavens, so the chapter spends a little less time quarreling with them and proportionally more helping writers decide questions of usage.

In Lesson 5 and 6, I've given a little more attention to the need to push grammatical complexity to the ends of sentences, in order to prepare students for the extended discussion in Lesson 8.

From Lesson 8 I have removed the discussion of quotations, to reappear in a new appendix. As Joe knew, it was at best a stretch to connect managing length with using quotations.

To Lesson 10 I have made significant revisions. Although I retained its structure and substance, many of the discussions have been changed. I have altered the account of the structure of introductions to a form that has proved better suited for writers encountering it for the first time.

From Lesson 12 I have removed the section on plagiarism, also to reappear in an appendix. Although plagiarism is an ethical issue, it connects only loosely with the ethics of style. But it connects quite closely to the material on quotations, much of which it duplicated and with which it now resides.

In a new appendix, I've collected and consolidated the materials on using sources. It now provides a coherent account of what a writer has to consider from first finding a source, to using it in her text, to citing it in her final bibliography.

I added, deleted, and revised several of the Quick Tips. These continue to offer practical advice about how to deal with common problems, now including the problem of *reading* difficult texts.

Finally, I've also done a lot of line editing. After thirty years of enduring endless iterations for everything we wrote together, I could not have done otherwise. And Joe would never forgive even the smallest infelicity that I intentionally left behind. As for the ones I unintentionally left?—well, he was the better craftsman.

What's the Same

This tenth edition aims at answering the same questions asked in the earlier ones:

- What is it in a sentence that makes readers judge it as they do?
- How do we diagnose our own prose to anticipate their judgments?
- How do we revise a sentence so that readers will think better of it?

This is how Joe explained what these questions mean to writers:

> The standard advice about writing ignores those questions. It is mostly truisms like *Make a plan, Don't use the passive, Think of your audience*—advice that most of us ignore as we wrestle ideas out onto the page. When I drafted this paragraph, I wasn't thinking about you; I was struggling to get my own ideas straight. I did know that I would come back to these sentences again and again (I didn't know that it would be for more than twenty-five years), and that it would be only then—as I revised—that I could think about you and discover the plan that fit my draft. I also knew that as I did so, there were some principles I could rely on. This book explains them.

Joe may not have thought, twenty-eight years ago, that he would be revising into the next century, but his lessons have always centered on revision.

No one drafts with total control, not me and not Joe (I know; I've seen his drafts). We cannot expect to be clear when caught up in the flow of our thoughts and words. Nor should we even try. Only after we step away can we imagine what it might be like for our readers, and even that is not enough. We need the cold light of analysis, of these principles, to predict when our readers will wish that we had written better and to know how to grant that wish. That was the genius of that original typescript and it remains the enduring genius of this book.

There is one more aspect of this book that remains the same: its personal voice. Joe is everywhere in the prose, from his distinctive brisk style to the ubiquitous *I*'s. The *I*'s are still there in this edition, but some of them were put there by me. I did not know how I could do otherwise. I hope that each of you, when you start on page 1, will forget the man who intruded into the text, and see and hear only Joe Williams.

PRINCIPLES, NOT PRESCRIPTIONS

The principles here may seem prescriptive, but that's not how they are intended. They are meant to help you predict how readers will judge your prose and then help you decide whether and how to revise it. As you try to follow those principles, you may write more slowly. That's inevitable. Whenever we reflect on what we write as we write it, we become self-conscious and lose the flow of that writing, sometimes to the point of near-paralysis. It passes. And you can keep these principles from gumming up your process if you remember that they have less to do with drafting than with revision. If there is a first principle of *drafting*, it is to ignore most of the advice about it.

SOME PREREQUISITES

To learn how to revise efficiently, though, you must know a few things:

- You should know a few grammatical terms: SUBJECT, VERB, NOUN, ACTIVE, PASSIVE, CLAUSE, PREPOSITION, and COORDINATION. All grammatical terms are capitalized the first time they appear and are defined in the text or in the Glossary.

- You have to learn new meanings for two familiar words: TOPIC and STRESS.

- You will have to learn a few new terms. Two are important: NOMINALIZATION and METADISCOURSE; three are useful: RESUMPTIVE MODIFIER, SUMMATIVE MODIFIER, and FREE MODIFIER. Some students object to learning new words, but the only way to avoid that is never to learn anything new.

Finally, if you read this book on your own, go slowly. It is not an amiable essay to read in a sitting or two. Take the lessons a few pages at a time, up to the exercises. Do the exercises, edit someone else's writing, then some of your own written a few weeks ago, then something you wrote that day.

An *Instruction Manual* is available for those who are interested in the scholarly and pedagogical thinking that has gone into *Style*.

GREGORY G. COLOMB

ACKNOWLEDGMENTS

GGC—

I want to think Ginny Blanford and everyone at Pearson Longman for the opportunity to continue what Joe Williams began. I share many of the debts Joe mentions in his acknowledgments, and I will let him name them himself. I owe Jon D'Errico for covering for me while I was squirreled away with this manuscript, and I owe my family an apology for having two book manuscripts due on the same day. Sandra, Robin, Karen, and Lauren are used to indulging these absences, but they know they are always in my heart.

JMW (FROM THE NINTH EDITION)—

So many have offered support and suggestions over the last twenty-five years, that I cannot thank you all. But again I begin with those English 194 students who put up with faintly dittoed pages (that tells you how many years ago this book was born) and with a teacher who at times was at least as puzzled as they.

I have learned from the undergraduate, graduate and professional students, and post-docs who have gone through the Little Red Schoolhouse writing program at the University of Chicago (a.k.a. Advanced Academic and Professional Writing). I am equally grateful to the graduate students who taught these principles and offered good feedback.

I have intellectual debts to those who broke ground in psycholinguistics, text linguistics, and functional sentence perspective. Those who keep up with such matters will recognize the influence of Charles Filmore, Jan Firbas, Nils Enkvist, Michael Halliday, Noam Chomsky, Thomas Bever, Vic Yngve, and others. The work of Eleanore Rosch has provided a rich explanation for why verbs should be actions and characters should be subjects. Her work in prototype semantics is a powerful theoretical basis for the kind of style urged here.

For reading earlier versions of this book, I thank Theresa Ammirati, Yvonne Atkinson, Margaret Batschelet, Nancy Barendse, Randy Berlin, Cheryl Brooke, Ken Bruffee, Christopher Buck,

Douglas Butturff, Donald Byker, Bruce Campbell, Elaine Chaika, Avon Crismore, Constance Gefvert, Darren Cambridge, Mark Canada, Paul Contino, Jim Garrett, Jill Gladstein, Karen Gocsik, Richard Grande, Jeanne Gunner, Maxine Hairston, George Hoffman, Rebecca Moore Howard, John Hyman, Sandra Jamieson, Richard Jenseth, Elizabeth Bourque Johnson, Julie Kalish, Seth Katz, Bernadette Longo, Ted Lowe, Brij Lunine, Richard McLain, Joel Margulis, Susan Miller, Linda Mitchell, Ellen Moody, Ed Moritz, Patricia Murray, Neil Nakadate, Janice Neuleib, Ann Palkovich, Matthew Parfitt, Donna Burns Philips, Mike Pownall, Peter Priest, John Ruszkiewicz, Margaret Shaklee, Nancy Sommers, Laura Bartlett Snyder, John Taylor, Mary Taylor, Bill Vande Kopple, Stephen Witte, Joseph Wappel, Alison Warriner, Wendy Wayman, Patricia Webb, and Kevin Wilson.

I am grateful for the feedback from the class taught by Stan Henning at the University of Wisconsin, Madison, and for the error in usage caught by Linda Ziff. I am particularly indebted to an exchange with Keith Rhodes about Lesson 12.

I am indebted to Christina Devlin for the Wesley quotation in Lesson 7 to James Vanden Bosch for the Montaigne quotation in the Glossary, and to Virginia Tufte's *The Syntax of Style* for the W.H. Gass quotation on p. 192. I thank Frederick C. Mish of the G. & C. Merriam Company for locating the best examples of three citations in Lesson 2, and Charles Bazerman, for leading me to the first paragraph of Crick and Watson's DNA paper in Lesson 7.

For several years, I have had the good fortune to work with a good colleague and friend whose careful thinking has helped me think better about many matters, both professional and personal, Don Freeman. Don's readings have saved me from more than a few howlers; I am indebted to him for the quote from William Blake in Lesson 8.

And again, those who contribute to my life more than I let them know: Oliver, Michele, and Eleanor; Chris and Ingrid; Dave, Patty, Owen, and Matilde; Megan, Phil, Lily and Calvin; and Joe, Christine, Nicholas, and Katherine. And at beginning and end still, Joan, whose patience and love flow more generously than I deserve.

IN MEMORIAM

Joseph Williams, 1933–2008
il miglior fabbro [the best craftsman]

On February 22, 2008 the world lost a great scholar and teacher and I lost a dear friend. For almost thirty years, Joe Williams and I taught together, researched together, wrote together, drank together, traveled together, and argued together and apart. When those "apart" arguments led to what in the last edition he called "our intemperate shouting matches," we grew closer—and wrote more thoughtfully—than ever. I knew his faults, but he was the best man I knew.

My epitaph for Joe—*il miglior fabbro*—puts him in exalted company: I take it from Dante, who applied it to the twelfth-century troubadour Arnaut Daniel, praised by Plutarch as the "Grand Master" of his craft. In the last century, T.S. Eliot famously said it of Ezra Pound. Of course, these poets were all known not for their clarity and grace but for their depth and difficulty. No matter, there have been none better than they at their craft, just as there have been none better than Joe at his. And Joe has the added distinction that his craft daily multiplies its good a thousand fold and more, in all those papers, reports, memos, and other documents that have served their readers better because of him.

PART ONE

Style as Choice

Have something to say, and say it as clearly as you can.
That is the only secret of style.
—MATTHEW ARNOLD

1

Understanding Style

> *Essentially style resembles good manners. It comes of endeavouring to understand others, of thinking for them rather than yourself—or thinking, that is, with the heart as well as the head.*
> —SIR ARTHUR QUILLER-COUCH

> *The great enemy of clear language is insincerity.*
> —GEORGE ORWELL

> *In matters of grave importance, style, not sincerity, is the vital thing.*
> —OSCAR WILDE

PRINCIPLES AND AIMS

This book rests on two principles: it is good to write clearly, and anyone can do it. The first is self-evident, especially to those who must read a lot of writing like this:

> An understanding of the causal factors involved in excessive drinking by students could lead to their more effective treatment.

But that second principle may seem optimistic to those who want to write clearly, but can't get close to this:

> We could more effectively treat students who drink excessively if we understood why they do so.

Of course, writing fails for reasons more serious than unclear sentences. We bewilder readers when we can't organize complex ideas coherently (an issue I address in Lesson 11). And they won't even read what we've written unless we motivate them to (an issue I address in Lesson 10). But once we've formulated our claims, organized supporting reasons, grounded them on sound evidence, and motivated readers to read attentively, we must still express it all clearly, a difficult task for most writers and a daunting one for many.

It is a problem that has afflicted generations of writers who have hidden their ideas not only from their readers, but sometimes even from themselves. When we read that kind of writing in government regulations, we call it *bureaucratese;* when we read it in legal documents, *legalese;* in academic writing that inflates small ideas into gassy abstractions, *academese*. Written carelessly or, worse, deliberately, it is in its extreme forms a language of exclusion that a democracy cannot tolerate. It is also a problem with a long history.

A SHORT HISTORY OF UNCLEAR WRITING

The Past

It wasn't until about the middle of the sixteenth century that writers decided that English was eloquent enough to replace Latin and French in serious discourse. But their first efforts were written in a style so complex that it defeated easy understanding:

> If use and custom, having the help of so long time and continuance wherein to [re]fine our tongue, of so great learning and experience which furnish matter for the [re]fining, of so good wits and judgments which can tell how to refine, have griped at nothing in all that time, with all that cunning, by all those wits which they won't let go but hold for most certain in the right of our writing, that then our tongue has no certainty to trust to, but write all at random.

> —Richard Mulcaster, *The First Part of the Elementary,* 1582

In the next century, English became the language of science. We might expect scientists to communicate the facts clearly and simply, but the complex style had spread to their writing as well. As one complained,

> Of all the studies of men, nothing may sooner be obtained than this vicious abundance of phrase, this trick of metaphors, this volubility of tongue which makes so great a noise in the world.

> —Thomas Sprat, *History of the Royal Society,* 1667

When this continent was settled, writers might have established a new, democratic prose style for a new, democratic nation. In fact, in 1776, the plain words of Thomas Paine's *Common Sense* helped inspire our Revolution:

> In the following pages I offer nothing more than simple facts, plain arguments, and common sense.

Sad to say, he sparked no revolution in our national prose style.
A half century later, James Fenimore Cooper complained about our writing:

> The love of turgid expressions is gaining ground, and ought to be corrected. One of the most certain evidences of a man of high breeding, is his simplicity of speech: a simplicity that is equally removed from vulgarity and exaggeration. . . . Simplicity should be the firm aim, after one is removed from vulgarity. . . . In no case, however, can one who aims at turgid language, exaggerated sentiments, or pedantic utterances, lay claim to be either a man or a woman of the world.
>
> —James Fenimore Cooper, *The American Democrat*, 1838

Unfortunately, in abusing that style, Cooper adopted it. Had he followed his own advice, he might have written,

> We should discourage those who promote turgid language. A well-bred person speaks simply, in a way that is neither vulgar nor exaggerated. No one can claim to be a man or woman of the world who deliberately exaggerates sentiments or speaks in ways that are turgid or pedantic.

About fifty years later, Mark Twain wrote what we now think is classic American prose. He said this about Cooper's style:

> There have been daring people in the world who claimed that Cooper could write English, but they are all dead now—all dead but Lounsbury [an academic who praised Cooper's style]. . . . [He] says that *Deerslayer* is a "pure work of art." . . . [But] Cooper wrote about the poorest English that exists in our language, and . . . the English of *Deerslayer* is the very worst tha[t] even Cooper ever wrote.

As much as we admire Twain's directness, few of us emulate it.

The Present

In the best-known essay on modern English style, "Politics and the English Language," George Orwell anatomized the turgid language of politicians, bureaucrats, academics, and other such windy speakers and writers:

> The keynote [of a pretentious style] is the elimination of simple verbs. Instead of being a single word, such as *break, stop, spoil, mend, kill,* a verb becomes a phrase, made up of a noun or adjective tacked on to some general-purposes verb such as *prove, serve, form, play, render.* In addition, the passive voice is wherever possible used in preference to the active, and noun constructions are used instead of gerunds (*by examination* of instead of *by examining*).

But as Cooper did, in abusing that style Orwell adopted it. He could have written more concisely:

> Pretentious writers avoid simple verbs. Instead of using one word, such as *break, stop, kill,* they turn the verb into a noun or adjective, then tack onto it a general-purpose verb such as *prove, serve, form, play, render.* Wherever possible, they use the passive voice instead of the active and noun constructions instead of gerunds (*by examination* instead of *by examining*).

If the best-known critic of a turgid style could not resist it, we ought not be surprised that politicians and academics embrace it. On the language of the social sciences:

> A turgid and polysyllabic prose does seem to prevail in the social sciences. . . . Such a lack of ready intelligibility, I believe, usually has little or nothing to do with the complexity of thought. It has to do almost entirely with certain confusions of the academic writer about his own status.
>
> —C. Wright Mills, *The Sociological Imagination*

On the language of medicine:

> It now appears that obligatory obfuscation is a firm tradition within the medical profession. . . . [Medical writing] is a highly skilled, calculated attempt to confuse the reader. . . . A doctor feels he might get passed over for an assistant professorship because he wrote his papers too clearly—because he made his ideas seem too simple.
>
> —Michael Crichton, *New England Journal of Medicine*

On the language of law:

> In law journals, in speeches, in classrooms and in courtrooms, lawyers and judges are beginning to worry about how often they have

been misunderstood, and they are discovering that sometimes they can't even understand each other.

—Tom Goldstein, *New York Times*

On the language of science:

There are times when the more the authors explain [about ape communication], the less we understand. Apes certainly seem capable of using language to communicate. Whether scientists are remains doubtful.

—Douglas Chadwick, *New York Times*

Generations of students have struggled with dense academic writing, many thinking they weren't smart enough to grasp a writer's deep ideas. Some have been right about that, but more could have blamed the writer's inability (or refusal) to write clearly. Many students, sad to say, give up; sadder still, others learn not only to read that style but to write it, inflicting it on the next generation of readers, thereby sustaining a 450-year-old tradition of unreadable writing.

SOME PRIVATE CAUSES OF UNCLEAR WRITING

If unclear writing has a long social history, it also has private causes. Michael Crichton mentioned one: some writers plump up their prose to impress those who think that complicated sentences indicate deep thinking. And in fact, when we want to hide the fact that we don't know what we're talking about, we typically throw up a tangle of abstract words in long, complex sentences.

Others write graceless prose not deliberately but because they are seized by the idea that good writing must be free of errors that only a grammarian can explain. They approach a blank page not as a space to explore ideas, but as a minefield to cross gingerly. They creep from word to word, concerned less with their readers' understanding than with their own survival. I address that issue in Lesson 2.

Others write unclearly because they freeze up, especially when they are learning to think and write in a new academic or professional setting. The afflicted include not just undergraduates taking their first course in economics or psychology, but graduate and professional students, new doctors and lawyers—anyone writing on a new topic for unfamiliar and therefore intimidating readers.

As we struggle to master new ideas, most of us write worse than we do when we write about things we understand better. For this, there is no remedy but experience.

But the biggest reason most of us write unclearly is that we cannot predict when readers will think our writing is unclear, much less what makes it so. What we write always seems clearer to us than to our readers, because we read into it what we want them to get out of it. And so instead of revising our writing to meet their needs, we call it done the moment it meets ours.

In all of this, of course, there is a great irony: we are likely to confuse others when we write about a subject that confuses us. But when we become confused as we read about a new subject written in a complex style, we too easily assume that its complexity signals deep thought, and so we try to imitate it, compounding our already confused writing.

This book shows you how to avoid both ends of that trap. You will learn how to recognize when others' writing is more complex than deep, how to recognize when others will say the same about your writing, and—when your writing is too complex—how to make it better.

On Writing and Reading

This is a book is about writing based on our ways of reading. Once we understand why readers judge a sentence to be dense and abstract, another clear and direct, we should know how to revise the one into the other. The problem is, we cannot judge our own writing as others will because we respond less to the words on the page than to the thoughts in our minds. We can avoid that solipsistic subjectivity only if we can figure out how what we have put *on the page* makes *our readers* feel as they do.

That's the main aim of this book: to show you what to look for *on the page*, what it is that makes readers think *This passage is too dense and difficult.*

Once you know that, you can help your readers by revising your sentences, paragraphs, and whole documents into something that will make them think not only *This writing is clear and direct* but, as importantly, *This is a writer I can trust, someone who wants to help me understand.*

Once you know what to look for on the page, you can also do something for yourself: The principles offered here also serve you as you read. When you encounter prose that seems difficult, you will know what to look for on the page to determine whether your difficulty comes from the necessary complexity of the material or the gratuitous complexity of the writing. If the latter, use these principles to help you mentally revise the abstract and indirect writing of others into something you can better understand (while giving yourself the silent satisfaction of knowing that you could have written it better).

ON WRITING AND REWRITING

A warning: if you think of the principles offered here as rules to follow *as you draft*, you may never finish anything. Most experienced writers get something down on paper or up on the screen as fast as they can. Then as they revise that first draft into something clearer, they understand their ideas better. And when they understand their ideas better, they express them more clearly, and the more clearly they express them, the better they understand them . . . and so it goes, ending only when they run out of energy, interest, or time.

For a fortunate few, that end comes weeks, months, even years after they begin. For most of us, though, the deadline is closer to tomorrow morning. And so we have to settle for prose that is less than perfect, but as good as we can make it. (Perfection may be the ideal, but it is the death of done.)

So use what you find here not as rules to impose on every sentence *as* you draft it, but as principles to help you identify already-drafted sentences likely to give your readers a problem, and then to revise those sentences quickly.

As important as clarity is, though, some occasions call for more:

> Now the trumpet summons us again—not as a call to bear arms, though arms we need; not as a call to battle, though embattled we are; but a call to bear the burden of a long twilight struggle, year in and year out, "rejoicing in hope, patient in tribulation," a struggle against the common enemies of man: tyranny, poverty, disease and war itself.
>
> —John F. Kennedy, Inaugural Address, January 20, 1961

Few of us are called upon to write a presidential address, but even on less lofty occasions, some of us take a private pleasure in writing a shapely sentence, even if no one will notice. If you enjoy not just writing a sentence but crafting it, you will find suggestions in Lesson 9.

In Lessons 10 and 11, I go beyond the clarity of individual sentences to discuss the coherence of a whole document. Writing is also a social act that might or might not serve the best interests of readers, so in Lesson 12, I address some issues about the ethics of style. In Appendix I, I discuss styles of punctuation. In Appendix II, I explain how to use and cite quotations and other material from sources.

Many years ago, H. L. Mencken wrote this:

> With precious few exceptions, all the books on style in English are by writers quite unable to write. The subject, indeed, seems to exercise a special and dreadful fascination over school ma'ams, bucolic college professors, and other such pseudoliterates. . . . Their central aim, of course, is to reduce the whole thing to a series of simple rules—the overmastering passion of their melancholy order, at all times and everywhere.

Mencken was right: no one learns to write well by rule, especially those who cannot see or feel or think. But I know that many do see clearly, feel deeply, and think carefully but cannot write sentences that make their thoughts, feelings, and visions clear to others. I also know that the more clearly we write, the more clearly we see and feel and think. Rules help no one do that, but some principles can.

Here they are.

Lesson

2

Correctness

*God does not much mind bad grammar, but He does not
take any particular pleasure in it.*
—ERASMUS

*No grammatical rules have sufficient authority to control the
firm and established usage of language. Established custom,
in speaking and writing, is the standard to which we must at
last resort for determining every controverted point in
language and style.*
—HUGH BLAIR

*English usage is sometimes more than mere taste,
judgment, and education—sometimes it's sheer luck, like
getting across the street.*
—E. B. WHITE

UNDERSTANDING CORRECTNESS

To a careful writer, nothing is more important than choice. For example, which of these sentences would you choose to write if you wanted readers to think you wrote clearly?

1. Lack of media support was the cause of our election loss.
2. We lost the election because the media did not support us.

10

Most of us choose (2).

Unlike clarity, though, correctness seems a matter not of choice, but of obedience. When the *American Heritage Dictionary* says that *irregardless* is "never acceptable" except for humor, our freedom to choose it seems limited at best. In matters of this kind, we choose not between better and worse, but between right and utterly, irredeemably, unequivocally Wrong. Which, of course, is no choice at all.

But that lack of choice does seem to simplify things: "Correctness" requires not sound judgment but only a good memory. If we remember that *irregardless* is always Wrong, we have nothing to choose. Some teachers and editors think we should memorize dozens of such "rules":

- Never begin a sentence with *and* or *but*.
- Never use double negatives.
- Never split INFINITIVES.

The truth is, however, more complicated. Some rules are real—if we ignore them, we risk being labeled at least unschooled: our VERBS must agree with SUBJECTS; our PRONOUNS must agree with their referents. (Capitalized words are defined in the Glossary.) There are many others. But many often repeated rules are less important than many think; some are not even real rules. And if you obsess over them all, you prevent yourself from writing quickly and clearly. That's why I address "correctness" now, before clarity, because I want to put it where it belongs—behind us.

RULES OF GRAMMAR AND THE BASIS OF THEIR AUTHORITY

Opinion is split on the social role of grammar rules. To some, they are just another device that the Ins use to control the Outs by stigmatizing their language and thereby suppressing their social and political aspirations. To others, the rules of Standard English have been so refined by generations of educated speakers and writers that they are now a force of nature and therefore must be observed by all the best writers of English.

Correctness as Historical Accident

Both views are correct, partly. For centuries, those governing our affairs have used grammatical "errors" to screen out those unwilling or unable to acquire the habits of the schooled middle class.

But the critics are wrong to claim that those rules were *devised* for that end. Standard forms of a language originate in accidents of geography and economic power. When a language has different regional dialects, that of the most powerful speakers usually becomes the most prestigious and the basis for a nation's "correct" writing.

Thus if some geographical accident had put Scotland closer to Europe than London is, and if its capital, Edinburgh, had become the center of Britain's economic, political, and literary life, we would speak and write less like Shakespeare and more like the Scottish poet Bobby Burns:

A ye wha are sae guid yourself	(All you who are so good yourselves
Sae pious and sae holy,	So pious and so holy,
Ye've nought to do but mark and tell	You've nothing to do but talk about
Your neebours' fauts and folly!	Your neighbors' faults and folly!)

Correctness as Unpredictability

Conservatives, on the other hand, are right that many rules of Standard English originated in efficient expression. For example, we no longer use all the endings that our verbs required a thousand years ago. We now omit present tense inflections in all but one context (and we don't need it there):

	1ST PERSON	2ND PERSON	3RD PERSON
Singular	I know + ø.	You know + ø.	She know + **S**.
Plural	We know + ø.	You know + ø.	They know + ø.

But those conservative critics are wrong when they claim that Standard English has been refined by the logic of educated speakers and writers, and so must by its very nature be socially and morally superior to the debased language of their alleged inferiors.

True, many rules of Standard English do reflect an evolution toward logical efficiency. But if by logical we mean regular and therefore predictable, then Standard English is in many ways *less* logical than nonstandard English. For example, the Standard English contraction in *I'm here, aren't I?* is *aren't*. But what could be more ungrammatical than the full form, *I am here, **are** I not*? Logically, we should contract *am* + *not* to *amn't*, which is in fact one historical source of the nonstandard *ain't* (the other is *are* + *not*). So the standard *aren't I* is less logical than the historically predictable but socially stigmatized *ain't I*. I could cite a dozen examples where the *violation* of a rule of Standard English reflects a logical mind making English grammar more consistent.

But it is, of course, the very *in*consistency of Standard English that makes its rules so useful to those who would use them to discriminate: to speak and write Standard English, we must either be born into it or invest years learning it (along with the values of its speakers).

Here's the point: Those determined to discriminate will seize on any difference. But our language seems to reflect the quality of our minds more directly than do our ZIP codes, so it's easy for those inclined to look down on others to think that grammatical "errors" indicate mental or moral deficiency. But that belief is not just factually wrong; in a democracy like ours, it is socially destructive. Yet even if *ain't* is logically correct, so great is the power of social convention that we avoid it, at least if we hope to be taken seriously when we write for serious purposes.

THREE KINDS OF RULES

These corrosive social attitudes about correctness have been encouraged by generations of grammarians who, in their zeal to codify "good" English, have confused three kinds of "rules."

Real Rules

Real rules define what makes English English: ARTICLES must precede NOUNS: *the book*, not *book the*. Speakers born into English don't think about these rules at all when they write, and violate them only when they are tired or distracted.

Social Rules

Social rules distinguish Standard English from nonstandard: *He doesn't have any money* versus *He don't have no money*. Schooled writers observe these rules as naturally as they observe the Real Rules and think about them only when they notice others violating them. The only writers who *self-consciously* try to follow them are those not born into Standard English who are striving to rise into the educated class.

Invented Rules

Finally, some grammarians have invented a handful of rules that they think we all *should* observe. These are the rules that the grammar police love to enforce and that too many educated writers obsess over. Most date from the last half of the eighteenth century:

> Don't split infinitives, as in *to **quietly** leave.*
>
> Don't end a sentence with a PREPOSITION.

A few date from the twentieth century:

> Don't use *hopefully* for *I hope,* as in ***Hopefully,*** *it won't rain.*
>
> Don't use *which* for *that,* as in *a car **which** I sold.*

For 250 years, grammarians have accused the best writers of violating rules like these, and for 250 years the best writers have ignored them. Which is lucky for the grammarians, because if writers did obey all the rules, grammarians would have to keep inventing new ones, or find another line of work. The fact is, none of these invented rules reflects the unselfconscious usage of our best writers.

In this lesson, we focus on this third kind of rule, the handful of invented ones, because only they vex those who already write Standard English.

Observing Rules Thoughtfully

It is, however, no simple matter to deal with these rules if you want to be thought of as someone who writes "correctly." You could choose the worst-case policy: follow all the rules all the time because sometime, someone will criticize you for something—for beginning a sentence with *and* or ending it with *up.*

But if you try to obey all the rules all the time, you risk becoming so obsessed with rules that you tie yourself in knots. And sooner or later, you will impose those rules—real or not—on others. After all, what good is learning a rule if all you can do is obey it?

The alternative to blind obedience is selective observance. But then you have to decide which rules to observe and which to ignore. And if you ignore an alleged rule, you may have to deal with someone whose passion for "good" grammar makes her see in your split infinitive a sign of moral corruption and social decay.

If you want to avoid being accused of "lacking standards," but refuse to submit to whatever "rule" someone can dredge up from ninth-grade English, you have to know more about these invented rules than the rule-mongers do. The rest of this lesson helps you do that.

TWO KINDS OF INVENTED RULES

We can sort most of these invented rules into two groups: Folklore and Elegant Options.

Folklore

These rules include those that most careful readers and writers ignore. You may not yet have had some of them inflicted on you, but chances are that you will. In what follows, the quotations that illustrate "violations" of these rules are from writers of considerable intellectual and scholarly stature or who, on matters of usage, are reliable conservatives (some are both). A check mark indicates acceptable Standard English, despite what some grammarians claim.

1. **"Don't begin sentences with *and* or *but*."** This passage ignores the "rule" twice:

   ✓ **But,** it will be asked, is tact not an individual gift, therefore highly variable in its choices? **And** if that is so, what guidance can a manual offer, other than that of its author's prejudices—mere impressionism?

   —Wilson Follett, *Modern American Usage: A Guide,*
   edited and completed by Jacques Barzun et al.

   Some inexperienced writers do begin too many sentences with *and*, but that is an error not in grammar but of style.

   Some insecure writers also think they should not begin a sentence with *because.* Allegedly not this:

   ✓ **Because** we have access to so much historical fact, today we know a good deal about changes within the humanities which were not apparent to those of any age much before our own and which the individual scholar must constantly reflect on.

   —Walter Ong, S. J., "The Expanding Humanities and the Individual
   Scholar," *Publication of the Modern Language Association*

   This folklore about *because* appears in no handbook, but it is gaining currency. It probably stems from advice aimed at avoiding sentence FRAGMENTS like this one:

   The plan was rejected. **Because** it was incomplete.

QUICK TIP: This rule about *because* has no basis in grammar, but it does reflect a small *stylistic* truth. In Lesson 5, we look at a principle of style that tells us to arrange the elements of sentences so that information that readers know comes *before* less familiar information (for a summary, skim pp. 68–70). It is a fact of English style that a SUBORDINATE CLAUSE beginning with *because* usually introduces new information:

> ✓ Some writers write graceless prose **because** they are seized by the idea that writing is good only when it's free of errors that only a grammarian can explain.

Reverse that order and you get a mildly awkward sentence:

> **Because** some writers are seized by the idea that writing is good only when it's free of errors that only a grammarian can explain, they write graceless prose.

When a *because*-clause introduces new information, as it usually does, it should not begin a sentence, but end it. That, however, is not a rule of grammar but a principle of style.

If you want to *begin* a sentence with a clause expressing familiar information about causation, introduce the clause with *since*, because *since* implies that the reader already knows what is in the clause:

> ✓ **Since** our language seems to reflect our quality of mind, it is easy for those inclined to look down on others to think that grammatical "errors" indicate mental or moral deficiency.

There are exceptions to this principle, but it's generally sound.

2. **"Use the RELATIVE PRONOUN *that*—not *which*—for restrictive clauses."** Allegedly, not this:

> ✓ Next is a typical situation **which** a practiced writer corrects "for style" virtually by reflex action.

> —Jacques Barzun, *Simple and Direct* (p. 69)

Yet just a few sentences before, Barzun himself (one of our most eminent intellectual historians and critics of style) had asserted,

> Us[e] *that* with defining [i.e. restrictive] clauses except when stylistic reasons interpose.

(In the sentence quoted above, no such reasons interpose.)

This "rule" is relatively new. It appeared in 1906 in Henry and Francis Fowler's *The King's English* (Oxford University Press). The Fowlers thought that the random variation between *that* and *which* to begin a restrictive clause was messy, so they just asserted that henceforth writers should (with some exceptions) limit *which* to *nonrestrictive* clauses.

A nonrestrictive clause, you may recall, modifies a noun naming a referent that you can identify unambiguously without the information in that clause. For example,

✓ ABCO Inc. ended its first bankruptcy, **which** it had filed in 1997.

A company can have only one first bankruptcy, so we can unambiguously identify the bankruptcy without the information in the following clause. We therefore call that clause *nonrestrictive*, because it does not further "restrict" or identify what the noun names. In that context, we put a comma before the modifying clause and begin it with *which*. That rule is based on historical and contemporary usage.

But, claimed the Fowlers, for restrictive clauses we should use not *which* but only *that*: For example,

✓ ABCO Inc. sold a product **that** [*not* **which**] made millions.

Since ABCO presumably makes many products, the clause *that made millions* "restricts" the product to the one that made millions, and so, said the Fowlers, it should begin with *that*.

Francis died in 1918, but Henry continued the family tradition with *A Dictionary of Modern English Usage* (Oxford University Press, 1926), where he made this wistful observation:

> Some there are who follow this principle now; but it would be idle to pretend that it is the practice either of most or of the best writers. (p. 635)

(For another allegedly incorrect *which*, see the passage by Walter Ong on p. 15.)

I confess I follow Fowler's advice, not because a restrictive *which* is an error, but because *that* has a softer sound. I do sometimes choose a *which* when it's within a word or two of a *that*, because I don't like the sound of two *that*s close together:

✓ We all have **that** one rule **that** we will not give up.

✓ We all have **that** one rule **which** we will not give up.

3. **"Use *fewer* with nouns you count, *less* with nouns you cannot."** Allegedly not this:

   ✓ I can remember no **less** than five occasions when the correspondence columns of *The Times* rocked with volleys of letters . . .

   > —Noel Gilroy Annan, Lord Annan, "The Life of the Mind in
   > British Universities Today," *American Council*
   > *of Learned Societies Newsletter*

   No one uses *fewer* with mass nouns (*fewer dirt*) but educated writers often use *less* with countable plural nouns (*less resources*).

4. **"Use *since* and *while* to refer only to time, not to mean *because* or *although*."** Most careful writers use *since* with a meaning close to *because* but, as mentioned above, with an added sense of 'What follows I assume you already know':

   ✓ **Since** asbestos is dangerous, it should be removed carefully.

   Nor do most careful writers restrict *while* to its temporal sense (*We'll wait while you eat*), but also use it with a meaning close to 'I assume you know what I state in this clause, but what I assert in the next will qualify it':

   ✓ **While** we agree on a date, we disagree about the place.

> *Here's the point:* If writers whom we judge to be competent regularly violate some alleged rule and most careful readers never notice, then the rule has no force. In those cases, it is not writers who should change their usage, but grammarians who should change their rules.

Elegant Options

These next "rules" complement the Real Rules: call them *Elegant Options*. Most readers do not notice when you observe a Real Rule, but does when you violates it (like that). On the other hand, few readers notice when you violate one of these optional rules, but some do when you observe it, because doing so makes your writing seem just a bit more self-consciously formal.

1. **"Don't split infinitives."** Purists condemn Dwight MacDonald, a linguistic archconservative, for this sentence (my emphasis in all the examples that follow).

✓ One wonders why Dr. Gove and his editors did not think of label-
ing *knowed* as substandard right where it occurs, and one suspects
that they wanted **to slightly conceal** the fact . . .

—"The String Untuned," *The New Yorker*

They would require

they wanted **to conceal slightly** the fact . . .

Infinitives are split so often that when you avoid splitting one,
careful readers may think you are trying to be especially correct,
whether you are or not.

2. **"Use *whom* as the OBJECT of a verb or preposition."** Purists
would condemn William Zinsser for this use of *who:*

✓ Soon after you confront this matter of preserving your identity,
another question will occur to you: "**Who** am I writing for?"

—*On Writing Well*

They would insist on

another question will occur to you: "For **whom** am I writing?"

Here is an actual rule: use *who* when it is the subject of a
verb *in its own clause*; use *whom* only when it is an object in
its own clause.

QUICK TIP: When a relative clause modifies a noun, the
correct form is *whom* if you can delete the relative pronoun
and still make sense:

✓ The committee chose someone **whom** they trusted.

✓ The committee chose someone [ ] they trusted.

If you cannot delete the *who/whom*, the correct form is *who:*

✓ The committee chose someone **who** earned their trust.

The committee chose someone [ ] earned their trust.

Two exceptions: (1) You cannot delete *whom* when it begins a
clause that is the object of a verb. In that case, you have to
depend on the grammar of the clause:

✓ The committee decided **whom** they should choose.

✓ The committee decided **who** was to be chosen.

(2) Always use *whom* as the object of a preposition:

> The committee chose someone **in whom** they had confidence.

3. **"Don't end a sentence with a preposition."** Purists condemn Sir Ernest Gowers, editor of Fowler's second edition, for this:

> ✓ The peculiarities of legal English are often used as a stick to beat the official **with.**
>
> —*The Complete Plain Words*

and insist on this:

> . . . a stick **with which** to beat the official.

The first is correct; the second is more formal. (Again, see the Ong passage on p. 15.) And when you choose to shift both the preposition and its *whom* to the left, your sentence seems more formal yet. Compare:

> ✓ The man I met **with** was the man I had written **to.**

> ✓ The man **with whom** I met was the man **to whom** I had written.

A preposition can, however, can end a sentence weakly (see pp. 85–86). George Orwell may have chosen to end this next sentence with *from* to make a sly point about English grammar, but I suspect it just ended up there (and note the "incorrect" *which*):

> [The defense of the English language] has nothing to do with . . . the setting up of a "standard English" **which** must never be departed **from.**
>
> —George Orwell, "Politics and the English Language"

This would have been less awkward and more emphatic:

> We do not defend English just to create a "standard English" whose rules we must always obey.

4. **"Use the singular with *none* and *any*."** *None* and *any* were originally singular, but today most writers use them as plural, so if you use them as singular, some readers will notice. The second sentence is a bit more formal than the first:

> ✓ **None** of the reasons **are** sufficient to end the project.

> ✓ **None** of the reasons **is** sufficient to end the project.

When you are under close scrutiny, you might choose to observe all these optional rules. Ordinarily, though, they are ignored by most careful writers, which is to say they are not rules at all, but rather stylistic choices that create a slightly formal tone. If you adopt the worst-case approach and observe them all, all the time, few readers will give you credit but many will notice how formal you seem.

Hobgoblins

For some unknown reason, a handful of items has become the object of particularly zealous abuse. There's no explaining why; none of them interferes with clarity or concision.

1. **"Never use *like* for *as* or *as if*."** Allegedly, not this:

   ✓ These operations failed **like** the earlier ones did.

   But this:

   ✓ These operations failed **as** the earlier ones did.

   Like became a SUBORDINATING CONJUNCTION in the eighteenth century when writers began to drop *as* from the conjunctive phrase *like as*, leaving just *like* as the conjunction. This process is called *elision*, a common linguistic change. It is telling that the editor of the second edition of Fowler's *Dictionary* (the one favored by conservatives) deleted *like* for *as* from Fowler's list of "Illiteracies" and moved it into the category of "Sturdy Indefensibles."

2. **"Don't use *hopefully* to mean 'I hope.'"** Allegedly, not this:

   ✓ Hopefully, it will not rain.

   But this:

   ✓ I hope that it will not rain.

   This "rule" dates from the middle of the twentieth century. It has no basis in logic or grammar and parallels the usage of other words that no one complains about, words such as *candidly, frankly, sadly,* and *happily:*

   ✓ Candidly, we may fail. (That is, *I am candid when I say we may fail.*)

   ✓ Seriously, we must go. (That is, *I am serious when I say we must go.*)

3. **"Don't use *finalize* to mean 'finish' or 'complete.'"** But *finalize* doesn't mean just 'finish.' It means 'to clean up the last few details,' a sense captured by no other word. Moreover, if we think *finalize* is bad because *-ize* is ugly, we would have to reject *nationalize, synthesize,* and *rationalize,* along with hundreds of other useful words.

4. **"Don't use *impact* as a verb, as in *The survey impacted our strategy*. Use it only as a noun, as in *The survey had an impact on our strategy*."** *Impact* has been a verb for 400 years, but on some people, historical evidence has none.

5. **"Don't modify absolute words such as *perfect, unique, final, or complete* with *very, more, quite,* and so on."** That rule would have deprived us of this familiar sentence:

   ✓ We the People of the United States, in order to form a **more perfect** union . . .

   (Even so, this is a rule worth following.)

6. **"Never ever use *irregardless* for *regardless* or *irrespective*."** However arbitrary this rule is, follow it. Use *irregardless* and some will judge you irredeemable.

Some Words That Attract Special Attention

A few words are so often confused with others that careful readers are likely to note when you correctly distinguish them—*flaunt* and *flout* for example. When you use them correctly, those who think the difference matters are likely to note that at least *you* know that *flaunt* means 'to display conspicuously' and that *flout* means 'to scorn a rule or standard.' Thus if you chose to scorn the rule about *flaunt* and *flout*, you would not flout your flaunting it, but flaunt your flouting it. Here are some others:

aggravate means 'to make worse.' It does not mean to 'annoy.' You can aggravate an injury but not a person.

anticipate means 'to prepare for a contingency.' It does not mean just 'expect.' You anticipate a question when you prepare its answer before it's asked; if you know it's coming but don't prepare, you only expect it.

anxious means 'uneasy' not 'eager.' You're eager to leave if you're happy to go. You're anxious about leaving if it makes you nervous.

blackmail means 'to extort by threatening to reveal damaging information.' It does not mean simply 'coerce.' One country cannot blackmail another with nuclear weapons when it only threatens to use them.

cohort means 'a group who attends on someone.' It does not mean a single accompanying person. When Prince Charles married his friend she became his 'consort'; his hangers-on are still his cohort.

comprise means 'to include all parts in a single unit.' It is not synonymous with *constitute*. The alphabet is not comprised *by* its letters; it comprises them. Letters *constitute* the alphabet, which is thus constituted by them.

continuous means 'without interruption.' It is not synonymous with *continual*, which means an activity continued through time, with interruptions. If you *continuously* interrupt someone, that person will never say a word because your interruption will never stop. If you *continually* interrupt, you let the other person finish a sentence from time to time.

disinterested means 'neutral.' It does not mean 'uninterested.' A judge should be disinterested in the outcome of a case, but not uninterested in it. (Incidentally, the original meaning of *disinterested* was 'to be uninterested.')

enormity means 'hugely bad.' It does not mean 'enormous.' In private, a belch might be enormous, but at a state funeral, it would also be an enormity.

fortuitous means 'by chance.' It does not mean 'fortunate.' You are fortunate when you fortuitously pick the right number in the lottery.

fulsome means 'sickeningly excessive.' It does not mean just 'much.' We all enjoy praise, except when it becomes fulsome.

notorious means 'known for bad behavior.' It does not mean 'famous.' Frank Sinatra was a famous singer but a notorious bully.

These days only a few readers still care about these distinctions, but they may be just those whose judgment carries weight when it matters most. It takes only a few minutes to learn to use these words in ways that testify to your precision, so it may be worth doing, especially if you also think their distinctions are worth preserving.

On the other hand, you get no extra points for correctly distinguishing *imply* and *infer, principal* and *principle, accept* and *except, capital* and *capitol, affect* and *effect, proceed* and *precede, discrete* and *discreet*. That's just expected of a schooled writer. Most careful readers also notice when a Latinate or Greek plural noun is used as a singular, so you might want to keep these straight, too:

Singular	datum	criterion	medium	stratum	phenomenon
Plural	data	criteria	media	strata	phenomena

Here's the point: You can't predict good grammar or correct usage by logic or general rule. You have to learn the rules one-by-one and accept the fact that some of them, probably most of them, are arbitrary and idiosyncratic.

A Problem: Pronouns and Gender Bias

Pronouns and Their Referents

We expect literate writers to make verbs agree with subjects:

> ✓ Our **reasons** ARE based on solid evidence.

We also expect their pronouns to agree with antecedents. Not this:

> Early **efforts** to oppose the hydrogen bomb failed because **it** ignored political issues. **No one** wanted to expose **themselves** to anti-Communist hysteria.

But this:

> ✓ Early **efforts** to oppose the hydrogen bomb failed because **they** ignored political issues. **No one** wanted to expose **himself** to anti-Communist hysteria.

There are, however, two problems with making pronouns agree with their referents.

First, do we use a singular or plural pronoun when referring to a noun that is singular in grammar but plural in meaning? For example, when we refer to singular nouns such as a *group, committee, staff, administration,* and so on, do we use a singular or plural verb? Some writers use a singular verb and pronoun when the group acts as a single entity:

> ✓ The **committee** HAS met but has not yet made **its** decision.

But they use a plural verb and pronoun when its members act individually:

> ✓ The **faculty** HAVE the memo, but not all of **them** have read it.

These days plurals are irregularly used in both senses (but the plural is the rule in British English).

Second, what pronoun do we use, *it* or *they,* to refer to pronouns such as *someone, everyone, no one* and to singular common nouns that signal no gender: *teacher, doctor, student?* We casually use *they:*

> **Everyone** knows **they** must answer for **their** actions.

> When **a person** is on drugs, it is hard to help **them.**

Formal usage requires a singular pronoun:

> ✓ **Everyone** realizes that **he** must answer for **his actions.**

But that rule raises the problem of biased language.

Gender and Biased Language

Common sense demands that we don't gratuitously offend readers, but if we reject *he* as a generic pronoun because it's biased and *they* because some readers consider it ungrammatical, we are left with only bad choices. Some writers choose a clumsy *he or she;* others choose a worse *he/she* or even *s/he.*

> If **a writer** ignores the ethnicity of **his or her** readers, **s/he** may respond in ways **the writer** would not expect to words that to **him or her** are innocent of bias.

Some writers substitute plurals for singulars:

> ✓ When **writers** ignore **their** readers' ethnicity, **they** may respond in ways **they** might not expect to words that are to **them** innocent of bias.

But in that sentence, *they, their,* and *them* are confusing, because they can refer either to writers or readers. To the careful ear, a sentence with singular nouns and pronouns seems a shade more precise:

> When a **writer** ignores **his** reader's ethnicity, **his reader** may respond in ways that **he** might not expect to words that are to **him** innocent of bias.

We can try a first person *we,*

> ✓ If **we** ignore the ethnicity of **our** readers, they may respond in ways **we** would not expect to words that to **us** are innocent of bias.

But *we* can also be ambiguous. We could also try impersonal abstraction, but that creates its own problem:

> Failure to consider ethnicity may lead to unexpected responses to words considered innocent of bias.

Finally, we can alternately use *he* and *she,* as I have. But that's not a perfect solution either, because some readers find *she* as stylistically intrusive as *he/she.* A reviewer in the *New York Times,* for example, wondered what to make of an author whom the reviewer charged with attempting to

> right history's wrongs to women by referring to random examples as "she," as in "Ask a particle physicist what happens when a quark is knocked out of a proton, and she will tell you . . .," which strikes this reader as oddly patronizing to women.

(We might wonder how it strikes women who happen to be particle physicists.)

For years to come, we'll have a problem with singular generic pronouns, and to some readers, any solution will be awkward. I suspect that eventually we will accept the plural *they* as a correct singular:

✓ **No one** should turn in **their** writing unedited.

Some claim that such compromises lead to lazy imprecision. Whatever the future, we have a choice now, and that's not a bad thing, because our choices define who we are.

Summing Up

We must write correctly, but if in defining correctness we ignore the difference between fact and folklore, we risk overlooking what is really important—the choices that make our writing dense and wordy or clear and concise. We are not precise merely because we get right *which* and *that* and avoid *finalize* and *hopefully*. Many who obsess on such details are oblivious to this more serious kind of imprecision:

> Too precise a specification of information processing requirements incurs the risk of overestimation resulting in unused capacity or inefficient use of costly resources or of underestimation leading to ineffectiveness or other inefficiencies.

That means,

✓ When you specify too precisely the resources you need to process information, you may overestimate. If you do, you risk having more capacity than you need or using costly resources inefficiently.

Both are grammatically precise, but who would choose to read more of the first?

I suspect that those who observe all the rules all the time do so not because they want to protect the integrity of the language or the quality of our culture, but to assert a style of their own. Some of us are straightforward and plain speaking; others take pleasure in a bit of elegance, in a touch of fastidiously self-conscious "class." It is an impulse we should not scorn, so long as it is not a pretext to discriminate and is subordinate to the more important matters to which we now turn—the choices that define not "good grammar," but clarity and grace.

PART TWO
Clarity

*Everything that can be thought at all
can be thought clearly.
Everything that can be said can be said clearly.*
—LUDWIG WITTGENSTEIN

*It takes less time to learn to write nobly than to
learn to write lightly and straightforwardly.*
—FRIEDRICH NIETZSCHE

Lesson

3

Actions

Suit the action to the word, the word to the action.
—William Shakespeare, *Hamlet*, 3.2

I am unlikely to trust a sentence that comes easily.
—William Gass

Understanding the Principles of Clarity

Making Judgments

We have words enough to praise writing we like: *clear, direct, concise,* and more than enough to abuse writing we don't: *unclear, indirect, abstract, dense, complex.* We can use those words to distinguish these two sentences:

1a. The cause of our schools' failure at teaching basic skills is not understanding the influence of cultural background on learning.

1b. Our schools have failed to teach basic skills because they do not understand how cultural background influences the way a child learns.

Most of us would call (1a) too complex, (1b) clearer, more direct. But those words don't refer to anything *in* those sentences; they describe how those sentences make us *feel*. When we say that (1a) is *unclear*, we mean that *we* have a hard time understanding it; we say it's *dense* when *we* struggle to read it.

The problem is to understand what is *in* those two sentences that makes us feel as we do. Only then can we rise above our too-good understanding of our own writing to know when our readers will think it needs revising. To do that, you have to know what counts as a well-told story. (To profit from this lesson and the next three, you must be able to identify verbs, SIMPLE SUBJECTS, and WHOLE SUBJECTS. See the Glossary.)

Telling Stories About Characters and Their Actions

This story has a problem:

> 2a. Once upon a time, as a walk through the woods was taking place on the part of Little Red Riding Hood, the Wolf's jump out from behind a tree occurred, causing her fright.

We prefer something closer to this:

> ✓ 2b. Once upon a time, Little Red Riding Hood was walking through the woods, when the Wolf jumped out from behind a tree and frightened her.

Most readers think (2b) tells its story more clearly than (2a), because it follows two principles:

- Its main characters are subjects of verbs.
- Those verbs express specific actions.

Those principles seem simple, but they need some explanation.

Principle of Clarity 1: Make main characters subjects. Look at the subjects in (2a). The simple subjects (boldfaced) are *not* the main characters (italicized):

> 2a. Once upon a time, as a **walk** through the woods was taking place on the part of *Little Red Riding Hood*, *the Wolf's* **jump** out from behind a tree occurred, causing *her* fright.

The subjects in that sentence do not name its characters; they name actions expressed in the abstract NOUNS *walk* and *jump:*

SUBJECT	VERB
a **walk** through the woods	was taking place
the *Wolf's* **jump** out from behind a tree	occurred

The whole subject of *occurred* does have a character *in* it: *the Wolf's jump,* but *the Wolf* is only attached to the simple subject *jump;* it is not *the* subject.

Contrast those abstract subjects with the concrete subjects (italicized and boldfaced) in (2b):

> 2b. Once upon a time, ***Little Red Riding Hood*** was walking through the woods, when ***the Wolf*** jumped out from behind a tree and frightened *her*.

The subjects and the main characters are now the same words:

SUBJECT/CHARACTER	VERB
Little Red Riding Hood	was walking
the Wolf	jumped

Principle of Clarity 2: Make important actions verbs. Now look at how the actions and verbs differ in (2a): its actions are not expressed in verbs but in abstract nouns (actions are boldfaced; verbs are capitalized):

> 2a. Once upon a time, as a **walk** through the woods WAS TAKING place on the part of Little Red Riding Hood, the Wolf's **jump** out from behind a tree OCCURRED, causing her **fright.**

Note how vague the verbs are: *was taking, occurred.* In (2b), the clearer sentence, the verbs name specific actions:

> ✓ 2b. Once upon a time, Little Red Riding Hood WAS WALKING through the woods, when the Wolf JUMPED out from behind a tree and FRIGHTENED her.

Here's the point: In (2a), the sentence that seems wordy and indirect, the two main characters, Little Red Riding Hood and the Wolf, are *not* subjects, and their actions—*walk, jump,* and *fright*—are *not* verbs. In (2b), the more direct sentence, those two main characters *are* subjects and their main actions *are* verbs. That's why we prefer (2b).

Fairy Tales and Writing for Grown-ups

Writing in college or on the job may seem distant from fairy tales, but it's not, because most sentences tell stories. Compare these two:

> 3a. The Federalists' argument in regard to the destabilization of government by popular democracy was based on their belief in the

tendency of factions to further their self-interest at the expense of the common good.

✓ 3b. The Federalists argued that popular democracy destabilized government, because they believed that factions tended to further their self-interest at the expense of the common good.

We can analyze those two sentences as we did the ones about Little Red Riding Hood and the Wolf.

Sentence (3a) feels dense for two reasons. First, its characters are not subjects. Its simple subject is *argument,* but the characters are *Federalists, popular democracy, government,* and *factions* (characters are italicized; the simple subject is boldfaced):

> 3a. *The Federalists'* **argument** in regard to the destabilization of *government* by *popular democracy* was based on *their* belief in the tendency of *factions* to further *their* self-interest at the expense of the common good.

Second, most of the actions (boldfaced) are not verbs (capitalized), but abstract nouns:

> 3a. The Federalists' **argument** in regard to the **destabilization** of government by popular democracy WAS BASED on their **belief** in the **tendency** of factions to FURTHER their self-interest at the expense of the common good.

Notice how long and complex is the whole subject of (3a) and how little meaning is expressed by its main verb *was based:*

WHOLE SUBJECT	VERB
The Federalists' argument in regard to the destabilization of government by popular democracy	was based

Readers think (3b) is clearer for two reasons: first, the actions (boldfaced) are verbs (capitalized):

> 3b. The Federalists ARGUED that popular democracy DESTABILIZED government, because they BELIEVED that factions TENDED TO FURTHER their self-interest at the expense of the common good.

Second, its characters (italicized) *are* subjects (boldfaced):

> 3b. The *Federalists* argued that *popular democracy* destabilized government, because *they* believed that *factions* tended to further *their* self-interest at the expense of the common good.

Note that all those subjects are short and specific:

WHOLE SUBJECT/CHARACTER	VERB/ACTION
the Federalists	argued
popular democracy	destabilized
they	believed
factions	tended to further

In the rest of this lesson, we look at actions and verbs; in the next, at characters and subjects.

VERBS AND ACTIONS

Our principle is this:

> *A sentence seems clear when its important actions are in verbs.*

Look at how sentences (4a) and (4b) express their actions. In (4a), actions (boldfaced) are not verbs (capitalized); they are nouns:

> 4a. Our **lack** of data PREVENTED **evaluation** of UN **actions** in **targeting** funds to areas most in **need** of **assistance.**

In (4b), on the other hand, the actions are almost all verbs:

> ✓ 4b. Because we LACKED data, we could not EVALUATE whether the UN HAD TARGETED funds to areas that most NEEDED **assistance.**

Readers will think your writing is dense if you use lots of abstract nouns, especially those derived from verbs and ADJECTIVES, nouns ending in *-tion, -ment, -ence,* and so on, *especially when you make those abstract nouns the subjects of verbs.*

A noun derived from a verb or adjective has a technical name: *nominalization.* The word illustrates its meaning: When we nominalize *nominalize,* we create the nominalization *nominalization.* Here are a few examples:

VERB	→	NOMINALIZATION	ADJECTIVE	→	NOMINALIZATION
discover	→	discovery	careless	→	carelessness
resist	→	resistance	different	→	difference
react	→	reaction	proficient	→	proficiency

We can also nominalize a verb by adding *-ing* (making it a GERUND):

She flies → her flying   We sang → our singing

Some nominalizations and verbs are identical:

hope → hope   result → result   repair → repair

We **REQUEST** that you **REVIEW** the data.

Our **request** IS that you DO a **review** of the data.

(Some actions also hide out in adjectives: *It is applicable* → *it applies.* Some others: *indicative, dubious, argumentative, deserving.*)

No element of style more characterizes turgid writing, writing that feels abstract, indirect, and difficult, than lots of nominalizations, especially as the subjects of verbs.

Here's the point: In grade school, we learned that subjects *are* characters (or "doers") and that verbs *are* actions. That's often true:

subject	verb	object
We	discussed	the problem.
doer	action	

But it is not true for this almost synonymous sentence:

subject	verb		
The problem	was	the topic	of our discussion.
		doer	action

We can move characters and actions around in a sentence, and subjects and verbs don't have to name any particular kind of thing at all. But when you match characters to subjects and actions to verbs in most of your sentences, readers are likely to think your prose is clear, direct, and readable.

Exercise 3.1

Analyze the subject/character and verb/action in these sentences:

There is opposition among many voters to nuclear power plants based on a belief in their threat to human health.

Many voters oppose nuclear power plants because they believe that such plants threaten human health.

Exercise 3.2

If you aren't sure whether you can distinguish verbs, adjectives, and nominalizations, practice on the list below. Turn verbs and adjectives into nominalizations, and nominalizations into adjectives and verbs. Remember that some verbs and nominalizations have the same form:

Poverty predictably CAUSES social problems.

Poverty IS a predictable **cause** of social problems.

analysis	believe	attempt	conclusion	evaluate
suggest	approach	comparison	define	discuss
expression	failure	intelligent	thorough	appearance
decrease	improve	increase	accuracy	careful
emphasize	explanation	description	clear	examine

Exercise 3.3

Create sentences using verbs and adjectives from Exercise 3.2. Then rewrite them using the corresponding nominalizations (keep the meaning the same). For example, using *suggest, discuss,* and *careful,* write:

I SUGGEST that we DISCUSS the issue CAREFULLY.

Then rewrite that sentence into its nominalized form:

My **suggestion** is that our **discussion** of the issue be done with **care**.

Only when you see how a clear sentence can be made unclear will you understand why it seemed clear in the first place.

DIAGNOSIS AND REVISION

You can use the principles of verbs as actions and subjects as characters to explain why your readers judge your prose as they do. But more important, you can also use them to identify and revise sentences that seem clear to you but not to your readers. Revision is a three-step process: diagnose, analyze, rewrite.

1. **Diagnose**

   a. Ignoring short (four- or five-word) introductory phrases, underline the first seven or eight words in each sentence.

      The outsourcing of high-tech work to Asia by corporations means the loss of jobs for many American workers.

b. Then look for two things:
  - Did you underline abstract nouns that are simple sub-jects (boldfaced)?

    The *outsourcing* of high-tech work to Asia by corporations means the loss of jobs for many American workers.

  - Did you reach beyond seven or eight words before get-ting to a verb?

    The outsourcing of high-tech work to Asia by corporations (10 words) **means** the loss of jobs for many American workers.

2. **Analyze**
   a. Decide who your main characters are, particularly the flesh-and-blood ones (more about this in the next lesson).

      The outsourcing of high-tech work to Asia by **corporations** means the loss of jobs for **many American workers.**

   b. Then look for the actions that those characters perform, es-pecially actions in nominalizations, those abstract nouns derived from verbs.

      The **outsourcing** of high-tech work to Asia by corporations means the **loss** of jobs for many American workers.

3. **Rewrite**
   a. If the actions are nominalizations, make them verbs.

      outsourcing → outsource   loss → lose

   b. Make the characters the subjects of those verbs.

      corporations outsource   American workers lose

   c. Rewrite the sentence with SUBORDINATING CONJUNCTIONS like *because, if, when, although, why, how, whether,* or *that.*

      ✓ Many middle-class American workers are losing their jobs, **because** corporations are outsourcing their high-tech work to Asia.

Some Common Patterns

You can quickly spot and revise five common patterns of nominalizations.

1. **The nominalization is the subject of an empty verb such as *be, seems, has,* etc.:**

   The **intention** of the committee IS to audit the records.

   a. Change the nominalization to a verb:

      intention → intend

   b. Find a character that would be the subject of that verb:

      The intention of **the committee** is to audit the records.

   c. Make that character the subject of the new verb:

      ✓ *The committee* INTENDS to audit the records.

2. **The nominalization follows an empty verb:**

   The *agency* CONDUCTED an **investigation** into the matter.

   a. Change the nominalization to a verb:

      investigation → investigate

   b. Replace the empty verb with the new verb:

      conducted → investigated

      ✓ The *agency* INVESTIGATED the matter.

3. **One nominalization is the subject of an empty verb and a second nominalization follows it:**

   Our **loss** in sales WAS a result of their **expansion** of outlets.

   a. Revise the nominalizations into verbs:

      loss → lose   expansion → expand

   b. Identify the characters that would be the subjects of those verbs:

      Our loss in sales was a result of **their** expansion of outlets.

   c. Make those characters subjects of those verbs:

      we lose   they expand

   d. Link the new CLAUSES with a logical connection:

     • To express simple cause: *because, since, when*
     • To express conditional cause: *if, provided that, so long as*
     • To contradict expected causes: *though, although, unless*

Our **loss** in sales	→	*We* LOST sales
was the result of	→	**because**
their **expansion** of outlets	→	*they* EXPANDED outlets

4. **A nominalization follows *there is* or *there are:***

   There IS no **need** for *our* further **study** of this problem.

   a. Change the nominalization to a verb:

   > need → need   study → study

   b. Identify the character that should be the subject of the verb:

   > There is no need for **our** further study of this problem.

   c. Make that character the subject of the verb:

   > no need → we need not   our study → we study

   > ✓ *We* **NEED** not **STUDY** this problem further.

5. **Two or three nominalizations in a row are joined by prepositions:**

   We did a **review** of the **evolution** of the brain.

   a. Turn the first nominalization into a verb:

   > review → review

   b. Either leave the second nominalization as it is or turn it into a verb in a clause beginning with *how* or *why:*

   > evolution of the brain → how the brain evolved

   > ✓ First, *we* **REVIEWED** the **evolution** of the *brain.*

   > ✓ First, *we* **REVIEWED** how *the brain* **EVOLVED**.

QUICK TIP: When you revise a complicated sentence, you will have more than one character-action clause. Decide how the clauses fit together, then try out these patterns: *X because Y; Since X, Y; If X, then Y; Although X, Y; X and/but/so Y.*

Some Happy Consequences

When you consistently rely on verbs to express key actions, your readers benefit in many ways:

1. Your sentences are more concrete, because they will have concrete subjects and verbs. Compare:

   There WAS an affirmative **decision** for **expansion.**

   ✓ *The Director* **DECIDED** to **EXPAND** the program.

2. Your sentences are more concise. When you use nominalizations, you have to add articles like *a* and *the* and prepositions
such as *of, by,* and *in.* You don't need them when you use verbs
and conjunctions (italicized):

> A **revision** *of* the program WILL RESULT *in* **increases** *in* our
> **efficiency** *in the* **servicing** *of* clients.

> ✓ *If* we REVISE the program, we CAN SERVE clients more EFFICIENTLY.

3. The logic of your sentences is clearer. When you nominalize
verbs, you link actions with fuzzy prepositions and phrases
such as *of, by,* and *on the part of.* But when you use verbs, you
link clauses with precise subordinating conjunctions such as
because, although, and *if:*

> Our more effective presentation of our study resulted in our suc-
> cess, despite an earlier start by others.

> ✓ **Although** others started earlier, we succeeded **because** we pre-
> sented our study more effectively.

4. Your sentence tells a more coherent story. This next sequence
of actions distorts their chronology. (The numbers refer to the
real sequence of events.)

> Decisions[4] in regard to administration[5] of medication despite in-
> ability[2] of an irrational patient appearing[1] in a Trauma Center to
> provide legal consent[3] rest with the attending physician alone.

When we revise those actions into verbs and reorder them, we
get a more coherent narrative:

> ✓ When a patient appears[1] in a Trauma Center and behaves[2] so irra-
> tionally that he cannot legally consent[3] to treatment, only the at-
> tending physician can decide[4] whether to medicate[5] him.

A COMMON PROBLEM SOLVED

You've probably had this experience: you think you've written
something good, but your reader thinks otherwise. You wonder
whether that person is just being difficult, but you bite your
tongue and try to fix it, even though you think it should already be
clear to anyone who can read Dr. Seuss. When that happens to me
(regularly, I might add), I almost always realize—eventually—that
my readers are right, that they see where my writing needs work
better than I do.

Why are we so often right about the writing of others and so
often wrong about our own? It is because we all read into our own

writing what we want readers to get out of it. That explains why two readers can disagree about the clarity of the same piece of writing: a reader who knows its content better is likely to think the passage is more clearly written than is a reader who knows less about it. Both are right. Degrees of clarity are in the eye of more or less informed beholders.

That is why we need to look at our own writing in a way that is almost mechanical, that sidesteps our too-good understanding of it. The quickest way is to underline the first seven or eight words of every sentence. If you don't see in those words a character as a subject and a verb as a specific action, you have a candidate for revision.

QUICK TIP: When you revise a longer piece of work, look first at those passages that were hard to write because you didn't fully understand your ideas. We all tend to write badly when we're unsure about what we want to say or how to say it.

Exercise 3.4

One sentence in each of these pairs is clear, expressing characters as subjects and actions as verbs; the other is indirect, with actions in nominalizations and characters often not in subjects. First, identify which is which. Then circle nominalizations and highlight verbs. If you are good at grammar, underline subjects. Then put a "c" over characters that seem to perform actions.

1a. Some people argue that atmospheric carbon dioxide does not elevate global temperature.
1b. There has been speculation by educators about the role of the family in improving educational achievement.
2a. Smoking during pregnancy may cause fetal injury.
2b. When we write concisely, readers understand easily.
3a. Researchers have identified the AIDS virus but failed to develop a vaccine to immunize those at risk.
3b. Attempts by economists at defining full employment have been met with failure.
4a. Complaints by editorial writers about voter apathy rarely offer suggestions about dispelling it.

4b. Although critics claim that children who watch a lot of television tend to become less able readers, no one has demonstrated that to be true.

5a. The loss of market share to Japan by domestic automakers resulted in the disappearance of hundreds of thousands of jobs.

5b. When educators discover how to use computer-assisted instruction, our schools will teach complex subjects more effectively.

6a. We need to know which parts of our national forests are being logged most extensively so that we can save virgin stands at greatest risk.

6b. There is a need for an analysis of library use to provide a reliable base for the projection of needed resources.

7a. Many professional athletes fail to realize that they are unprepared for life after stardom because their teams protect them from the problems that the rest of us adjust to every day.

7b. Colleges now have an understanding that yearly tuition increases are impossible because of strong parental resistance to the soaring cost of higher education.

Exercise 3.5

Now revise the nominalized sentences in Exercise 3.4 into sentences with verbs. Use its paired verbal version as a model. For example, if the verbal sentence begins with *when*, begin your revision with *when:*

Sentence to revise: 2a. **Smoking** during pregnancy may lead to fetal **injury.**

Model: 2b. When we WRITE concisely, readers UNDERSTAND more easily.

Your revision: 2a. When pregnant women SMOKE . . .

Exercise 3.6

Revise these next sentences so that the nominalizations are verbs and characters are their subjects. In (1) through (5), characters are italicized and nominalizations are boldfaced.

1. *Lincoln's* **hope** was for the **preservation** of the Union without war, but the *South's* **attack** on Fort Sumter made war an **inevitability.**

2. **Attempts** were made on the part of the *president's aides* to assert *his* **immunity** from a *congressional* subpoena.

3. There were **predictions** by *business executives* that the *economy* would experience a quick **revival.**

4. *Your* **analysis** of *my* report omits any data in **support** of *your* **criticism** of *my* **findings.**

5. The *health care industry's* **inability** to exert cost **controls** could lead to the *public's* **decision** that *congressional* **action** is needed.

In sentences 6 through 10, the character are italicized; find the actions and revise.

6. A *papal* appeal was made to the world's rich *nations* for assistance to those facing the threat of *African* starvation.

7. Attempts at explaining increases in *voter* participation in this year's elections were made by *several candidates.*

8. The agreement by the *class* on the reading list was based on the assumption that there would be tests on only certain selections.

9. There was no independent *business-sector* study of the cause of the sudden increase in the trade surplus.

10. An understanding as to the need for controls over drinking on campus was recognized by *fraternities.*

In 11 through 15, only the nominalizations are boldfaced; find or invent the characters and revise.

11. There is **uncertainty** at the CIA about North Korean **intentions** as to **cessation** of missile **testing.**

12. Physical **conditioning** of the team is the **responsibility** of the coaching staff.

13. **Contradictions** among the data require an **explanation.**

14. The Dean's **rejection** of our proposal was a **disappointment** but not a **surprise** because our **expectation** was that a **decision** had been made.

15. Their **performance** of the play was marked by **enthusiasm** but lacked intelligent **staging.**

Exercise 3.7

Revise these sentences. At the end of each is a hint. For example:

Congress's **reduction** of the deficit resulted in the **decline** of interest rates. [because]

✓ Interest rates DECLINED because Congress REDUCED the deficit.

1. The use of models in teaching prose style does not result in improvements of clarity and directness in student writing. [Although we use . . .]

2. Precision in plotting the location of building foundations enhances the possibility of its accurate reconstruction. [When we precisely plot . . .]

3. Any departures by the members from established procedures may cause termination of membership by the Board. [If members . . .]

4. A student's lack of socialization into a field may lead to writing problems because of his insufficient understanding about arguments by professionals in that field. [When . . ., . . ., because . . .]

5. The successful implementation of a new curriculum depends on the cooperation of faculty with students in setting achievable goals within a reasonable time. [To implement . . ., . . .]

Two Qualifications

Useful Nominalizations

I have so relentlessly urged you to turn nominalizations into verbs that you might think you should never use one. But in fact, you can't write well without them. The trick is to know which to keep and which to revise. Keep these:

1. **A nominalization as a short subject refers to a previous sentence:**

   ✓ **These arguments** all depend on a single unproven claim.

   ✓ **This decision** can lead to positive outcomes.

   Those nominalizations link one sentence to another in a cohesive flow, an issue I'll discuss in more detail in Lesson 5.

2. **A short nominalization replaces an awkward *The fact that:***

   The fact that she ACKNOWLEDGED the problem impressed me.

   ✓ Her **acknowledgment** of the problem impressed me.

   But then, why not this:

   ✓ *She* IMPRESSED me when *she* ACKNOWLEDGED the problem.

3. **A nominalization names what would be the OBJECT of the verb:**

   I accepted *what she* REQUESTED [that is, *She requested **something***].

   ✓ I accepted her **request.**

   This kind of nominalization feels more concrete than an abstract one. However, contrast *request* above with this next sentence, where *request* is more of an action:

   Her **request** for **assistance** CAME after the deadline.

   ✓ She REQUESTED **assistance** after the deadline.

4. **A nominalization refers to a concept so familiar to your readers that to them, it is a virtual character (more about this in the next lesson):**

✓ Few problems have so divided us as **abortion** on **demand.**

✓ The Equal Rights **Amendment** was an issue in past **elections.**

✓ **Taxation** without **representation** did not spark the American **Revolution.**

Those nominalizations name familiar concepts: *abortion* on *demand, amendment, election, taxation, representation, revolution.* You must develop an eye for distinguishing nominalizations expressing a common idea from those that you can revise into a verb:

There is a **demand** for a **repeal** of the **inheritance** tax.

✓ We DEMAND that Congress REPEAL the **inheritance** tax.

CLARITY, NOT SIMPLEMINDEDNESS

Your readers want you to write clearly, but not in Dick-and-Jane sentences. This was written by a student aspiring to academic sophistication:

> After Czar Alexander II's emancipation of Russian serfs in 1861, many freed peasants chose to live on communes for purposes of cooperation in agricultural production as well as for social stability. Despite some communes' attempts at economic and social equalization through the strategy of imposing low economic status on the peasants, which resulted in their reduction to near poverty, a centuries-long history of social distinctions even among serfs prevented social equalization.

In his struggle to write clearly, he revised that paragraph into something that sounds as if it were written by a 12-year-old:

> In 1861, Czar Alexander II emancipated the Russian serfs. Many of them chose to live on agricultural communes. There they thought they could cooperate with one another in agricultural production. They could also create a stable social structure. The leaders of some of these communes tried to equalize the peasants economically and socially. As one strategy, they tried to impose on all a low economic status. That reduced them to near poverty. However, the communes failed to equalize them socially. This happened because even serfs had made social distinctions among themselves for centuries.

Some argue that all sentences should be short, no more than 20 or so words. But most mature ideas are too complicated to express in Dick-and-Jane sentences. In Lessons 8 and 9 we look at ways to revise too-short, too-simple sentences into a style that is readable but still complex enough to communicate complex ideas. When that student applied those principles to his primer-style sentences, he produced this:

> After Russian serfs were emancipated by Czar Alexander II in 1861, many chose to live on agricultural communes, hoping they could cooperate in working the land and establish a stable social structure. At first, some who led the communes tried to equalize the new peasants socially and economically by imposing on everyone a low economic status, a strategy that reduced them to near poverty. But the communes failed to equalize them socially because the serfs had for centuries observed their own social distinctions.

Those sentences are long but clear, because the writer consistently aligned major characters with subjects and actions with verbs.

SUMMING UP

We can represent these principles graphically. As we read, we mentally integrate two levels of sentence structure. One is a relatively fixed grammatical sequence of subject and verb (the empty box is for everything that follows the verb):

Fixed	Subject	Verb	————

The other level of sentence structure is based on its characters and their actions. They have no fixed order, but readers prefer them matched to subjects and verbs. We can graphically combine those principles:

Fixed	Subject	Verb	————
Variable	Character	Action	————

Keep in mind that readers want to see characters not just *in* a subject, as in these two:

The *president's* veto of the bill infuriated Congress.

The veto of the bill by *the president* infuriated Congress.

Instead, they want to see the character *as* the subject, like this:

✓ When *the president*$_{\text{subject}}$ VETOED$_{\text{verb}}$ the bill, *he*$_{\text{subject}}$ INFURIATED$_{\text{verb}}$ Congress.

When you frustrate those expectations, you make readers work harder than they should have to. So keep these principles in mind as you revise:

1. Express actions in verbs:

    The **intention** of the committee is improvement of morale.

    ✓ The committee INTENDS to improve morale.

2. Make the subjects of those verbs the characters associated with those actions.

    A decision by **the dean** in regard to the funding of the program by **the department** is necessary for adequate **staff** preparation.

    ✓ **The staff** CAN PREPARE adequately, only after **the dean** DECIDES whether **the department** WILL FUND the program.

3. Don't revise these nominalizations:

    a. They refer to a previous sentence:

    ✓ **These arguments** all depend on a single unproven claim.

    b. They replace an awkward *The fact that*:

    The fact that she strenuously objected impressed me.

    ✓ **Her strenuous objections** impressed me.

    c. They name what would be the object of a verb:

    I do not know **what she INTENDS.**

    ✓ I do not know **her intentions.**

    d. They name a concept so familiar to your readers that it is a virtual character:

    ✓ Few problems have so divided us as **abortion** on **demand.**

    ✓ The Equal Rights **Amendment** was an issue in past **elections.**

4

Characters

*Whatever is translatable in other and simpler words of the same
language, without loss of sense or dignity, is bad.*
—Samuel Taylor Coleridge

When character is lost, all is lost.
—Anonymous

UNDERSTANDING THE IMPORTANCE
OF CHARACTERS

Readers think sentences are clear and direct when they see key
actions in their verbs. Compare (1a) with (1b):

1a. The CIA feared the president would recommend to Congress that
it reduce its budget.

1b. The CIA had fears that the president would send a recommendation to Congress that it make a reduction in its budget.

Sentence (1a) is a third shorter than (1b), but some readers don't
think it's much clearer.
But now compare (1b) and (1c):

1b. The CIA had fears that the president would send a recommendation to Congress that it make a reduction in its budget.

1c. The fear of the CIA was that a recommendation from the president to Congress would be for a reduction in its budget.

Every reader thinks that (1c) is less clear than either (1a) or (1b).

The reason is this: In both (1a) and (1b), important characters are short, specific subjects of verbs (characters are italicized, subjects boldfaced, verbs capitalized):

1a. *The* **CIA** FEARED *the* **president** WOULD RECOMMEND to *Congress* that *it* REDUCE its budget.

1b. *The* **CIA** HAD fears that *the* **president** WOULD SEND a recommendation to *Congress* that *it* MAKE a reduction in its budget.

But the two subjects in (1c) are not concrete characters, but abstractions (boldfaced).

1c. The **fear** of the *CIA* WAS that a **recommendation** from the *president* to *Congress* WOULD BE for a **reduction** in its budget.

The different verbs in (1a) and (1b) make some difference, but the abstract subjects in (1c) make a bigger one.

Here's the point: Readers want actions in verbs, but even more they want characters as subjects. We create a problem for readers when for no good reason we do not name characters in subjects, or worse, delete them entirely, like this:

1d. There was fear that there would be a recommendation for a budget reduction.

Who fears? Who recommends? Who reduces? It is important to express actions in verbs, but the *first* principle of a clear style is this: Make the subjects of most of your verbs *the main* characters in your story.

Diagnosis and Revision

Finding and Relocating Characters

To get characters into subjects, you have to know two things:

1. where you should look for characters
2. what you should do when you find them (or don't)

For example, this sentence feels indirect and impersonal.

Governmental intervention in fast-changing technologies has led to the distortion of market evolution and interference in new product development.

We can diagnose that sentence:

1. **Underline the first seven or eight words:**

   <u>Governmental intervention in fast-changing technologies has led</u> to the distortion of market evolution and interference in new product development.

   In those first words, readers want to see characters as the subjects of verbs. But in that example, they don't.

2. **Find the main characters.** They may be POSSESSIVE PRONOUNS attached to nominalizations, objects of prepositions (particularly *by* and *of*), or only implied. In that sentence, one main character is in the adjective *governmental;* the other, *market,* is in the object of a preposition: *of market evolution.*

3. **Skim the passage for actions involving those characters, particularly actions buried in nominalizations.** Ask *Who is doing what?*

governmental **intervention**	→	*government* **intervenes**
distortion	→	*[government]* **distorts**
market **evolution**	→	*markets* **evolve**
interference	→	*[government]* **interferes**
development	→	*[market]* **develops**

   To revise, reassemble those new subjects and verbs into a sentence, using conjunctions such as *if, although, because, when, how,* and *why:*

   ✓ **When** a *government* INTERVENES in fast-changing technologies, *it* DISTORTS how *markets* EVOLVE and INTERFERES with their ability to DEVELOP new products.

   Be aware that just as actions can be in adjectives (*reliable* → *rely*), so can characters:

   Medieval *theological* debates often addressed issues considered trivial by modern *philosophical* thought.

   When you find a character implied in an adjective, revise in the same way:

   ✓ *Medieval theologians* often debated issues that *modern philosophers* consider trivial.

> **QUICK TIP:**   The first step in diagnosing a dense style is to look at subjects. If you do not see main characters there expressed in a few short, concrete words, you have to look for them. They can be in objects of prepositions, in possessive pronouns, or in adjectives. Once you find them, look for actions they are involved in.
>
> ### When you are writing:
> Make those characters the subjects of verbs naming those actions. Then string together those character-action pairs into complete sentences.
>
> ### When you are reading:
> Focusing on the characters, try to retell the story in the sentences, one action at a time. If that fails, list character-action pairs and rewrite the sentences yourself.

Reconstructing Absent Characters

Readers have the biggest problem with sentences devoid of *all* characters:

> A decision was made in favor of doing a study of the disagreements.

That sentence could mean either of these, and more:

> We decided that I should study why they disagreed.
>
> I decided that you should study why he disagreed.

The writer may know who is doing what, but readers might not and so usually need help.

Sometimes we omit characters to make a general statement:

> Research strategies that look for more than one variable are of more use in understanding factors in psychiatric disorder than strategies based on the assumption that the presence of psychopathology is dependent on a single gene or on strategies in which only one biological variable is studied.

But when we try to revise that into something clearer, we have to invent characters, then decide what to call them. Do we use *one* or *we*, or name a generic "doer"?

> ✓ If *one/we/researchers* are to understand what causes psychiatric disorder, *one/we/they* should use research strategies that look for more than one

variable rather than assume that a single gene is responsible for a psychopathology or adopt a strategy in which *one/we/they* study only one biological variable.

To most of us, *one* feels stiff, but *we* may be ambiguous because it can refer just to the writer, or to the writer and others but not the reader, or to the reader and writer but not others, or to everyone. But if you avoid both nominalizations and vague pronouns, you can slide into PASSIVE verbs (I'll discuss them in a moment):

> To understand what makes patients vulnerable to psychiatric disorders, strategies that look for more than one variable SHOULD BE USED rather than strategies in which a gene IS ASSUMED a gene causes psychopathology or only one biological variable IS STUDIED.

QUICK TIP: When you are explaining a complicated issue to someone involved in it, imagine sitting across the table from that person, saying *you* as often as you can:

> Taxable intangible property includes financial notes and municipal bonds. A one-time tax of 2% on its value applies to this property.

> ✓ **You** have to pay tax on **your** intangible property, including **your** financial notes and municipal bonds. On this property, **you** pay a one-time tax of 2%.

If *you* seems not appropriate, change it to a character that is:

> **Taxpayers** have to pay tax on their intangible property, including **their** financial notes and municipal bonds. **They** pay . . .

Abstractions as Characters

So far, I've discussed characters as if they had to be flesh-and-blood people. But we might have solved the problem of the previous example with a different kind of character, the abstraction *study:*

> ✓ To understand what causes psychiatric disorder, *studies* should look for more than one variable rather than adopt a strategy in which *they* test only one biological variable or assume that a single *gene* is responsible for a psychopathology.

Now the sentence is clear, but appropriately professional.

You can tell stories whose main characters are abstractions, including nominalizations, so long as you make them the subjects of a series of sentences that tell a story. Here's a story about a character called *freedom of speech*, two nominalizations.

✓ No right is more basic to a free society than **freedom of speech.**
Free speech served the left in the 1960s when it protested the Vietnam
War, and **it** is now used by the right when it claims that speech
includes contributions to political organizations. **The doctrine of**
free speech has been embraced by all sides to protect themselves
against those who would silence unpopular views. As a legal concept,
it arose . . .

The phrase *freedom of speech* (or its equivalents *free speech* and *it*)
is a virtual character because it is so familiar and because it is the
subject of a series of sentences.

But when you do use abstractions as characters, you can create
a problem. A story about an abstraction as familiar as *free speech* is
clear enough, but if you surround a less familiar abstract character
with a lot of other abstractions, readers may feel that your writing
is unnecessarily dense and complex.

For example, few of us are familiar with *prospective* and *immediate*
intention, so most of us are likely to struggle with a story about them,
especially when those terms are surrounded by other abstractions (actions are boldfaced; human characters are italicized):

The **argument** is this. The cognitive component of **intention** exhibits
a high degree of **complexity.** **Intention** is temporally divisible into
two: prospective **intention** and immediate **intention**. The cognitive
function of prospective **intention** is the **representation** of a *subject's*
similar past **actions**, *his* current situation, and *his* course of future
actions. That is, the cognitive component of prospective **intention** is
a **plan**. The cognitive function of immediate **intention** is the
monitoring and **guidance** of ongoing bodily **movement**.

—Myles Brand, *Intending and Acting*

We can make that passage clearer if we tell it from the point
of view of flesh-and-blood characters (they are italicized; "de-
nominalized" verbs are boldfaced and capitalized):

✓ *I* ARGUE this about intention. It has a complex cognitive component
that *we* can divide into two temporal kinds: prospective and immediate. *We* use prospective intention to REPRESENT how *we* have ACTED in
our past and present and how *we* will ACT in the future. That is, *we*
use the cognitive component of prospective intention to help *us* PLAN.
We use immediate intention to MONITOR and GUIDE *our* bodies as *we*
MOVE them.

But have I made this passage say something that the writer didn't mean? Some argue that any change in form changes meaning. In this case, the writer might offer an opinion, but only his readers could decide whether the two passages have different meanings, because at the end of the day, a passage means only what a careful and competent reader thinks it does.

Here's the point: Most readers want the subjects of verbs to name flesh-and-blood characters. But often, you must write about abstractions. When you do, turn them into virtual characters by making them the subjects of verbs that tell a story. If readers are familiar with your abstractions, no problem. But when they are not, avoid using lots of other abstract nominalizations around them. When you revise an abstract passage, you may have a problem if the hidden characters are "people in general." Try a general term for whoever is doing the action, such as *researchers, social critics, one,* and so on. If not, try *we.* But the fact is, unlike many other languages, English has no good solution for naming a generic "doer."

Exercise 4.1

Before you revise these next sentences, diagnose them. Look at the first six or seven words (ignore short introductory phrases). Then revise so that each has a specific character as subject of a specific verb. To revise, you may have to invent characters. Use *we, I,* or any other word that seems appropriate.

1. In recent years, the appearance of new interpretations about the meaning of the discovery of America has led to a reassessment of Columbus's place in Western history.

2. A decision about forcibly administering medication in an emergency room setting despite the inability of an irrational patient to provide legal consent is usually an on-scene medical decision.

3. Tracing transitions in a well-written article provides help in efforts at improving coherence in writing.

4. Resistance has been growing against building mental health facilities in residential areas because of a belief that the few examples of improper management are typical.

5. With the decline in network television viewing in favor of cable and rental DVDs, awareness is growing at the networks of a need to revise programming.

CHARACTERS AND PASSIVE VERBS

More than any other advice, you probably remember *Write in the active voice, not in the passive.* That's not bad advice, but it has exceptions.

When you write in the active voice, you typically put

- the agent or source of an action in the subject
- the goal or receiver of an action in a DIRECT OBJECT:

	subject	verb	object
Active:	I	lost	the money
	character/agent	action	goal

The passive differs in three ways:

1. The subject names the goal of the action.
2. A form of *be* precedes a verb in its PAST PARTICIPLE form.
3. The agent or source of the action is after the verb in a *by-*phrase or dropped entirely:

	subject	be + verb	prepositional phrase
Passive:	The money	was lost	[by me].
	goal	action	character/agent

The terms *active* and *passive,* however, are ambiguous, because they can refer not only to those two grammatical constructions but to how a sentence makes you *feel.* We call a sentence *passive* if it feels flat, regardless of whether its verb is actually in the passive voice. For example, compare these two sentences.

We can manage the problem if we control costs.

Problem management requires cost control.

Grammatically, both sentences are in the active voice, but the second *feels* passive, for three reasons:

- Neither of its actions—*management* and *control*—are verbs; both are abstract nominalizations.
- The subject is *problem management,* an abstraction.
- The sentence lacks flesh-and-blood characters entirely.

To understand why we respond to those two sentences as we do, we have to distinguish the technical, grammatical meanings of *active* and *passive* from their figurative, impressionistic meanings. In what follows, I discuss grammatical passives.

Choosing between Active and Passive

Some critics tell us to avoid the passive everywhere because it adds a couple of words and often deletes the agent, the "doer" of the action. But in fact, the passive is often the better choice. To choose between active and passive, you have to answer three questions:

1. **Must your readers know who is responsible for the action?** Often, we don't say who does an action because we don't know or readers won't care. For example, we naturally choose the passive in these sentences:

   ✓ The president **WAS RUMORED** to have considered resigning.

   ✓ Those who **ARE FOUND** guilty can **BE FINED**.

   ✓ Valuable records should always **BE KEPT** in a safe.

   If we do not know who spread rumors, we cannot say, and no one doubts who finds people guilty or fines them or who should keep records safe. So those passives are the right choice.

   Sometimes, of course, writers use the passive when they don't want readers to know who is responsible for an action, especially when the doer is the writer. For example,

   > Because the test was not done, the flaw was uncorrected.

   I will discuss the issue of intended impersonality in Lesson 12.

2. **Would the active or passive verb help your readers move more smoothly from one sentence to the next?** We depend on the beginning of a sentence to give us a context of what we know before we read what's new. A sentence confuses us when it opens with information that is new and unexpected. For example, in this next passage, the subject of the second sentence gives us new and complex information (boldfaced), before we read more familiar information that we recall from the previous sentence (italicized):

   > We must decide whether to improve education in the sciences alone or to raise the level of education across the whole curriculum. **The weight given to industrial competitiveness as opposed to the value we attach to the liberal arts** _{new information} WILL DETERMINE _{active verb} *our decision.* _{familiar information}

In the second sentence, the verb *determine* is in the active voice, *will determine* our decision. But we could read the sentence more easily if it were passive, because the passive would put the short, familiar information (*our decision*) first and the new and complex information last, the order we all prefer:

✓ We must decide whether to improve education in the sciences alone or raise the level of education across the whole curriculum. *Our decision*_{familiar information} WILL BE DETERMINED_{passive verb} **by the weight we give to industrial competiveness as opposed to the value we attach to the liberal arts.** _{new information}

I discuss where to put old and new information in a sentence in the next lesson.

3. **Would the active or passive give readers a more consistent and appropriate point of view?** The writer of this next passage reports the end of World War II in Europe from the point of view of the Allies. To do so, she uses active verbs to make the Allies a consistent sequence of subjects:

✓ By early 1945, *the Allies* HAD essentially DEFEATED _{active} Germany; all that remained was a bloody climax. *American, French, British, and Russian forces* HAD BREACHED _{active} its borders and WERE BOMBING _{active} it around the clock. But *they* HAD not yet SO DEVASTATED _{active} Germany as to destroy its ability to resist.

Had she wanted to explain history from the German point of view, she would have used passive verbs to make Germany the subject/character:

✓ By early 1945, *Germany* HAD essentially BEEN DEFEATED; _{passive} all that remained was a bloody climax. *Its borders* HAD BEEN BREACHED, _{passive} and *it* WAS BEING BOMBED _{passive} around the clock. *It* HAD not BEEN SO DEVASTATED, _{passive} however, that *it* could not RESIST. _{active}

Some writers switch from one character to another for no apparent reason. Avoid this:

By early 1945, *the Allies* had essentially defeated Germany. *Its borders* had been breached, and *they* were bombing it around the clock. *Germany* was not so devastated, however, that *the Allies* would meet with no resistance. Though *Germany's population* was demoralized, *the Allies* still attacked German cities from the air.

Pick a point of view and stick to it.

Here's the point: Many writers use the passive verb too often, but it has important uses. Use it in these contexts:

- You don't know who did an action, readers don't care, or you don't want them to know.

- You want to shift a long and complex bundle of information to the end of its sentence, especially when it also lets you move to its beginning a chunk of information that is shorter, more familiar, and therefore easier to understand.

- You want to focus your readers' attention on one or another character.

Exercise 4.2

In the following, change all active verbs into passives, and all passives into actives. Which sentences improve? Which do not? (In the first two, active verbs that could be passive are italicized; verbs already passive are boldfaced.)

1. Independence is **gained** by those on welfare when skills are **learned** that the marketplace *values*.

2. Different planes of the painting are **noticed,** because their colors are **set** against a background of shades of gray that are **laid** on in layers that cannot be **seen** unless the surface is **examined** closely.

3. In this article, it is argued that the Vietnam War was fought to extend influence in Southeast Asia and was not ended until it was made clear that the United States could not defeat North Vietnam unless atomic weapons were used.

4. Science education will not be improved in this nation to a level sufficient to ensure that American industry will be supplied with skilled workers and researchers until more money is provided to primary and secondary schools.

5. The first part of Bierce's "An Occurrence at Owl Creek Bridge" is presented in a dispassionate way. In the first paragraph, two sentinels are described in detail, but the line, "It did not appear to be the duty of these two men to know what was occurring at the center of the bridge" takes emotion away from them. In paragraph 2, a description is given of the surroundings and spectators, but no feeling is betrayed because the language used is neutral and unemotional. This entire section is presented as devoid of emotion even though it is filled with details.

The "Objective" Passive vs. *I/We*

Some scholarly writers claim that they should not use a first-person subject, because they need to create an objective point of view, something like this:

> Based on the writers' verbal intelligence, prior knowledge, and essay scores, their essays **were analyzed** for structure and evaluated for richness of concepts. The subjects **were** then **divided** into a high- or low-ability group. Half of each group **was** randomly **assigned** to a treatment group or to a placebo group.

Contrary to that claim, academic and scientific writers use the active voice and the first-person *I* and *we* regularly. These next passages come from articles in respected journals:

✓ This paper is concerned with two problems. How can **we** best handle in a transformational grammar certain restrictions that . . ., To illustrate, **we** may cite . . ., **we** shall show . . .

✓ Since the pituitary-adrenal axis is activated during the acute phase response, **we** have investigated the potential role . . . Specifically, **we** have studied the effects of interleukin-1 . . .

Here are the first few words from several consecutive sentences from *Science*, a journal of great prestige:

✓ **We** examine . . ., **We** compare . . ., **We** have used . . ., Each has been weighted . . ., **We** merely take . . ., They are subject . . ., **We** use . . ., Efron and Morris describe . . ., **We** observed . . ., **We** might find . . .

> —John P. Gilbert, Bucknam McPeek, and Frederick Mosteller,
> "Statistics and Ethics in Surgery and Anesthesia," *Science*

It is not true that academic writers always avoid the first person *I* or *we*.

Passives, Characters, and Metadiscourse

When academic writers do use the first person, however, they use it in certain ways. Look at the verbs in the passages above. There are two kinds:

• One kind refers to research activities: *examine, observe, measure, record, use.* Those verbs are usually in the passive voice: *The subjects were observed . . .*

• The other kind of verb refers not to the subject matter or the research, but to the writer's own writing and thinking: *cite, show, inquire.* These verbs are often active and in the first person: *We will show* . . . They are examples of what is called METADISCOURSE. Metadiscourse is the language you use when you refer not to the substance of your ideas, but to yourself, your reader, or your writing:

- your thinking and act of writing: *We/I will explain, show, argue, claim, deny, suggest, contrast, add, expand, summarize* . . .

- your readers' actions: *consider now, as you recall, look at the next example* . . .

- the logic and form of what you have written: *first, second; to begin; therefore, however, consequently* . . .

Metadiscourse appears most often in introductions, where writers announce their intentions. They typically use the first person: *I claim that* . . . , *I will show* . . . , *We begin by* . . . , and again at the end, when they summarize: *I have argued* . . . , *I have shown* . . .

On the other hand, scholarly writers rarely use the first person to describe specific actions they performed as *part* of their research:

> To determine if monokines elicited an adrenal steroidogenic response, **I** ADDED preparations of . . .

The writer of the original sentence used a passive verb, *were added*, to name an action that anyone can perform, not just the writer:

> To determine if monokines elicited a response, **preparations** . . . WERE ADDED.

A passive sentence like that, however, can create a problem: its writer dangled a modifier. You dangle a modifier when an introductory phrase has an *implied* subject that differs from the *explicit* subject in the following or preceding clause. In that example, the implied subject of the infinitive verb *determine* is *I* or *we: I determine* or *we determine*.

> [So that **I** could] determine if monokines elicited a response, preparations WERE ADDED.

But that implied subject, *I*, differs from the *explicit* subject of the clause it introduces—***preparations*** *were added*. When the two differ, the modifier dangles. Writers of scientific prose use this pattern so often, though, that it has become standard usage in their community.

I might note that this impersonal "scientific" style is a modern development. In his "New Theory of Light and Colors" (1672),

Sir Isaac Newton wrote this charming first-person account of an experiment:

> I procured a triangular glass prism, to try therewith the celebrated phenomena of colors. And for that purpose, having darkened my laboratory, and made a small hole in my window shade, to let in a convenient quantity of the sun's light, I placed my prism at the entrance, that the light might be thereby refracted to the opposite wall. It was at first a very pleasing diversion to view the vivid and intense colors produced thereby.

QUICK TIP: Some teachers prohibit the use of *I* everywhere in the writing of their students not because it is wrong, but because inexperienced writers begin too many sentences with *I think . . ., I believe . . .*, and so on. Others forbid *I* because they want to discourage students from writing a narrative account of their thinking: *First I read . . ., Then I considered . . .* On those two occasions, follow their advice.

Here's the point: Some writers and editors avoid the first person by using the passive everywhere, but deleting an *I* or *we* doesn't make a researcher's thinking more objective. We know that behind those impersonal sentences are still flesh-and-blood people doing, thinking, and writing. In fact, the first-person *I* and *we* are common in scholarly prose when used with verbs that name actions unique to the writer.

Exercise 4.3

The verbs in 1 through 4 below are passive, but two could be active because they are metadiscourse verbs that would take first-person subjects. Revise the passive verbs that should be changed into active verbs. Then go through each sentence again and revise nominalizations into verbs where appropriate.

1. It is believed that a lack of understanding about the risks of alcohol is a cause of student bingeing.
2. The model has been subjected to extensive statistical analysis.

3. Success in exporting more crude oil for hard currency is suggested here as the cause of the improvement of the Russian economy.

4. The creation of a database is being considered, but no estimate has been made in regard to the potential of its usefulness.

The verbs in 5 through 8 are active, but some of them should be passive because they are not metadiscourse verbs. Revise in other ways that seem appropriate.

5. In Section IV, I argue that the indigenous peoples engaged in overcultivation of the land leading to its exhaustion as a food-producing area.

6. Our intention in this book is to help readers achieve an understanding not only of the differences in grammar between Arabic and English but also the differences in worldview as reflected by Arabic vocabulary.

7. To make an evaluation of changes in the flow rate, I made a comparison of the current rate with the original rate on the basis of figures I had compiled with figures that Jordan had collected.

8. We performed the tissue rejection study on the basis of methods developed with our discovery of increases in dermal sloughing as a result of cellular regeneration.

Exercise 4.4

In these sentences, change passive verbs into actives only where you think it will improve the sentence. If necessary, invent a rhetorical situation to account for your choice of active or passive. (Different answers are correct for this one.)

1. Your figures were analyzed to determine their accuracy. Results will be announced when it is thought appropriate.

2. Home mortgage loans now are made for thirty years. With the price of housing at inflated levels, those loans cannot be paid off in a shorter time.

3. The author's impassioned narrative style is abandoned and a cautious treatment of theories of conspiracy is presented. But when the narrative line is picked up again, he invests his prose with the same vigor and force.

4. Many arguments were advanced against Darwinian evolution in the nineteenth century because basic assumptions about our place in the world were challenged by it. No longer were humans defined as privileged creatures but rather as a product of natural forces.

5. For many years, federal regulations concerning wiretapping have been enforced. Only recently have looser restrictions been imposed on the circumstances that warrant it.

In these sentences, change passives to actives where appropriate and change nominalizations into verbs. Invent characters where necessary.

6. It is my belief that the social significance of smoking receives its clearest explication through an analysis of peer interaction among adolescents. In particular, studies should be made of the manner in which interactive behavior is conditioned by social class.

7. These directives are written in a style of maximum simplicity as a result of an attempt at more effective communication with employees with limited reading skills.

8. The ability of the human brain to arrive at solutions to human problems has been undervalued because studies have not been done that would be considered to have scientific reliability.

Exercise 4.5

The excerpt below is from an actual letter from the chancellor of a state university to parents of students. Except for the second word, *you,* why is the first part so impersonal? Why is the last part more personal? Change the first part so that you name in subjects whoever performs an action. Then change the second part to eliminate all characters. How do the two parts now differ? Have you improved the letter? This exercise raises the question of deliberate misdirection, an issue we'll cover in Lesson 12.

> As you probably have heard, the U of X campus has been the scene of a number of incidents of racial and sexual harassment over the last several weeks. The fact that similar incidents have occurred on campuses around the country does not make them any less offensive when they take place here. Of the ten to twelve incidents that have been reported since early October, most have involved graffiti or spoken insults. In only two cases was any physical contact made, and in neither case was anyone injured.
>
> U of X is committed to providing its students with an environment where they can live, work, and study without fear of being taunted or harassed because of their race, gender, religion, or ethnicity. I have made it clear that bigotry and intolerance will not be permitted and that U of X's commitment to diversity is unequivocal. We are also taking steps to improve security in campus housing. We at U of X are proud of this university's tradition of diversity . . .

NOUN + NOUN + NOUN

One more stylistic choice does not directly involve characters and actions, but we discuss it here because it can distort a sentence so that the form of an idea fails to match the grammar of its expression. It is the long compound noun phrase:

> Early *childhood thought disorder misdiagnosis* often results from unfamiliarity with recent *research literature* describing such conditions. This paper is a review of seven recent studies in which are findings of particular relevance to *pre-adolescent hyperactivity diagnosis* and to *treatment modalities* involving *medication maintenance level evaluation procedures*.

Some grammarians claim we should never modify one noun with another, but that would rule out common phrases such as *stone wall, student center, space shuttle,* and many other useful terms.

But strings of nouns feel lumpy, so avoid them, especially ones you invent. When you find a compound noun of your own invention, revise, especially when it includes nominalizations. Reverse the order of words and find prepositions to connect them:

1	2	3	4	5
early	childhood	thought	disorder	misdiagnosis
misdiagnose	disordered	thought	in early	childhood
5	4	3	1	2

Re-assembled, it looks like this:

> Physicians misdiagnose[5] disordered[4] thought[3] in young[1] children[2] because they are unfamiliar with recent literature on the subject.

If, however, a long compound noun includes a technical term in your field, keep that part of the compound and unpack the rest:

> Physicians misdiagnose[5] thought disorders[3,4] in young[1] children[2] because they are unfamiliar with recent literature on the subject.

Exercise 4.6

Revise the compound noun phrases in 1 through 4.

1. The plant safety standards committee discussed recent air quality regulation announcements.
2. Diabetic patient blood pressure reduction may be brought about by renal depressor application.

3. The goal of this article is to describe text comprehension processes and recall protocol production.

4. On the basis of these principles, we may now attempt to formulate narrative information extraction rules.

In these, unpack compound nouns and revise nominalizations.

5. This paper is an investigation into information processing behavior involved in computer human cognition simulation.

6. Enforcement of guidelines for new automobile tire durability must be a Federal Trade Commission responsibility.

7. The Social Security program is a monthly income floor guarantee based on a lifelong contribution schedule.

8. Based on training needs assessment reviews and on office site visits, there was the identification of concepts and issues that can be used in our creation of an initial staff questionnaire instrument.

A LAST POINT: THE PROFESSIONAL VOICE

Every group expects its members to show that they accept its values by adopting its distinctive voice. The apprentice banker must learn not only to think and look like one, but to speak and write like one, as well. Too often, though, aspiring professionals think they join the club only when they write in the club's most complex technical language. It is an exclusionary style that erodes the trust a civil society depends on, especially in a world where information and expertise are now the means to power and control.

It is true that some research can never be made clear to intelligent lay readers—but less often than many researchers think. Here is an excerpt from Talcott Parsons, a social scientist who was as revered for his influence on his field as he was ridiculed for the opacity of his prose.

> Apart from theoretical conceptualization there would appear to be no method of selecting among the indefinite number of varying kinds of factual observation which can be made about a concrete phenomenon or field so that the various descriptive statements about it articulate into a coherent whole, which constitutes an "adequate," a "determinate" description. Adequacy in description is secured insofar as determinate and verifiable answers can be given to all the scientifically important questions involved. What questions are important is largely determined by the logical structure of the generalized conceptual scheme which, implicitly or explicitly, is employed.

We can make that clearer to moderately well-educated readers:

> Without a theory, scientists have no way to select from everything they could say about a subject only that which they can fit into a coherent whole that would be an "adequate" or "determinate" description. Scientists describe something "adequately" only when they can verify answers to all the questions they think are important. They decide what questions are important based on their implicit or explicit theories.

And we could make even it more concise:

> Whatever you describe, you need a theory to fit its parts into a whole. You need a theory to decide even what questions to ask and to verify their answers.

My versions lose the nuances of Parsons's passage and the last one loses some of its content, but his excruciating density numbs all but his most masochistically dedicated readers. Most readers would accept the tradeoff.

Here's the point: When you read or write a style that seems complex, you must determine whether it needs to be so complex to express complex ideas precisely. A difficult style can needlessly complicate complex ideas as easily as simple ones. Einstein said that everything should be made as simple as possible, but no simpler. Accordingly, a style should be as complex as necessary, *but no more*.

If you detect a needlessly complex style **when you read**, look for characters and actions so that you can unravel for yourself the complexity the writer needlessly inflicted on you. **When you write**, use the same tools to detect when you are guilty of gratuitous complexity and, if you are, revise. When you do, you follow the Writer's Golden Rule: Write to others as you would have others write to you.

Summing Up

1. Readers judge prose to be clear when subjects of sentences name characters and verbs name actions.

Fixed	Subject	Verb	———
Variable	Character	Action	———

2. If you tell a story in which you make abstract nominalizations its main characters and subjects, use as few other nominalizations as you can:

> A *nominalization* is a **replacement** of a verb by a noun, often resulting in **displacement** of characters from subjects by nouns.

> ✓ When *a nominalization* REPLACES a verb with a noun, *it* often DISPLACES characters from subjects.

3. Use a passive if the agent of an action is self-evident:

> *The voters* REELECTED the president with 54 percent of the vote.

> ✓ *The president* WAS REELECTED with 54 percent of the vote.

4. Use a passive if it lets you replace a long subject with a short one:

> Research demonstrating the soundness of our reasoning and the need for action SUPPORTED *this decision.*

> ✓ *This decision* WAS SUPPORTED BY research demonstrating the soundness of our reasoning and the need for action.

5. Use a passive if it gives your readers a coherent sequence of subjects:

> ✓ By early 1945, *the Axis nations* had BEEN essentially DEFEATED; all that remained was a bloody climax. *The German borders* had BEEN BREACHED, and both *Germany and Japan* were being bombed around the clock. *Neither country*, though, had BEEN so DEVASTATED that *it* could not RESIST.

6. Use an active verb if it is a metadiscourse verb:

> The terms of the analysis must BE DEFINED.

> ✓ We must DEFINE the terms of the analysis.

7. When possible, rewrite long compound noun phrases:

> We discussed the **board**[1] **candidate**[2] **review**[3] **meeting**[4] **schedule**[5].

> ✓ We discussed the **schedule**[5] of **meetings**[4] to **review**[3] **candidates**[2] for the **board**[1].

5

Cohesion and Coherence

*If he would inform, he must advance regularly from Things
known to things unknown, distinctly without Confusion,
and the lower he begins the better. It is a common Fault in
Writers, to allow their Readers too much knowledge: They
begin with that which should be the Middle, and skipping
backwards and forwards, 'tis impossible for any one but he
who is perfect in the Subject before, to understand their Work,
and such an one has no Occasion to read it.*
—BENJAMIN FRANKLIN

*The two capital secrets in the art of prose composition are
these: first, the philosophy of transition and connection; or the
art by which one step in an evolution of thought is made to arise
out of another: all fluent and effective composition depends on the
connections; secondly, the way in which sentences are made to
modify each other; for the most powerful effects in written
eloquence arise out of this reverberation, as it were, from each
other in a rapid succession of sentences.*
—THOMAS DE QUINCEY

Understanding Coherence

So far, I've discussed clarity as if we could achieve it just by mapping characters and actions onto subjects and verbs. But readers need more than individually clear sentences before they think a whole passage seems *coherent*. These two passages, for example, say much the same thing but feel very different:

> 1a. The basis of our American democracy—equal opportunity for all—is being threatened by college costs that have been rising fast for the last several years. Increases in family income have been significantly outpaced by increases in tuition at our colleges and universities during that period. Only the children of the wealthiest families in our society will be able to afford a college education if this trend continues. Knowledge and intellectual skills, in addition to wealth, will divide us as a people, when that happens. Equal opportunity and the egalitarian basis of our democratic society could be eroded by such a divide.

> ✓ 1b. In the last several years, college costs have been rising so fast that they are now threatening the basis of our American democracy— equal opportunity for all. During that period, tuition has significantly outpaced increases in family income. If this trend continues, a college education will soon be affordable only by the children of the wealthiest families in our society. When that happens, we will be divided as a people not only by wealth, but by knowledge and intellectual skills. Such a divide will erode equal opportunity and the egalitarian basis of our democratic society.

The first seems choppy, even disorganized; the second seems to "hang together" better.

But like the word *clarity*, the words *choppy* and *disorganized* refer not to the words on the page, but to how we *feel* about them. What is it about the *arrangement* of words in (1a) that makes us feel we are moving through it in fits and starts? Why does (1b) seem to flow more easily? We base those judgments on two aspects of word order:

- We judge sequences of sentences to be *cohesive* depending on how each sentence ends and the next begins.

- We judge a whole passage to be *coherent* depending on how all the sentences in a passage cumulatively begin.

I'll discuss cohesion and one kind of coherence in this lesson, then say more about coherence in Lesson 11.

COHESION: A SENSE OF FLOW

In Lesson 4, we devoted a few pages (53–61) to that familiar advice, *Avoid passives*. If we always did, we would choose the active verb in sentence (2a) over the passive in (2b):

> 2a. The collapse of a dead star into a point perhaps no larger than a marble CREATES _{active} a black hole.

> 2b. A black hole IS CREATED _{passive} by the collapse of a dead star into a point perhaps no larger than a marble.

But we might choose otherwise when we put those sentences into this passage:

> ¹Some astonishing questions about the nature of the universe have been raised by scientists studying black holes in space. ²ᵃ/ᵇ[_____].
> ³So much matter compressed into so little volume changes the fabric of space around it in puzzling ways.

Here's the active sentence there:

> 1a. ¹Some astonishing questions about the nature of the universe have been raised by scientists studying black holes in space. ²ᵃThe collapse of a dead star into a point perhaps no larger than a marble creates a black hole. ³So much matter compressed into so little volume changes the fabric of space around it in puzzling ways.

And here's the passive:

> 1b. ¹Some astonishing questions about the nature of the universe have been raised by scientists studying black holes in space. ²ᵇA black hole is created by the collapse of a dead star into a point perhaps no larger than a marble. ³So much matter compressed into so little volume changes the fabric of space around it in puzzling ways.

Our sense of "flow" calls not for (2a), the sentence with the active verb, but for (2b), the one with the passive.

The reason is clear: the last four words of the first sentence introduce an important character—*black holes in space*. But with sentence (2a), the next concepts we hit are *collapsed stars* and *marbles*, information that seems to come out of nowhere:

> ¹Some astonishing questions about the nature of the universe have been raised by scientists studying <u>black holes in space</u>. ²ᵃ<u>The collapse of a dead star into a point perhaps no larger than a marble</u> creates . . .

If we follow sentence (1) with (2b), the sentence with the passive verb, we feel those sentences connect more smoothly, because now the first words in (2b) repeat what we just read at the end of (1):

> ¹. . . studying black holes in space. ²ᵇA black hole is created by the collapse of a dead star into <u>a point perhaps no larger than a marble</u>. ³<u>So much matter compressed into so little volume</u> changes the fabric of space around it in puzzling ways. . . .

Note that the passive also lets us put at the *end* of sentence (2b) words that connect it to the *beginning* of sentence (3):

> ¹. . . black holes in space. ²ᵇ<u>A black hole</u> is created by the collapse of a dead star into **a point perhaps no larger than a marble**. ³**So much matter compressed into so little volume** changes the fabric of space around it in puzzling ways.

Here's the point: Sentences are *cohesive* when the last few words of one set up information that appears in the first few words of the next. That's what gives us our experience of flow. And in fact, that's the biggest reason the passive is in the language: to let us arrange sentences so that they flow from one to the next easily. We can integrate that insight with our principles about subject and characters, and verbs and actions.

Fixed			
Variable	Familiar		
Fixed	Subject	Verb	———
Variable	Character	Action	———

Diagnosis and Revision

That principle of reading suggests two principles of writing. They are mirror images. The first is this:

1. **Begin sentences with information familiar to your readers.**
   Readers get that familiar information from two sources:
   - First, they remember words from the sentences they just read.

That's why the beginning of (2b) coheres with the end of (1) and why the beginning of (3) coheres with the end of (2b):

[1]. . . questions about the nature of the universe have been raised by scientists studying [black holes in space. [2b]A black hole] is created by the collapse of a dead star into [a point perhaps no larger than a marble. [3]So much matter compressed into so little volume] changes the fabric of space . . .

- Second, readers bring to a sentence a general knowledge of its subject. We would not have been surprised, for example, if the next sentence in that paragraph about black holes had begun like this:

. . . changes the fabric of space around it in puzzling ways. [4]Astronomers have reported that . . .

The word *Astronomers* did not appear in the preceding sentences, but since we are reading about space and black holes, we wouldn't be surprised by a reference to them.

The second principle is the flip side of the first.

2. **End sentences with information that readers cannot anticipate.** Readers always prefer to read what's easy before what's hard, and what's familiar and simple is easier to understand than what's new and complex.

You can see when others fail to observe the old-before-new principle more easily than when you do, because after you've worked on your own sentences for a while, everything in them seems familiar— to you. But hard as it is to distinguish old from new in your own writing, you have to try, because readers want to begin sentences with information that is familiar to *them,* and only then move on to information that is new.

Here's the point: In every *sequence* of sentences you write, you have to balance principles that make individual sentences clear and principles that make a passage cohesive. *But in that tradeoff, give priority to helping readers create a sense of cohesive flow.* That means starting sentences with familiar information. Fortunately, the principle of old before new cooperates with the principle of characters as subjects. Once you mention your main characters, readers take them as familiar information. So when characters are up front, so is familiar information.

QUICK TIP: Writers often refer to something in a previous sentence with words such as *this, these, that, those, another, such, second,* or *more.* When you use any of those signals, try to put them at or close to the beginning of a sentence:

> How to calculate credits for classes taken in a community colleges is **another** issue that we must consider.

> ✓ **Another** issue that we must consider is how to calculate credits for classes taken in a community college.

Exercise 5.1

Revise these two passages to improve their old-new flow by putting old information first in each sentence. In (1), I boldface the words that I feel are old information.

1. Two aims—the recovery of the American economy and the modernization of America into a military power—were **in the president's mind when he assumed his office.** The drop in unemployment figures and inflation, and the increase in the GNP testifies to **his success in the first.** But our increased involvement in international conflict without any clear set of political goals indicates **less success with the second.** Nevertheless, increases in the military budget and a good deal of saber rattling **pleased the American voter.**

2. The components of Abco's profitability, particularly growth in Asian markets, will be highlighted in our report to demonstrate its advantages versus competitors. Revenue returns along several dimensions—product type, end-use, distribution channels, etc.—will provide a basis for this analysis. Likely growth prospects of Abco's newest product lines will depend most on its ability in regard to the development of distribution channels in China, according to our projections. A range of innovative strategies will be needed to support the introduction of new products.

COHERENCE: A SENSE OF THE WHOLE

When you create cohesive flow, you take the first step toward helping readers think your prose hangs together. But they will judge you to be a competent writer only when they feel that your writing is not just cohesive but *coherent*. It's easy to confuse the words *cohesion* and *coherence* because they sound alike.

- Think of *cohesion* as pairs of sentences fitting together in the way two pieces of a jigsaw puzzle do (recall the black hole sentences).
- Think of *coherence* as seeing what all the sentences in a piece of writing add up to, the way all the pieces in a puzzle add up to the picture on the box.

This next passage has good cohesive flow because we move from one sentence to the next without a hitch:

> Sayner, Wisconsin, is the snowmobile capital of the world. The buzzing of snowmobile engines fills the air, and their tank-like tracks crisscross the snow. The snow reminds me of Mom's mashed potatoes, covered with furrows I would draw with my fork. Her mashed potatoes usually make me sick—that's why I play with them. I like to make a hole in the middle of the potatoes and fill it with melted butter. This behavior has been the subject of long chats between me and my analyst.

Though we move from sentence to sentence easily, that passage as a whole is incoherent. (It was created by six different writers, one of whom wrote the first sentence, with the other five sequentially adding one sentence, knowing only the immediately preceding one.) It is incoherent for three reasons:

1. The subjects of the sentences are entirely unrelated.
2. The sentences share no common "themes" or ideas.
3. The paragraph has no one sentence that states what the whole passage supports or explains.

I will discuss that second point in the next lesson and the third one in Lesson 11. The rest of this lesson focuses on the first point, shared subjects.

Subjects, Topics, Grammar, and Coherence

For five hundred years, English teachers have defined *subject* in two ways:

1. the "doer" of the action
2. what a sentence is "about," its main topic

In Lessons 3 and 4, we saw why that first definition doesn't work: the subjects of many sentences are actions: *The **explosion** was loud.*

But also flawed is that second definition: *A subject is what a sentence is about.* It is flawed because often, the subject of a sentence doesn't state its main topic, the idea that the rest of the sentence "comments" on. That "topicalizing" function can be performed by other parts of a sentence.

For example, none of the main subjects in these sentences names their topics.

- The main subject of this sentence (italicized) is *it,* but the topic of the sentence is *your claim,* the object of the preposition *for:*

  It is impossible for **your claim** to be proved.

- The subject of this sentence is *I,* but its topic is *this question,* the object of *to:*

  In regard to **this question,** *I* believe more research is needed.

- The subject of this sentence is *it,* but its topic is *our proposal,* the subject of a verb in a subordinate clause:

  It is likely that **our proposal** will be accepted.

- The subject of this sentence is *no one,* but its topic is *such results,* a direct object shifted to the front for emphasis:

  Such results *no one* could have predicted.

QUICK TIP: When you start to **read** a passage whose ideas you expect to be difficult, skim it quickly to find its main characters. Then think about those characters before you begin reading carefully. What do you know about them? What other ideas do you associate with them? What would you expect to read about them? The more sharply you have characters in mind as you read, the more easily you will understand stories about them.

Diagnosing and Revising Topics

As with other issues of clarity, you can't predict how readers will judge the flow of your writing just by reading it, because you know it too well. You must analyze it more objectively. This passage feels choppy, out of focus, even disorganized:

> Consistent ideas toward the beginnings of sentences help readers understand what a passage is generally about. A sense of coherence arises when a sequence of topics comprises a narrow set of related ideas. But the context of each sentence is lost by seemingly random shifts of topics. Unfocused paragraphs result when that happens.

Here's how to diagnose its problems and revise it. You can diagnose and revise your own writing in the same way.

1. **Diagnose**

   a. Underline the first seven or eight words of every sentence in a passage, stopping when you hit a verb.

   b. If you can, underline the first five or six words of every clause in those sentences.

   > <u>Consistent ideas toward the beginnings of sentences</u>, especially in their subjects, help readers understand what a passage is generally about. <u>A sense of coherence</u> arises when a sequence of topics comprises a narrow set of related ideas. But <u>the context of each sentence</u> is lost by seemingly random shifts of topics. <u>Unfocused, even disorganized paragraphs</u> result when <u>that</u> happens.

2. **Analyze**

   a. Do the underlined words constitute a relatively small set of topics that name related ideas? Even if *you* see how they are related, will your readers? For that passage, the answer is no.

   b. Do the underlined words name the most important characters, real or abstract? Again, the answer is no.

3. **Rewrite**

   a. In most (not necessarily all) of your sentences, use subjects to name their topics.

   b. Put those subjects close to the beginning of the sentences.

Here is that passage revised, with the new topics boldfaced:

> **Readers** understand what a passage is generally about when **they** see consistent ideas toward the beginnings of sentences, especially in their subjects. **They** feel a passage is coherent when **they** read a sequence of topics that focuses on a narrow set of related ideas. But when **topics** seem to shift randomly, **readers** lose the context of each sentence. When **that** happens, **they** feel they are reading paragraphs that are unfocused and even disorganized.

QUICK TIP: When you start to draft a new section of your paper, list the characters you intend to write about. Include not just flesh-and-blood characters, but important concepts as well. *Before* you draft, think about each character for a moment. Try to picture the people or things on your list. What are they like? For a concept, think about the ideas you associate with it. Then as you draft, try to put those characters into the subjects of most of your sentences. If you do not mention one of those characters for several sentences, you may have gotten off track.

AVOIDING DISTRACTIONS AT THE BEGINNING OF A SENTENCE

It is hard to begin a sentence well. Readers want to get to a topic/subject quickly, but too often we begin sentences in ways that keep readers from getting there. It's called *throat clearing.* Throat-clearing typically begins with metadiscourse that connects a sentence to the previous one, with transitions such as *and, but, therefore:*

And therefore . . .

We then add a second kind of metadiscourse that expresses our attitude toward what is coming, words such as *fortunately, perhaps, allegedly, it is important to note, for the most part,* or *politically speaking:*

And therefore, it is important to note . . .

Then we indicate time, place, or manner:

And therefore, it is important to note that, in Eastern states since 1980 . . .

Only then do we get to the topic/subject:

And, therefore, it is important to note that, in Eastern states since 1980, **acid rain** has become a serious problem.

When you open several sentences like that, your readers have a hard time seeing not just what each sentence is about, but their cumulative focus that makes a whole passage coherent. When you find a sentence with lots of words before its subject/topic, revise:

✓ Since 1980, therefore, acid rain has become a political problem in the Eastern states.

> ***Here's the point:*** When you begin sentences, choose your topics carefully. Make most of them subjects of your sentences. They should be short, concrete, familiar words, and more often than not, they should name the main characters in your story. Most important, keep them consistent: do not vary your subjects for the sake of variety. Your topics should tell your readers what a passage is globally "about."

INTEGRATING THE PRINCIPLES

We can bring together these principles about old and new and strings of consistent topics with the principles about characters as subjects and actions as verbs (I'll fill in the empty boxes in Lesson 6):

Fixed	Topic		
Variable	Familiar		
Fixed	Subject	Verb	————
Variable	Character	Action	————

Exercise 5.2

Revise these passages to give them consistent topic strings. First determine the characters, then their actions. Then start each sentence with a character, and let the sentence take you where it wants to go. In (1), words that could be consistent subject/topics are boldfaced.

1. **Vegetation** covers the earth, except for those areas continuously covered with ice or utterly scorched by continual heat. Richly fertilized plains and river valleys are places where **plants** grow most richly, but also at the edge of perpetual snow in high mountains. The ocean and its edges as well as in and around lakes and swamps are **densely vegetated**. The cracks of busy city sidewalks have **plants** in them as well as in seemingly barren cliffs. Before humans existed, the earth was covered with **vegetation**, and the earth will have **vegetation** long after evolutionary history swallows us up.

2. The power to create and communicate a new message to fit a new experience is not a competence animals have in their natural states. Their genetic code limits the number and kind of messages that they can communicate. Information about distance, direction, source, and richness of pollen in flowers constitutes the only information that can be communicated by bees, for example. A limited repertoire of messages delivered in the same way, for generation after generation, is characteristic of animals of the same species, in all significant respects.

3. The importance of language skills in children's problem-solving ability was stressed by Jones (1985) in his paper on children's thinking. Improvement in nonverbal problem solving was reported to have occurred as a result of improvements in language skills. The use of previously acquired language habits for problem articulation and activation of knowledge previously learned through language are thought to be the cause of better performance. Therefore, systematic practice in the verbal formulation of nonlinguistic problems prior to attempts at their solution might be an avenue for exploration in the enhancement of problem solving in general.

Two Qualifications

Alleged Monotony

At this point, you may be conflicted by that common advice *Vary how you begin your sentences*. That's a bad idea, especially when you change subjects just to make them different. You may think a passage is monotonous if you see the same topic in several of its sentences *in your own prose*. But your readers are less likely to notice, because they will be focusing on your ideas.

On the other hand, you might revise if you find you have used exactly the same words for the same topics in exactly the same positions. This passage goes over the top in that kind of consistency:

> **"Moral climate"** is created when an objectivized moral standard for treating people is accepted by others. **Moral climate** results from norms of behavior that are accepted by society whereby if people conform they are socially approved of, or if they don't they are shunned. In this light, **moral climate** acts as a reason to refrain from saying or doing things that the community does not support. **A moral climate** encourages individuals to conform to a moral standard and apply that standard to their own circumstances.

In such passages, you can vary a few of the words that refer to a repeated topic:

> **"Moral climate"** is created. . . . **This climate** results. . . . In this light, **morality** acts. . . . **A moral climate** encourages. . . .

Be cautious, though: Most writers change topics too often.

Faked Cohesion

Some writers try to fake coherence by lacing their prose with conjunctions like *thus, therefore, however,* and so on, regardless of whether they signal real logical connections. An example:

> Because the press is the major medium of interaction between the president and the people, how it portrays him influences his popularity. **Therefore,** it should report on the president objectively. Both reporters and the president are human, **however,** subject to error and favoritism. **Also,** people act differently in public than they do in private. **Hence,** to understand a person, it is important to know the whole person, his environment, upbringing, and education. **Indeed,** from the correspondence with his family, we can learn much about Harry S. Truman, our thirty-third president.

Experienced writers use these connecting devices, but they depend more on the logical flow of their ideas. They are especially careful not to overuse words like *and, also, moreover, another,* and so on, words that say simply *Here's one more thing*. You need a *but* or *however* when you contradict or qualify what you just said, and you can use a *therefore* or *consequently* to wind up a line of reasoning. But avoid using words like these more than a few times a page. Your readers don't need them when your sentences are cohesive and the passage they constitute is coherent.

Exercise 5.3

Revise these passages to give them more consistent topic strings. First, decide who the main characters should be, then make them the subjects of verbs expressing important actions. In the first passage, I boldface topics so that you can see how inconsistent they are.

1. **Some potential threats** exist in the modern mass communications media, though there are many significant advantages. If **a powerful minority** should happen to control it, **public opinion** could be manipulated through biased reporting. And while

---

a wide knowledge of public affairs is a great advantage that results from national coverage, **divisiveness and factionalism** can be accentuated by connecting otherwise isolated, local conflicts into a single larger conflict as a result of showing that **conflicts about the same issues** are occurring in different places. It will always be true, of course, that **human nature** produces differences of opinion, but **the threat of faction and division** may be reinforced when **national coverage** publicizes uninformed opinions. According to some, **education** can suppress faction when **the true nature of conflicts** reaches the public through the media, but **history** has shown that as **much coverage** is given to people who encourage conflict as to people who try to remove conflict.

2. Some sort of palace revolt or popular revolution plagued seven of eight reigns of the Romanov line after Peter the Great. In 1722, achievement by merit was made the basis of succession when the principle of heredity was terminated by Peter. This resulted in many tsars' not appointing a successor before dying, including Peter. Ivan VI was less than two months old when appointed by Czarina Anna, but Elizabeth, daughter of Peter the Great, defeated Anna and ascended to the throne in 1741. Succession not dependent upon authority resulted in the boyars' regularly disputing who was to become sovereign. Male primogeniture became the law in 1797 when Paul I codified the law of succession. But conspirators strangled him (one of whom was probably his son, Alexander I).

3. Many issues other than science, domestic politics in particular, faced Truman when he was considering the Oppenheimer committee's recommendation to stop the hydrogen bomb project. A Sino-Soviet bloc had been proclaimed by Russia and China, so the Cold War was becoming an issue. Support for Truman's foreign policy was shrinking among Republican leaders in Congress. And the first Russian atom bomb test made the public demand a strong response from him. Truman's conclusion that he could not afford letting the public think that Russia had been allowed to be first in developing the most powerful weapon yet was an inevitable one. The risk in the Oppenheimer recommendation was worth taking according to some historians, but the political issues that Truman had to face were too powerful to ignore.

Exercise 5.4

The point of this exercise is to see that simply by changing subjects, you change the feel of a passage. In his essay, "Stranger in the Village," the African-American writer James Baldwin reflects on his relationship to European Christianity. In the first sentence of his essay, he makes the cathedral at Chartres the topic and a metaphorical character:

> **The cathedral at Chartres,** I have said, says something to the people of this village which **it** cannot say to me, but it is important to understand that **this cathedral** says something to me which **it** cannot say to them.

But in the second sentence, he switches the topic/subjects to the villagers, then to himself:

> Perhaps **they** are struck by the power of the spires, the glory of the windows; but **they** have known God, after all, longer than I have known him, and in a different way, and I am terrified . . .

Nothing forced him to choose those topics. He could have written this:

> I have said that I hear something from the cathedral at Chartres that **the people** of this village do not hear, but it is important to understand that . . .

Experiment with Baldwin's passage by changing its topics. First, focus on Baldwin (as above). Then revise a second time, focusing on the people of Chartres, then a third time focusing on the architecture. How does the feel of the passage change? Why did Baldwin make the choices he did, do you think? (No one can know the right answer.) Here is his passage. I boldface topics; you will not be able to change them all.

> **The cathedral at Chartres,** I have said, says something to the people of this village which **it** cannot say to me, but it is important to understand that **this cathedral** says something to me which **it** cannot say to them. Perhaps **they** are struck by the power of the spires, the glory of the windows; but **they** have known God, after all, longer than I have known him, and in a different way, and I am terrified by the slippery bottomless well to be found in the crypt, down which **heretics** were hurled to death, and by the obscene, inescapable gargoyles jutting out of the stone and seeming to say that **God and the devil** can never be divorced. I doubt that **the villagers** think of the devil when **they** face a cathedral because **they** have never been identified with the devil. But I must accept the status which **myth,** if nothing else, gives me in the West before I can hope to change the myth.

What does this exercise suggest about "natural" connections between characters and subjects? What does it imply about how we understand who's responsible for what actions? How much can a writer control how we decide who's responsible for the real action in the world? Which is more accurate, *I am teaching you* or *you are learning from me*? Does it matter? We return to these questions in Lesson 12.

SUMMING UP

We can sum up this lesson in this model:

Fixed	Topic	
Variable	Familiar	
Fixed	Subject	Verb	————
Variable	Character	Action	————

It represents two principles:

1. Begin sentences with subjects that communicate old information, information that your readers are familiar with:

   > The number of dead in the Civil War exceeded all other wars in American history combined. A reason for the lingering animosity between North and South today is **the memory of this terrible carnage**.

   > ✓ Of all the wars in American history, none has exceeded the Civil War in the number of dead. **The memory of this terrible carnage** is one reason for the lingering animosity between North and South today.

2. Through a series of sentences, keep your topics short and reasonably consistent:

   > **Competition by Asian companies with American companies in the Pacific** is the first phase of this study. **Labor costs and the ability to introduce new products quickly in particular** are examined. **A plan that will show American industry how to restructure its facilities** will be developed from this study.

   > ✓ In the first phase of this study, **we** examine how **Asian companies** compete with American companies in the Pacific region. **We** examine in particular their labor costs and ability to introduce new products quickly. **We** develop from this study a **plan** that will show **American industry** how to restructure its facilities.

Lesson

6

Emphasis

*"Begin at the beginning," the King said, gravely, "and go on
till you come to the end; then stop."*
—LEWIS CARROLL

Beginning and end shake hands with each other.
—GERMAN PROVERB

In the end is my beginning.
—T. S. ELIOT

All's well that ends well.
—WILLIAM SHAKESPEARE

UNDERSTANDING HOW SENTENCES END

If you consistently write sentences whose subjects/topics name a
few central characters and then join them to strong verbs, you'll
likely get the rest of the sentence right, and in the process create a
passage that is both cohesive and coherent. But if the first few
words of a sentence are worth special attention, so are the last
few, because how you end a sentence determines how readers
judge both its clarity and its strength. In this lesson, we address
clarity first, then strength, then how the right emphasis on the
right words can contribute to coherence.

When readers build up momentum in the first nine or ten words of a sentence, they get through complicated material that follows more easily. Compare:

> 1a. A sociometric and actuarial analysis of Social Security revenues and disbursements for the last six decades to determine changes in projecting deficits is the subject of this study.

> ✓ 1b. In this study, we analyze Social Security's revenues and disbursements for the last six decades, using sociometric and actuarial criteria to determine changes in projecting deficits.

As we start (1a), we struggle to understand its technical terms at the same time we are hacking through a subject twenty-two words long. In (1b), we go through just five words to get past a subject and verb and twelve more before we hit a term that might slow us up. By that point we have enough momentum to carry us through the complexity to its end. In short, in (1a), we hit the complexity at the beginning; in (1b), we don't hit it until near the end, where we can handle it better.

Complex Meaning

In Lesson 5 we saw that readers prefer sentences whose beginnings are grammatically simple, with any grammatical complexity at the end. Another kind of complexity is in the meanings of words, especially technical terms. Compare these two passages:

> 3a. The role of calcium blockers in the control of cardiac irregularity can be seen through an understanding of the role of calcium in the activation of muscle cells. The regulatory proteins actin, myosin, tropomyosin, and troponin make up the sarcomere. The energy-producing, or ATPase, protein myosin makes up its thick filament, while actin, tropomyosin, and troponin make up its thin filament. Interaction of myosin and actin triggers muscle contraction.

> ✓ 3b. When a muscle contracts, it uses calcium. If we can understand how calcium affects muscle contraction, we can explain how the drugs called "calcium blockers" control cardiac irregularity. The basic unit of muscle contraction is the sarcomere. It has two filaments, one thin and one thick. Those filaments consist of four proteins that regulate contraction: actin, tropomyosin, and troponin in the thin filament and myosin in the thick one. Muscles contract when a protein in the thin filament, actin, interacts with the protein in the thick filament, myosin, an energy-producing or ATPase protein.

Both passages use the same technical terms, but (3b) is clearer to those who know nothing about the chemistry of muscles.

Those passages differ in two ways. First, information that is only implicit in (3a) is stated explicitly in (3b):

> 3a. The regulatory proteins actin, myosin, tropomyosin, and troponin make up the sarcomere. The energy-producing, or ATPase, protein myosin makes up. . . .

> ✓ 3b. The basic unit of muscle contraction is the sarcomere. It has two filaments, one thin and one thick. Those filaments consist of. . . .

More important, I moved the technical terms from the beginning of the sentences in (3a) to the end of the sentences in (3b). Note how almost all the technical terms in (3a) are toward the beginnings of their sentences:

> 3a. The role of **calcium blockers** in the control of **cardiac irregularity** can be seen through an understanding of the role of calcium in the activation of muscle cells.

> The **regulatory proteins actin, myosin, tropomyosin, and troponin** make up the **sarcomere**.

> The **energy-producing, or ATPase, protein myosin** makes up its thick filament, while **actin, tropomyosin, and troponin** make up its thin filament.

> **Interaction of myosin and actin** triggers muscle contraction.

In (3b), those technical terms appear at the ends of their sentences:

> . . . uses **calcium.**

> . . . "calcium blockers" control **cardiac irregularity**

> . . . is the **sarcomere.**

> . . . **actin, tropomyosin, and troponin** in the thin filament and **myosin** in the thick one.

> . . . **myosin**, an **energy-producing or ATPase protein.**

These principles work for prose intended even for professional readers. In this next passage, from the *New England Journal of Medicine*, the writer deliberately uses metadiscourse to construct the second sentence just to get a new technical term at its end:

> The incubation of peripheral-blood lymphocytes with a lymphokine, interleukin-2, generates lymphoid cells that can lyse fresh, noncultured, natural-killer-cell-resistant tumor cells but not normal cells. *We term these cells* **lymphokine-activated killer (LAK) cells.**

Here's the point: Your readers want you to use the end of your sentences to help them manage two kinds of difficulty:

- long and complex phrases and clauses
- new information, particularly unfamiliar technical terms

In general, your sentences should begin with elements that are relatively short: a short introductory phrase or clause, followed by a short, concrete subject, followed by a verb expressing a specific action. After the verb, the sentence can go on for several lines, if it is well constructed (see Lessons 8 and 9). The general principle is to carry the reader not from complexity to simplicity, but from simplicity to complexity. We can integrate that principle with our others:

Fixed	Topic	
Variable	Short, simple, familiar	Long, complex, new
Fixed	Subject	Verb	———
Variable	Character	Action	———

ANOTHER NEW TERM: *STRESS*

In the last lesson, we said that an important position in the *psychological* geography of a sentence is its first few words, because they name the topic of a sentence, its *psychological* as opposed to subject (see pp. 72–75). In this lesson, I've been discussing the end of a sentence in general, but its last few words are particularly important. You can sense that when you hear your voice rise at the end of a sentence to emphasize one syllable more strongly than the others:

   . . . more strongly than the ó-thers.

We have the same experience when reading silently.

   We'll call this most emphatic part of a sentence its *stress* and add it to our last box. How you manage the emphasis in that stress position helps establish the voice readers hear in your prose, because if you

end a sentence on words that carry little meaning, your sentence will
seem to end weakly.

> Global warming could raise sea levels to a point where much of the
> world's low-lying coastal areas would disappear, **according to most
> atmospheric scientists.**

> ✓ According to most atmospheric scientists, global warming could raise
> sea levels to a point where much of the world's low-lying coastal areas
> **would disappear.**

Fixed	Topic		Stress
Variable	Short, simple, familiar	Long, complex, new	
Fixed	Subject	Verb	———
Variable	Character	Action	———

In Lesson 4, we saw how to revise subject/topics to create different
points of view (pp. 54–56). You can create different stylistic effects
by managing how you end your sentences.

Compare these next passages. One was written to blame an
American president for being weak with Iran on arms control. The
other is a revision that stresses Iran. The ends of the sentences tell
you which is which:

> 1a. The administration has blurred an issue central to nuclear arms
> control, **the issue of verification.** Irresponsible charges, innuendo,
> and leaks have submerged **serious problems with Iranian compli-
> ance.** The objective, instead, should be not to exploit these concerns
> in order to further poison our relations, repudiate existing agree-
> ments, or, worse still, terminate arms control altogether, but to **insist
> on compliance and clarify questionable behavior.**

> 1b. The issue of verification—so central to nuclear arms control—has
> been **blurred by the administration.** Serious problems with Iranian
> compliance have been submerged in **irresponsible charges, innuendo,
> and leaks.** The objective, instead, should be to clarify questionable
> behavior and insist on compliance—not to exploit these concerns in
> order to **further poison our relations, repudiate existing agree-
> ments, or, worse still, terminate arms control altogether.**

> *Here's the point:*   Just as you look at the first few words of
> your sentences for focus, you can look at the last few words
> for emphasis. You can revise a sentence to emphasize particular
> words that you want readers to hear stressed and thereby
> note as particularly significant.

DIAGNOSIS AND REVISION

If you have managed your subjects and topics well, you will almost
by default emphasize the right words at the end of your sentences.
But there are some ways to revise just for that purpose.

Four Tactical Revisions

1. **Trim the end.**

   Sociobiologists claim that our genes control our social behavior **in
   the way we act in situations we are in every day.**

   Since *social behavior* means *the way we act in situations . . . ,*
   we drop everything after *behavior:*

   ✓ Sociobiologists claim that our genes **control our social behavior.**

2. **Shift peripheral ideas to the left.**

   The data offered to prove ESP are too weak, **for the most part.**
   ✓ **For the most part,** the data offered to prove ESP are **too weak.**

   Particularly avoid ending with anticlimactic metadiscourse:

   Job opportunities in computer programming are getting scarcer, **it
   must be remembered.**
   ✓ **It must be remembered** that job opportunities in computer programming are getting scarcer.

3. **Shift new information to the right.**   A more common way to
   manage stress is by moving new information to the end of a
   sentence.

   Questions about the ethics of withdrawing intravenous feeding
   are *more difficult* [than something just mentioned].
   ✓ *More difficult* [than something just mentioned] are **questions
   about the ethics of withdrawing intravenous feeding.**

4. **Avoid repeating words at the end.** This is a fine point: a
sentence can end flatly if you repeat a word that you used just a
few words before at the end of a sentence, because the voice we
hear in our mind's ear trails off at the end of such a sentence. If
you read aloud the preceding sentence and this one, you can
hear how the repetition causes a drooping sound at the end of
each sentence. To avoid that kind of flat ending, rewrite or use
a pronoun instead of repeating the word. For example:

> A sentence will seem to end flatly if you use a word at its end that
> you used just a few words before, because when you repeat that
> word your voice trials off. Instead of repeating the noun, use a
> **pronoun.** The reader will at least hear emphasis on the word just
> **before it**.

Five Syntactic Devices to Emphasize the Right Words

There are several syntactic devices that let you manage where in a
sentence you stress units of new information.

1. **Passives (for the last time).** A passive verb lets you flip a subject and object. In the next two sentences, we revise the active
verb into a passive to get the concept of genes influencing
behavior closer to the stress position:

> Some sociobiologists claim that **our genes** influence active aspects
> of behavior that we think are learned. **Our genes,** for example,
> seem to determine . . .

> ✓ Some sociobiologists claim that aspects of behavior that we think
> are learned are in fact influenced _{passive} **by our genes. Our genes,**
> for example, seem to determine . . .

As we've seen, the passive is in the language so that we can get
old and new information in the right order.

2. ***There.*** Some editors discourage *there is/there are* constructions as wordy, but they let you shift a subject to after its verb
to emphasize it. Compare:

> **Several syntactic devices** let you manage where in a sentence
> you locate units of new information.

> ✓ *There are* **several syntactic devices** that let you manage where in
> a sentence you locate units of new information.

Experienced writers commonly begin a paragraph or section with
there to introduce new topics and concepts that they develop in
sentences that follow (for more on introducing new concepts, see
Lesson 11). Used too often, of course, it seems weak and wordy.

3. ***What*-shift.** This is another device that shifts a part of the sentence to the right, thereby emphasizing it more:

> We need a monetary policy that would end fluctuations in money supply, unemployment, and inflation.
>
> ✓ **What** we need **is** a monetary policy that would end fluctuations in money supply, unemployment, and inflation.

4. ***It*-shift.** When you have a subject consisting of a long NOUN CLAUSE, you can move it to the end of the sentence and start with an *it:*

> **That oil prices would be set by OPEC** once seemed inevitable.
>
> ✓ *It* once seemed inevitable **that oil prices would be set by OPEC.**

5. ***Not only X, but Y (as well).*** In this next pair, note how the *but* emphasizes the last element of the pair:

> We must clarify these issues and **develop trust.**
>
> ✓ We must *not only* clarify these issues, *but* **develop trust.**

Unless you have reason to emphasize the negative, end with the positive:

> The point is to highlight our success, **not to emphasize our failures.**
>
> ✓ The point is not to emphasize our failures but **to highlight our success.**

One characteristic of especially elegant prose is how writers use a handful of special rhetorical figures to end their sentences. I will discuss those devices in Lesson 9.

QUICK TIP: You can easily check whether you have stressed the right words by reading your sentences aloud: As you speak the last few words, raise your voice and tap the table with your fingers. If you've stressed the wrong words, your voice and table thumping will feel wrong:

> It is sometimes possible to represent a complex idea in a simple sentence, but more often you cannot represent it in that kind of sentence.

If you've stressed the right words, your voice and table thumping will feel right:

> It is sometimes possible to represent a complex idea in a simple sentence, but MORE **OF**TEN YOU CAN**NOT**.

Exercise 6.1

Revise these sentences to emphasize the right words. In the first three, I boldfaced what I think should be stressed. Then eliminate wordiness, nominalizations, etc.

1. The President's tendency **to rewrite the Constitution** is the biggest danger to the nation, in my opinion, at least.

2. A new political philosophy that could affect our society **well into the twenty-first century** may emerge from these studies.

3. There are **limited** opportunities for faculty to work with individual students in large American colleges and universities.

4. Building suburban housing developments in floodplains has led to the existence of extensive and widespread flooding and economic disaster in parts of our country in recent years, it is now clear.

5. The teacher who makes an assignment of a long final term paper at the end of the semester and who then gives only a grade and nothing else such as a critical comment is a common object of complaint among students at the college level.

6. Renting textbooks rather than buying them for basic required courses such as mathematics, foreign languages, and English, whose textbooks do not go through yearly changes, is feasible, however, economically speaking.

Exercise 6.2

Revise these passages so that their sentences begin with appropriate topics and end with appropriate emphasis.

1. The story of King Lear and his daughters was a popular one during the reign of Queen Elizabeth. At least a dozen available books offered the story to anyone wishing to read it, by the time Elizabeth died. The characters were undeveloped in most of these stories, however, making the story a simple narrative that stated an obvious moral. When he began work on *Lear,* perhaps his greatest tragedy, Shakespeare must have had several versions of this story available to him. He turned the characters into credible human beings with complex motives, however, even though they were based on the stock figures of legend.

2. Whether the date an operation intends to close down might be part of management's "duty to disclose" during contract bargaining is the issue here, it would appear. The minimization of conflict is the central rationale for the duty that management has to bargain in good faith. In order to allow the union to put forth proposals on behalf of its members, companies are obligated to disclose major changes in an operation during bargaining, though the case law is scanty on this matter.

3. Athens' catastrophic Sicilian Invasion is the most important event in Thucydides' *History of the Peloponnesian War.* Three-quarters of the history is devoted to setting up the invasion because of this. Through the step-by-step decline in Athenian society that Thucydides describes, we can see how he chose to anticipate the Sicilian Invasion. The inevitability that we associate with the tragic drama is the basic reason for the need to anticipate the invasion.

This next passage will seem difficult because it deals with a subject you probably know little about; even so, you can make it more readable by putting the technical terms at the end of each sentence and the familiar language at the beginning.

4. Mucosal and vascular permeability altered by a toxin elaborated by the vibrio is a current hypothesis to explain this kind of severe condition. Changes in small capillaries located near the basal surface of the epithelial cells, and the appearance of numerous microvesicles in the cytoplasm of the mucosal cells are evidence in favor of this hypothesis. Hydrodynamic transport of fluid into the interstitial tissue and then through the mucosa into the lumen of the gut is believed to depend on altered capillary permeability.

Revise this next passage to stress its most important numbers.

5. Changes in revenues are as follows. An increase to $56,792 from $32,934, a net increase of approximately 73 percent, was realized July 1–August 31 in the Ohio and Kentucky areas. In the Indiana and Illinois areas there was in the same period a 10 percent increase of $15,370, from $153,281 to $168,651. However, a decrease to $190,580 from $200,102, or 5 percent, occurred in the Wisconsin and Minnesota regions in almost the same period of time.

Topics, Themes, Emphasis, and Coherence

There is one more function performed by the stress of certain sentences, one that helps readers think a whole passage is coherent. As we saw in the last lesson, readers take the clearest topic to be a short noun phrase that comes early in a sentence, usually as its subject. That's why most of us judge this next paragraph to be unfocused: its sentences do not open from any consistent point of view:

1a. Great strides in the early and accurate diagnosis of Alzheimer's disease have been made in recent years. Not too long ago, senility in an older patient who seemed to be losing touch with reality was often confused with Alzheimer's. Genetic clues have become the basis of newer and more reliable tests in the last few years, however. The risk of human tragedy of another kind, though, has resulted from the increasing accuracy of these tests: predictions about susceptibility to Alzheimer's have become possible, long before the appearance of any overt symptoms. At that point, an apparently healthy person could be devastated by such an early diagnosis.

If we revise that passage so that its topics form a consistent topic string, we also make it more coherent (topics are boldfaced):

> ✓ 1b. In recent years, **researchers** have made great strides in the early and accurate diagnosis of Alzheimer's disease. Not too long ago, when **a physician** examined an older patient who seemed out of touch with reality, **she** had to guess whether the **person** was senile or had Alzheimer's. In the past few years, however, **physicians** have been able to use new and more reliable tests focusing on genetic clues. But in **the accuracy of these new tests** lies the risk of another kind of human tragedy: **physicians** may be able to predict Alzheimer's long before its overt appearance, but **such an early diagnosis** could psychologically devastate an apparently healthy person.

The passage now focuses on just two topics: researcher/physicians and testing/diagnosis.

But there is one more revision that would make that passage even more of a whole:

> **Put key words in the stress position of the *first* sentence of a passage in order to emphasize the key ideas that form a connecting thread through the rest of a passage.**

The first sentence now stresses advances in diagnosis: . . . *the early and accurate diagnosis of Alzheimer's disease*. But the point in this passage is not about diagnosis, but about its risks. That concept, however, does not appear until we are more than halfway through that paragraph.

Readers would grasp the point of that passage better if all of its key concepts appeared in the first sentence, *specifically toward its end, in its stress position*. Readers read the opening sentence or two of a paragraph to find the key concepts that the paragraph will repeat and develop, *and they specifically look for those concepts in the last few words of that opening, introductory, framing sentence*.

Here is a new first sentence for the Alzheimer's paragraph that would help readers focus on the key concepts not just of *Alzheimer's* and *new diagnoses*, but of *new problem* and *informing those most at risk*.

> In recent years, researchers have made great strides in the early and accurate diagnosis of Alzheimer's disease, but those **diagnoses** have

raised **a new problem** about **informing those most at risk who show no symptoms of it**.

We can call those key concepts that thread through a passage its *themes*.

Look at the highlighted words in the passage below one more time:

- The boldfaced words are all about testing.
- The italicized words are all about mental states.
- The capitalized words are all about a new problem.

Each of those concepts is announced toward the end of a new opening sentence, especially the theme of the new problem.

> ✓ 1b. In recent years, researchers have made great strides in the early and accurate **diagnosis** of *Alzheimer's disease,* but those **diagnoses** have raised A NEW PROBLEM about INFORMING THOSE *MOST AT RISK* WHO SHOW *NO SYMPTOMS OF IT.* Not too long ago, when a physician examined an older patient who seemed *out of touch with reality,* she had to **guess** whether that person had *Alzheimer's* or was *only senile.* In the past few years, however, physicians have been able to use **new and more reliable tests** focusing on genetic clues. But in the accuracy of these **new tests** lies the RISK OF ANOTHER KIND OF HUMAN TRAGEDY: physicians may be able to **predict** *Alzheimer's* long before its overt appearance, but such an early **diagnosis** could PSYCHOLOGICALLY DEVASTATE AN APPARENTLY HEALTHY PERSON.

That passage now "hangs together" not for just one reason, but for three:

- Its topic string consistently focuses on physicians and diagnosis.
- Threading through it are strings of words that focus on the themes of (1) tests, (2) mental conditions, and (3) a new problem.
- *And no less important, the passage helps us notice those themes by emphasizing them at the end of its opening sentence.*

This principle applies to sentences that introduce fairly long paragraphs (two or three sentence introductory, transitional, and other kinds of paragraphs follow different patterns). It also applies to sentences that introduce passages of any length, even to a whole document: *locate at the end of an introductory sentence words that announce the key themes that you intend to develop in the rest of the passage.* We will return to this matter in Lesson 11.

Here's the point: We depend on concepts running through a passage to create a sense of its coherence. You help readers identify those concepts in two ways:

- Repeat some of them as topics of sentences, creating a consistent topic string.
- Repeat others as themes elsewhere in a passage, creating consistent thematic threads.

Readers are more likely to notice those key themes if you emphasize them at the end of the sentence that introduces the passage.

QUICK TIP: For a paragraph more than five or six sentences long, underline the sentence that you think best introduces, sets up, frames the rest of the paragraph. If you can't do that quickly, your paragraph probably has a problem. If you can, circle the important words of that introductory segment. Those words should sound like a title for the paragraph. If they do not, your readers may have a problem. We will return to this matter in Lesson 11.

Exercise 6.3

Here are a paragraph and three opening sentences that might introduce it. Which introductory sentence best sets up the ideas that follow? Assume that the reader would be already familiar with the characters—Russian rulers. The best of the three sentences will in its last few words highlight the new themes that the writer wants us to associate with those rulers.

1. The next century the situation changed, because disputes over succession to the throne caused some sort of palace revolt or popular revolution in **seven out of eight reigns of the Romanov line after Peter the Great.**

2. The next century the situation changed, because after Peter the Great seven out of eight reigns of the Romanov line were **plagued by turmoil over disputed succession to the throne.**

3. Because turmoil over disputed succession to the throne plagued seven out of eight reigns of the Romanov line after Peter the Great, **the situation changed in the next century.**

The problems began in 1722, when Tsar Peter the Great passed a law of succession that terminated the principle of succession by heredity and required the sovereign to appoint a successor when he died. But because many of the tsars, including Peter, died before they named successors, those who aspired to rule had no authority by appointment, and so their succession was often disputed by the boyars, lower-level aristocrats. There was turmoil even when successors were appointed. In 1740, Ivan VI was adopted by Czarina Anna Ivanovna and named as her successor at age two months, but his succession was challenged by Elizabeth, daughter of Peter the Great. In 1741, she defeated Anna and ascended to the throne herself. In 1797 Paul tried to eliminate these disputes by codifying a law: primogeniture in the male line. But turmoil continued. Paul was strangled by conspirators, one of whom was probably his son, Alexander I.

SUMMING UP

1. Use the end of a sentence to introduce long, complex, or otherwise difficult-to-process material, particularly unfamiliar technical terms and new information.

> **A determination of involvement of lipid-linked saccharides in the assembly of oligosaccharide chains of ovalbumin *in vivo*** was the principal aim of this study. ***In vitro* and *in vivo* studies utilizing oviduct membrane preparations and oviduct slices and the antibiotic tunicamycin** were undertaken to accomplish this.

> ✓ The principal aim of this study was to determine how **lipid-linked saccharides are involved in the assembly of oligosaccharide chains of ovalbumin *in vivo*.** To accomplish this, studies were undertaken *in vitro* and *in vivo*, **utilizing the antibiotic tunicamycin on preparations of oviduct membrane and on oviduct slices.**

2. Use the stress position at the very end to emphasize words that you want your readers to hear emphasized in their minds' ear:

> The administration has blurred an issue central to arms control, **the issue of verification.** Irresponsible charges, innuendo, and leaks have submerged **serious problems with Iranian compliance.**

The issue of verification—so central to arms control—has been **blurred by the administration.** Serious problems with Iranian compliance have been submerged in **irresponsible charges, innuendo, and leaks.**

3. Use the stress of a sentence that introduces a passage to announce the key themes that the rest of the passage will develop:

In recent years, researchers have made great strides in the early and accurate **diagnosis** of *Alzheimer's disease,* but those **diagnoses** have raised A NEW PROBLEM about INFORMING THOSE *MOST AT RISK* WHO SHOW *NO SYMPTOMS OF IT.* Not too long ago, when a physician examined an older patient who seemed out of touch with reality, she had to **guess** whether that person was senile or had *Alzheimer's.* In the past few years, however, they have been able to use **new and more reliable tests** focusing on genetic clues. But in the accuracy of these **new tests** lies the RISK OF ANOTHER KIND OF HUMAN TRAGEDY: physicians may be able to **predict** *Alzheimer's* long before its overt appearance, but such an early **diagnosis** could PSYCHOLOGICALLY DEVASTATE AN APPARENTLY HEALTHY PERSON.

SUMMARY: PART 2

A simple English sentence is more than the sum of its words; it is a system of systems.

Fixed	Topic		Stress
Variable	Short, simple, familiar	:	Long, complex, new
Fixed	Subject	Verb	————
Variable	Character	: Action	: ————

Readers prefer sentences with these characteristics:

1. They want sentences to get to the subject of a main clause quickly, so avoid opening more than a few sentences with long, complex phrases and subordinate clauses.

2. They want sentences that get past the subject of a main clause to a verb quickly, so do this:

   a. Keep subjects short and, if you can, concrete—ideally flesh-and-blood characters.

   b. Open sentences with familiar information.

3. They want verbs that name specific actions, so do not bury actions in abstract nouns.

4. Readers deal with complexity more easily at the end of a sentence, so put there information that they will find least familiar, most complex, most difficult to understand.

5. Readers are confused when in a series of sentences each opens with a different subject, so through a passage, focus on a few topics that define what that passage is centrally "about."

6. Readers understand the ideas in a passage more easily when they can connect them to a few key concepts, so thread through a passage the themes that signal its most important ideas.

In short, write sentences that get to a short, concrete, familiar subject quickly, join that subject to a verb that names a specific action, and keep your subjects consistent. Readers want to see those patterns not just in the main clause of a sentence, but in every subordinate clause as well.

PART THREE

Grace

There are two sorts of eloquence; the one indeed scarce
deserves the name of it, which consists chiefly in
laboured and polished periods, an over-curious and
artificial arrangement of figures, tinseled over with a
gaudy embellishment of words. . . . The other sort of
eloquence is quite the reverse to this, and which may be
said to be the true characteristic of the holy Scriptures;
where the eloquence does not arise from a laboured and
farfetched elocution, but from a surprising mixture of
simplicity and majesty.
—LAURENCE STERNE

Concision

*I write for those who judge of books, not by the quantity,
but by the quality of them: who ask not how long,
but how good they are? I spare both my reader's time
and my own, by couching my sense
in as few words as I can.*
—JOHN WESLEY

*Often I think writing is sheer paring away of oneself
leaving always something thinner, barer, more meager.*
—F. SCOTT FITZGERALD

*The ability to simplify means to eliminate the unnecessary
so that the necessary may speak.*
—HANS HOFMANN

To a Snail: If "compression is the first grace of style," you have it.
—MARIANNE MOORE

UNDERSTANDING CONCISION

You get close to clarity when you match your characters and actions
to your subjects and verbs, and closer yet when you get the right
characters into topics and the right words under stress. But readers

may still think your prose is a long way from graceful if it's anything
like this:

> In my personal opinion, it is necessary that we should not ignore the
> opportunity to think over each and every suggestion offered.

That writer matched characters with subjects, and actions with
verbs, but in too many words: opinion is always personal, so we
don't need *personal,* and since this statement is opinion, we don't
need *in my opinion. Think over* and *not ignore* both mean *consider.*
Each and every is redundant. And suggestion is by definition offered.
In fewer words:

> ✓ We should consider each suggestion.

Though not elegant, that sentence at least has style's first grace—
compression, or as we'll call it, *concision.* Concision, though, is only
a start. You must still make your sentences shapely. In this lesson,
I focus on concision; in the next, on shape.

DIAGNOSIS AND REVISION

Five Principles of Concision

When I edited that sentence about suggestions, I followed five
principles:

1. Delete words that mean little or nothing.
2. Delete words that repeat the meaning of other words.
3. Delete words implied by other words.
4. Replace a phrase with a word.
5. Change negatives to affirmatives.

Here they are again, with details:

1. **Delete meaningless words.** Some words are verbal tics that
   we use as unconsciously as we clear our throats:

kind of	actually	particular	really	certain	various
virtually	individual	basically	generally	given	practically

   > Productivity **actually** depends on **certain** factors that **basically**
   > involve psychology more than **any particular** technology.
   > ✓ Productivity depends on psychology more than on technology.

2. **Delete doubled words.** Early in the history of English, writers got into the habit of pairing a French or Latin word with a native English one, because foreign words sounded more learned. Most paired words today are just redundant. Among the common ones:

full and complete	hope and trust	any and all
true and accurate	each and every	basic and fundamental
hopes and desires	first and foremost	various and sundry

3. **Delete what readers can infer.** This redundancy is common but hard to identify, because it comes in so many forms.

Redundant Modifiers Often, the meaning of a word implies others, especially its modifier:

Do not try to *predict* **future** events that will **completely** *revolutionize* society, because **past** *history* shows that it is the **final** *outcome* of minor events that **unexpectedly** *surprises* us more.

✓ Do not try to predict revolutionary events, because history shows that the outcome of minor events surprises us more.

Some common redundancies:

terrible tragedy	various different	free gift
basic fundamentals	future plans	each individual
final outcome	true facts	consensus of opinion

Redundant Categories Every word implies its general category, so you can usually cut a word that names it. Compare (the category is boldfaced):

During that *period* **of time,** the *membrane* **area** became *pink* **in color** and *shiny* **in appearance.**

✓ During that *period,* the *membrane* became *pink* and *shiny.*

In doing that, you may have to change an adjective into an ADVERB:

The holes must be aligned in an *accurate* **manner.**

✓ The holes must be aligned *accurately.*

Sometimes you change an adjective into a noun:

The county manages the *educational* **system** and *public recreational* **activities.**

✓ The county manages *education* and *public recreation.*

Here are some general nouns (boldfaced) often used redundantly:

large in **size**   round in **shape**   honest in **character**

unusual in **nature**   of a strange **type**   **area** of mathematics

of a bright **color**   at an early **time**   in a confused **state**

General Implications This kind of wordiness is even harder to spot because it can be so diffuse:

Imagine someone trying to learn the rules for playing the game of chess.

Learn implies *trying, rules* implies *playing the game, chess* is a *game.* So more concisely,

Imagine learning the rules of chess.

4. **Replace a phrase with a word.** This redundancy is especially difficult to fix, because you need a big vocabulary and the wit to use it. For example:

As you carefully read what you have written to improve wording and catch errors of spelling and punctuation, the thing to do before anything else is to see whether you could use sequences of subjects and verbs instead of the same ideas expressed in nouns.

That is,

✓ As you edit, first replace nominalizations with clauses.

I compressed five phrases into five words:

carefully read what you have written   →   edit

the thing to do before anything else   →   first

use X instead of Y   →   replace

nouns instead of verbs   →   nominalizations

sequences of subjects and verbs   →   clauses

I can offer no principle that tells you when to replace a phrase with a word, much less give you the word. I can point out only that you often can, and that you should be alert for opportunities to do so—which is to say, try.

Here are some common phrases (boldfaced) to watch for. Note that some of these let you turn a nominalization into a verb (both italicized):

We must explain **the reason for** the *delay* in the meeting.

✓ We must explain **why** the meeting is *delayed*.

Despite the fact that the data were checked, errors occurred.
✓ **Even though** the data were checked, errors occurred.

In the event that you finish early, contact this office.
✓ **If** you finish early, contact this office.

In a situation where a class closes, you may petition to get in.
✓ **When** a class closes, you may petition to get in.

I want to say a few words **concerning the matter of** money.
✓ I want to say a few words **about** money.

There is a need for more careful *inspection* of all welds.
✓ You **must** *inspect* all welds more carefully.

We **are in a position** to make you an offer.
✓ We **can** make you an offer.

It is possible that nothing will come of this.
✓ Nothing **may** come of this.

Prior to the *end* of the training, apply for your license.
✓ **Before** training *ends,* apply for your license.

We have noted a **decrease/increase in the number of** errors.
✓ We have noted **fewer/more** errors.

5. **Change negatives to affirmatives.** When you express an idea in a negative form, not only must you use an extra word: *same → not different,* but you also force readers to do a kind of algebraic calculation. These two sentences, for example, mean much the same thing, but the affirmative is more direct:

   Do not write in the negative.   →   Write in the affirmative.

You can rewrite most negatives, some formulaically:

not different	→	similar	not many	→	few
not the same	→	different	not often	→	rarely
not allow	→	prevent	not stop	→	continue
not notice	→	overlook	not include	→	omit

Do not translate a negative into an affirmative if you want to emphasize the negative. (Is that such a sentence? I could have written, *Keep a negative sentence when . . .*)

Some verbs, prepositions, and conjunctions are implicitly negative:

Verbs	*preclude, prevent, lack, fail, doubt, reject, avoid, deny, refuse, exclude, contradict, prohibit, bar*
Prepositions	*without, against, lacking, but for, except*
Conjunctions	*unless, except when*

You can baffle readers if you combine *not* with these negative words. Compare these:

> **Except** when you have **failed** to submit applications **without** documentation, benefits will **not** be **denied.**

✓ You will receive benefits only if you submit your documents.

✓ To receive benefits, submit your documents.

And you baffle readers completely when you combine explicitly and implicitly negative words with passives and nominalizations:

> There should be **no** submission of payments **without** notification of this office, **unless** the payment does **not** exceed $100.

> Do not **submit** payments if you have not **notified** this office, unless you are **paying** less than $100.

Now revise the negatives into affirmatives:

✓ If you pay more than $100, notify this office first.

Exercise 7.1

Prune the redundancy from these sentences.

1. Critics cannot avoid employing complex and abstract technical terms if they are to successfully analyze literary texts and discuss them in a meaningful way.
2. Scientific research generally depends on fully accurate data if it is to offer theories that will allow us to predict the future in a plausible way.
3. In regard to desirable employment in teaching jobs, prospects for those engaged in graduate-school-level studies are at best not certain.
4. Notwithstanding the fact that all legal restrictions on the use of firearms are the subject of heated debate and argument, it is necessary that the general public not stop carrying on discussions pro and con in regard to them.

5. Most likely, a majority of all patients who appear at a public medical clinical facility do not expect special medical attention or treatment, because their particular health problems and concerns are often not major and for the most part can usually be adequately treated without much time, effort, and attention.

Where appropriate, change the following negatives to affirmatives, and do any more editing you think useful.

6. Except when expenses do not exceed $250, the Insured may not refuse to provide the Insurer with receipts, checks, or other evidence of costs.

7. There is no possibility in regard to a reduction in the size of the federal deficit if reductions in federal spending are not introduced.

8. Do not discontinue medication unless symptoms of dizziness and nausea are not present for six hours.

9. No one should be prevented from participating in cost-sharing educational programs without a full hearing into the reasons for his or her not being accepted.

10. No agreement exists on the question of an open or closed universe, a dispute about which no resolution is likely as long as a computation of the total mass of the universe has not been done.

11. So long as taxpayers do not engage in widespread refusal to pay taxes, the government will have no difficulty in paying its debts.

12. No alternative exists in this country to the eventual development of tar sand, oil shale, and coal as sources of fuel, if we wish to stop being energy dependent on imported oil.

13. Not until a resolution between Catholics and Protestants in regard to the authority of papal supremacy is reached will there be a start to a reconciliation between these two Christian religions.

Exercise 7.2

Here are two actual sentences from two "free" offers.

You will not be charged our first monthly fee unless you don't cancel within the first thirty days.

To avoid being charged your first monthly fee, cancel your membership before your free trial ends.

Which is less clear? Why might it have been written like that? Revise it.

QUICK TIP: Try deleting every adverb and every adjective before a noun, then restore *only* those that readers need to understand the passage. In this passage, which must be restored?

> At the heart of the argument culture is our habit of seeing issues and ideas as ~~absolute and irreconcilable~~ principles ~~continually~~ at war. To move beyond this ~~static and limiting~~ view, we can remember the ~~Chinese~~ approach to yin and yang. They are ~~two~~ principles, yes, but they are conceived not as ~~irreconcilable polar~~ opposites but as elements that coexist and should be brought into balance ~~as much as possible~~. As ~~sociolinguist~~ Suzanne Wong Scollon notes, "Yin is always present in and changing into yang and vice versa." How can we translate this ~~abstract~~ idea into ~~daily~~ practice?
>
> —from Deborah Tannen, *The Argument Culture*

A Particular Kind of Redundancy: Metadiscourse

Lesson 4 described metadiscourse as language that refers to the following:

- the writer's intentions: *to sum up, candidly, I believe*
- directions to the reader: *note that, consider now, as you see*
- the structure of the text: *first, second, finally, therefore, however*

Everything you write needs metadiscourse, but too much buries your ideas:

> The last point I would like to make is that in regard to men-women relationships, it is important to keep in mind that the greatest changes have occurred in how they work together.

Only nine of those thirty-four words address men-women relationships:

> men-women relationships . . . greatest changes . . . how they work together.

The rest is metadiscourse:

> The last point I would like to make is that in regard to . . . it is important to keep in mind that . . .

When we prune the metadiscourse, we tighten the sentence:

> The greatest changes in men-women relationships have occurred in how they work together.

Now that we see what the sentence says, we can make it still more direct:

> ✓ Men and women have changed their relationships most in how they work together.

Some teachers and editors urge us to cut all metadiscourse, but everything we write needs some. You have to read with an eye to how good writers in your field use it, then do likewise.

There are, however, some types that you can usually cut.

Metadiscourse That Attributes Your Ideas to a Source   Don't announce that something has been *observed, noticed, noted,* and so on; just state the fact:

> High divorce rates **have been observed** to occur in areas that **have been determined to have** low population density.
>
> ✓ High divorce rates occur in areas with low population density.

Metadiscourse That Announces Your Topic   The boldface phrases tell your reader what your sentence is "about":

> **This section introduces another** problem, that of noise pollution. **The first thing to say about it is** that noise pollution exists not only . . .

Readers catch the topic more easily if you reduce the metadiscourse:

> ✓ **Another** problem is noise pollution. **First,** it exists not only . . .

Two other constructions call attention to a topic, usually mentioned at least once in the text previous to it:

> **In regard to** a vigorous style, the most important feature is a short, concrete subject followed by a forceful verb.
>
> **So far as** China's industrial development **is concerned,** it will take only a few years to equal that of Japan.

But you can usually work those topics into a subject:

> ✓ **The most important feature of a vigorous style** is a short, concrete subject followed by a forceful verb.
>
> ✓ **China** will take only a few years to equal Japan's industrial development.

Metadiscourse That Hedges and Intensifies   Another kind of metadiscourse reflects the writer's certainty about what she is claiming. This kind of metadiscourse comes in two flavors, *hedges* and *intensifiers*. Hedges qualify your certainty; intensifiers increase it. Both can be redundant, but they influence how readers judge your character, because they signal how well you balance caution and confidence.

Hedges   These are common hedges:

Adverbs	*usually, often, sometimes, almost, virtually, possibly, allegedly, arguably, perhaps, apparently, in some ways, to a certain extent, somewhat, in some/certain respects*
Adjectives	*most, many, some, a certain number of*
Verbs	*may, might, can, could, seem, tend, appear, suggest, indicate*

Some readers think all hedging is not just redundant, but mealy-mouthed. This is:

> There **seems to be some** evidence to **suggest** that **certain** differences between Japanese and Western rhetoric **could** derive from historical influences **possibly** traceable to Japan's cultural isolation and Europe's history of cross-cultural contacts.

On the other hand, only a fool or someone with massive historical evidence would make an assertion as flatly certain as this:

> This evidence **proves** that Japanese and Western rhetorics differ because of Japan's cultural isolation and Europe's history of cross-cultural contacts.

In most academic writing, we more often state claims closer to this (note my own hedging; compare the more assertive, *In academic writing, we state claims like this*):

> ✓ This evidence **suggests** that **aspects** of Japanese and Western rhetoric differ because of Japan's cultural isolation and Europe's history of cross-cultural contacts.

The verbs *suggest* and *indicate* let you state a claim about which you are less than 100 percent certain, but confident enough to propose:

> ✓ The evidence **indicates** that some of these questions remain unresolved.
> ✓ These data **suggest** that further studies are necessary.

Even confident scientists hedge. This next paragraph introduced the most significant breakthrough in the history of genetics, the discovery of the double helix of DNA. If anyone was entitled to be assertive, it was Crick and Watson. But they chose to be diffident (note, too, the first person *we;* hedges are boldfaced):

> We **wish to suggest a** [not *the*] structure for the salt of deoxyribose nucleic acid (D.N.A.) . . . A structure for nucleic acid has already been proposed by Pauling and Corey . . . **In our opinion,** this structure is unsatisfactory for two reasons: (1) **We believe** that the material which gives the X-ray diagrams is the salt, not the free acid . . . (2) **Some** of the van der Waals distances **appear** to be too small.
>
> —J. D. Watson and F. H. C. Crick,
> "Molecular Structure of Nucleic Acids"

Without the hedges, their claim would be more concise but more aggressive. Compare this (I boldface the stronger words, but most of the aggressive tone comes from the *absence* of hedges):

> We ~~wish to suggest~~ **state here** ~~a~~ **the** structure for the salt of deoxyribose nucleic acid (D.N.A.) . . . A structure for nucleic acid has already been proposed by Pauling and Corey . . . ~~In our opinion~~, [T]his structure is unsatisfactory for two reasons: (1) ~~We believe that~~ [T]he material which gives the X-ray diagrams is the salt, not the free acid . . . (2) ~~Some of~~ [T]he van der Waals distances ~~appear to be~~ **are** too small.

Intensifiers These are common intensifiers:

Adverbs	*very, pretty, quite, rather, clearly, obviously, undoubtedly, certainly, of course, indeed, inevitably, invariably, always, literally*
Adjectives	*key, central, crucial, basic, fundamental, major, principal, essential*
Verbs	*show, prove, establish, as you/we/everyone knows/can see, it is clear/obvious that*

The most common intensifier is the absence of a hedge. In this case, less is more. The first sentence below has no intensifiers at the blanks, but neither does it have any hedges, and so it seems like a strong claim:

> _____ Americans believe that the federal government is _____ intrusive and _____, authoritarian.

✓ **Many** Americans believe that the federal government is **often** intrusive and **increasingly** authoritarian.

Confident writers use intensifiers less often than they use hedges because they want to avoid sounding as assertive as this:

> For a century now, **all** liberals have argued against **any** censorship of art, and **every** court has found their arguments so **completely** persuasive that **not** a person **any** longer remembers how they were countered. As a result, today, censorship is **totally** a thing of the past.

Some writers think that kind of aggressive style is persuasive. Quite the opposite: If you state a claim moderately, readers are more likely to consider it thoughtfully:

> For **about** a century now, **many** liberals have argued against censorship of art, and **most** courts have found their arguments persuasive **enough** that **few** people **may** remember **exactly** how they were countered. As a result, today, censorship is **virtually** a thing of the past.

Some claim that a passage hedged that much is wordy and weak. Perhaps. But it does not come on like a bulldozer. It leaves room for a reasoned and equally moderate response.

QUICK TIP: When most readers read a sentence that begins with something like *obviously, undoubtedly, it is clear that, there is no question that,* and so on, they reflexively think the opposite.

Here's the point: You need some metadiscourse in everything you write, especially metadiscourse that guides readers through your text, words such as *first, second, therefore, on the other hand,* and so on. You also need some metadiscourse that hedges your certainty, words such as *perhaps, seems, could,* and so on. The risk is in using too many.

Exercise 7.3

Here are sentences that announce a topic rather than state a thesis. Delete the metadiscourse and rewrite what remains. Then decide whether the full statement makes a claim that readers would want to read about. For example:

> In this study, I examine the history of Congressional legislation regarding the protection of children in the workplace.

First, delete the metadiscourse:

> . . . the history of Congressional legislation regarding the protection of children in the workplace.

Then rewrite what is left into a full sentence:

> ✓ Congress has legislated the protection of children in the workplace.

That appears to be a self-evident, uninteresting claim.

1. This essay will survey research in schemata theory as applied to the pedagogy of mathematical problem solving.
2. I will analyze Frost's use of imagery of seasons in his longer poems published at the end of his career.
3. The methodological differences between English and American histories of the War of 1812 resulting in radically differing interpretations of the cause of the conflict are the topic of this study.
4. In this essay, I analyze the mistaken assumption underlying Freud's interpretation of dreams.
5. We will consider scientific thinking and its historical roots in connection with the influence of Egypt on Greek thought.
6. This article discusses needle sharing among drug users.
7. The relationship between birth order and academic success will be explored.
8. I intend to address the problem of the reasons for the failure and success of trade embargoes in this century.

Exercise 7.4

Edit these for both unnecessary metadiscourse and redundancy.

1. But on the other hand, we can perhaps point out that there may always be TV programming to appeal to our most prurient and, therefore, lowest interests.
2. In this particular section, I intend to discuss my position about the possible need to dispense with the standard approach to plea bargaining. I believe this for two reasons. The first reason is that there is the possibility of letting hardened criminals avoid receiving their just punishment. The second reason is the following: plea bargaining seems to encourage a growing lack of respect for the judicial system.
3. Turning now to the next question, there is in regard to wilderness area preservation activities one basic principle when attempting to formulate a way of approaching decisions about unspoiled areas to be set aside as not open to development for commercial exploitation.

4. It is my belief that in regard to terrestrial-type snakes, an assumption can be made that there are probably none in unmapped areas of the world surpassing the size of those we already have knowledge of.

5. Depending on the particular position that one takes on this question, the educational system has taken on a degree of importance that may be equal to or perhaps even exceed the family as a major source of transmission of social values.

Productive Redundancy

Learning by Writing   Some teachers think any redundancy signals mental laziness. But we almost inevitably fall into redundancy when we write about a subject that we are just learning. We signal membership in a community by what we say and how we say it, but a surer sign is knowing what to leave unsaid—our community's common knowledge. Unfortunately, learning what not to say takes time.

Here, for example, is a paragraph by a good undergraduate writer (I checked). But he was writing his first paper in a new community, law school:

> It is my opinion that the ruling of the lower court concerning the case of *Haslem v. Lockwood* should be upheld, thereby denying the appeal of the plaintiff. The main point supporting my point of view on this case concerns the tenet of our court system which holds that in order to win his case, the plaintiff must prove that he was somehow wronged by the defendant. The burden of proof rests on the plaintiff. He must show enough evidence to convince the court that he is in the right.

To his legal writing teacher, everything after the first comma was redundant: It is a given that if a court upholds a ruling, it denies the appeal; that the plaintiff can win only if he proves a defendant has wronged him; that the plaintiff has the burden of proof; that the plaintiff has to provide evidence. But at this early stage in his career, this writer was still learning his community's obvious knowledge, and so could not resist rehearsing it.

Metadiscourse about Thinking   Just as "belaboring the obvious" signals a writer new to a field, so does using metadiscourse to narrate one's thinking. When we are comfortable thinking through familiar problems, we don't have to narrate how we do it. But when we are inexperienced, we often feel compelled to tell a story about what we thought and did.

Look again at that paragraph by the first-year law student. Not only did he belabor the obvious, he recorded some of his thinking. I boldface metadiscourse and italicize the self-evident:

> **It is my opinion that** *the ruling of the lower court concerning* the case of Haslem v. Lockwood should be upheld, *thereby denying the appeal of the plaintiff.* **The main point supporting my point of view on this case concerns** *the tenet of our court system which holds that in order to win his case, the plaintiff must prove that he was somehow wronged by the defendant. The burden of proof rests on the plaintiff. He must show enough evidence to convince the court that he is in the right.*

When we delete the narrative and the obvious, we are left with something leaner:

> *Haslem* should be affirmed, because plaintiff failed to meet his burden of proof.

QUICK TIP: Once you have drafted a paper, read it once simply to see whether you have organized it as a narrative of your thinking. Most readers aren't interested in how you thought through an issue; they want to see the results of your having done it.

Concise, Not Terse

Having stressed concision so strongly, I must now step back. Readers don't like flab, but neither do they like a style so terse that it's all gristle and bone. Here is some amiable advice from the most widely read book on style, the third edition of Strunk and White's *The Elements of Style:*

> Revising is part of writing. Few writers are so expert that they can produce what they are after on the first try. Quite often you will discover, on examining the completed work, that there are serious flaws in the arrangement of the material, calling for transpositions. When that is the case, a word processor can save you time and labor as you rearrange the manuscript. You can select material on the screen and move it to a more appropriate spot, or, if you cannot find the right spot, move the material to the end of the manuscript until you decide whether to delete it. Some writers find that working with the printed copy of the manuscript helps them to visualize the process of changes; others prefer to revise entirely on screen. Above all, do not be afraid to experiment with what you have written. Save both the revised and the original versions; you can always use the computer to restore the

manuscript to its original condition, should that course seem best. Remember, it is no sign of weakness or defeat that your manuscript needs major surgery. This is a common occurrence in all writing, and among the best writers. (199 words)

We can shorten that paragraph just by erasing its redundancy:

Revising is part of writing. Few writers ~~are so expert that they can~~ produce what they are after on the first try. ~~Quite~~ Often you will discover, ~~on examining the completed work, that there are serious~~ flaws in the arrangement of the material, ~~calling for transpositions~~. When that is the case, a word processor can save ~~you~~ time ~~and labor~~ as you rearrange the manuscript. You can ~~select material on the screen and~~ move [material] to a more appropriate spot, or, if you cannot find the right spot, move the material to the end of the manuscript until you decide whether to delete it. Some writers find that working with the printed ~~copy of the~~ manuscript helps them ~~to~~ visualize ~~the process of~~ changes; others prefer to revise ~~entirely~~ on screen. Above all, ~~do not be afraid to~~ experiment ~~with what you have written.~~ Save ~~both~~ the revised and the original versions; you can always ~~use the computer to~~ restore the manuscript to its original condition, ~~should that course seem best. Remember,~~ It is no sign of weakness ~~or defeat~~ that your manuscript needs ~~major~~ surgery. This is ~~a~~ common ~~occurrence~~ in all writing, and among the best writers. (140 words.)

With some rewording, we can cut that version by another third (revisions are italicized):

Revising is part of writing, because few writers ~~produce what they are after on the first try~~ *write perfect first drafts. If you use a word processor and find* ~~Often you will discover serious~~ flaws in *your* arrangement, ~~of the material. When that is the case, a word processor can save time as you rearrange the manuscript.~~ You can ~~select material on the screen and~~ move material to a more appropriate spot, or if you cannot find *one* ~~the right spot,~~ to the end ~~of the manuscript~~ until you decide whether to delete it. Some writers find ~~that working with~~ the printed manuscript helps them ~~to~~ visualize changes; others revise on the screen. Above all, experiment. Save ~~both the revised and~~ the original version; you can always ~~restore the manuscript~~ go back to it ~~its original condition. Remember,~~ It is no sign of weakness that your manuscript needs surgery. This is common to all writing, and among the best writers. (101 words)

And if we cut to the bone, we can cut that in half:

Most writers revise because few write a perfect first draft. If you work on a computer, you can rearrange the parts by moving them around. If you save the original, you can always go back to it. Even great writers revise, so if your manuscript needs surgery, it signals no weakness. (51 words)

But in boiling down that original paragraph to a quarter of its original length, I've bleached out its garrulous charm, a tradeoff that many readers would reject.

I can't tell you when you've written so concisely that your readers think you are terse, even abrupt. That's why you should listen to what readers say about your writing. They know what you never can: how it feels to be your reader.

SUMMING UP

You need more than concision to guarantee grace, but when you clear away deadwood, you can see the shape of a sentence more clearly.

1. Redundant pairs

   If and when we can define our final aims and goals, each and every member of our group will be ready and willing to offer aid and assistance.

   ✓ If we define our goals, we will all be ready to help.

2. Redundant modifiers

   In the business world of today, official governmental red tape seriously destroys initiative among individual businesses.

   ✓ Government red tape destroys business initiative.

3. Redundant categories

   In the area of education, tight financial conditions are forcing school boards to cut nonessential expenses.

   ✓ Tight finances are forcing school boards to cut nonessentials.

4. Meaningless modifiers

   Most students generally find some kind of summer work.

   ✓ Most students find summer work.

5. Obvious implications

   Energy used to power industries and homes will in years to come cost more money.

   ✓ Energy will eventually cost more.

6. A phrase for a word

> A sail-powered craft that has turned on its side or completely over must remain buoyant enough so that it will bear the weight of those individuals who were aboard.

> ✓ A capsized sailboat must support those on it.

7. Indirect negatives

> There is no reason not to believe that engineering malfunctions in nuclear energy systems cannot be anticipated.

> ✓ Malfunctions in nuclear energy systems will surprise us.

8. Excessive metadiscourse

> It is almost certainly the case that totalitarian systems cannot allow a society to have what we would define as stable social relationships.

> ✓ Totalitarianism prevents stable social relationships.

9. Hedges and intensifiers

The only principle here is the Goldilocks rule: not too much, not too little, but just right. That's little help, but this is a matter where you have to develop and then trust your ear.

Too certain:	In my research, **I prove** that people with a gun in their home use it to kill themselves or a family member instead of to protect themselves from an intruder.
Too uncertain:	**Some** of my recent research **seems** to **imply** that there **may** be a **risk** that **certain** people with a gun in their homes **could** be **more prone** to use it to kill themselves or a family member than to protect themselves from **possible** intruders.
Just right?	My research **indicates** that people with a gun in their homes **are more likely** to use it to kill themselves or a family member than they are to protect themselves from an intruder.

8

Shape

The structure of every sentence is a lesson in logic.
—JOHN STUART MILL

Sentences in their variety run from simplicity to complexity, a progression not necessarily reflected in length: a long sentence may be extremely simple in construction—indeed must be simple if it is to convey its sense easily.
—SIR HERBERT READ

A long complicated sentence should force itself upon you, make you know yourself knowing it.
—GERTRUDE STEIN

You never know what is enough until you know what is more than enough.
—WILLIAM BLAKE

UNDERSTANDING THE SHAPE OF SENTENCES

If you can write clear and concise sentences, you have achieved much. But if you can't write a clear sentence longer than twenty words or so, you're like a composer who can write only jingles. Despite those who advise against long sentences, you cannot communicate every complex idea in a short one: you have to know how to write a sentence that is both long and clear.

Consider, for example, this sentence:

> In addition to differences in ethnicity or religion that have for centuries plagued Sunnis, Shiites, and Kurds, explanations of the causes of their distrust must include all of the other social, economic, and cultural conflicts that have plagued them that are rooted in a troubled history that extends 1300 years into the past.

Even if that idea needs all those fifty-three words (it doesn't), they could be arranged into a more shapely sentence.

We can start revising by editing the abstractions into character/subjects and action/verbs and then break the sentence into shorter ones:

> Historians have tried to explain why Sunnis, Shiites, and Kurds distrust one another today. Many have claimed that the sources of conflict are age-old differences in ethnicity or religion. But they must study all the other social, economic, and cultural conflicts that have plagued them through their 1300 years of troubled history.

But those sentences are choppy, almost immature. We need something like this:

> ✓ To explain why Sunnis, Shiites, and Kurds distrust one another to-day, historians must study not only age-old differences of ethnicity and religion, but all the other social, economic, and cultural conflicts that have plagued their 1300 years of troubled history.

That sentence is forty-one words long, but it doesn't sprawl. So it can't be length alone that makes a sentence ungainly. In this lesson, I focus on how to write sentences that are long and complex but also clear and shapely.

DIAGNOSIS AND REVISION

As with other issues of style, you can see sprawl in the writing of others more easily than in your own, so you have to diagnose your prose in ways that sidestep your intractable subjectivity.

Start by picking out sentences longer than two lines and reading them aloud. If in reading one of your long sentences you feel that you are about to run out of breath before you come to a place where you can pause to integrate all of its parts into a whole that communicates a single conceptual structure [breathe], you have found a sentence, like this one, that your readers would likely want you to revise. Or if your sentence, because of one interruption after another, seems to stop and start, your readers are, if they are typical, likely to judge that your sentence, as this one does, lurches from one part to the next.

Readers get a sense of shapeless length from four things:

- The sentence does not begin with its *point*.
- It takes readers too long to get to the verb in the main clause.
- After the verb, they have to slog through a shapeless sprawl of tacked-on subordinate clauses.
- They are stopped by one interruption after another.

Making the Point Clear

Here is a basic principle of style: Readers want a sentence to begin with a segment that is short, clear, and easy to grasp. So far, we've focused on short, concrete subjects followed by a specific verb.

But we can extend that principle. Compare these sentences:

A new sales initiative that has created a close integration between the garden and home products departments has made significant improvements to the services that Acme offers.

✓ Acme has significantly improved its services with a new sales initiative that closely integrates the garden and home products departments.

The second seems clearer for all the reasons we've discussed: it opens with a short, concrete subject followed by a verb naming a specific action.

But the revised sentence does something else for readers. It now opens with a short main clause that states its *point*: Acme has improved its services. That short, crisp point is then followed by details that support and explain it.

You can't break out a point in every sentence, especially short ones. But when you write a long, complex sentence, look for its point, the statement that you most want readers to grasp. When you find it, put it at the beginning of the sentence, then add to it the longer, more complex material. That's the first step in writing a well-shaped sentence.

Revising Long Openings

Some sentences seem to take forever to get started:

Since most undergraduate students change their fields of study at least once during their college careers, many more than once, first-year students who are not certain about their program of studies should not load up their schedules to meet requirements for a particular program.

That sentence takes thirty-one words to get to its main verb, *should not load up*. Here are two rules of thumb about beginning a sentence:

1. **Get to the subject of the main clause quickly.** Avoid beginning more than a few sentences with long introductory phrases and clauses.

2. **Get to the verb and object quickly.** Avoid long, abstract subjects and interruptions between subjects and verbs and between verbs and their objects.

Rule of Thumb 1: Get to the subject quickly   We have a problem with sentences that open with long introductory phrases and clauses, because as we read them, we have to keep in mind that the subject and verb of a main clause are still to come, and that load on our memory hinders easy understanding.

Compare these. In the first, we have to read and understand seventeen words while holding in mind that we have yet to reach the main subject and verb. In the second, we get past the subject and verb of the first clause in just three words:

> **Since most undergraduate students change their major fields of study at least once during their college careers,** *first-year students* who are not certain about the program of studies they want to pursue SHOULD NOT LOAD UP their schedules to meet requirements for a particular program.

> ✓ **First-year students** SHOULD NOT LOAD UP their schedules with requirements for a particular program if they are not certain about the program of studies they want to pursue, because **most** CHANGE their major fields of study at least once during their college careers.

If you open with a long introductory clause, try moving it to the end of its sentence or turning it into a sentence of its own.

Occasionally, you have to start a sentence with a subordinate clause, especially if it's an *if*-clause, because *if*-clauses usually refer to ideas already known and so must appear early in a sentence (see pp. 68–70):

> ✓ If we are to limit this spread of nuclear weapons, we must guarantee the security of nations wanting to arm themselves against their neighbors.

Rule of Thumb 2: Get past the verb and object quickly   Readers also want to get past the main subject to its verb and object.

Therefore,

- keep subjects short
- avoid interrupting the subject-verb connection
- avoid interrupting the verb-object connection

Revise Long Subjects into Short Ones Start by underlining whole subjects. If you find a subject longer than seven or eight words that includes a nominalization, try turning the nominalization into a verb and finding a subject for it (review pp. 29–37):

> **Abco Inc.'s *understanding* of the drivers of its profitability in the Asian market for small electronics** helped it pursue opportunities in Africa.

> ✓ **Abco Inc.** was able to pursue opportunities in Africa because it understood what drove profitability in the Asian market for small electronics.

A subject can also be long if it includes a long RELATIVE CLAUSE:

> A company **that focuses on hiring the best personnel and then trains them not just for the work they are hired to do but for higher-level jobs** IS likely to earn the loyalty of its employees.

Try turning the relative clause into an introductory subordinate clause beginning with *when* or *if*:

> ✓ **When a company focuses on hiring the best personnel and then trains them not just for the work they are hired to do but for higher-level jobs,** it is likely to earn the loyalty of its employees.

But if the introductory clause turns out to be as long as that one, try moving it to the end of its sentence, especially if (1) the main clause is short and the point of the sentence and (2) the moveable clause expresses newer and more complex information that supports or elaborates on the main clause.

> ✓ A company is likely to earn the loyalty of its employees **when it focuses on hiring the best personnel and then trains them not just for the work they are hired to do but for higher-level jobs.**

Or better yet, perhaps, turn it into a sentence of its own.

> ✓ Some companies focus on hiring the best personnel and then train them not just for the work they are hired to do but for higher-level jobs later. **Such companies are likely to earn the loyalty of their employees.**

Avoid Interrupting the Subject-Verb Connection You also frustrate readers when you interrupt the connection between a subject and verb, like this:

> Some scientists, **because they write in a style that is impersonal and objective,** do not easily communicate with laypeople.

That *because*-clause after the subject forces us to hold our mental breath until we reach the verb, *do not easily communicate.* Move the interruption to the beginning or end of its sentence, depending on whether it connects more closely to what precedes or follows it.

✓ Because some scientists write in a style that is impersonal and objective, they do **not easily communicate with laypeople. This lack of communication** damages . . .

✓ Some scientists do not easily communicate with laypeople because they write in **a style that is impersonal and objective. It is a kind of style** filled with passives and . . .

We mind short interruptions less:

✓ Some scientists **deliberately** write in a style that is impersonal and objective.

Avoid interrupting the verb-object connection We also like to get past the verb to its object quickly. This sentence doesn't let us do that:

> We must develop, **if we are to become competitive with other companies in our region,** a core of knowledge regarding the state of the art in effective industrial organizations.

Move the interrupting element to the beginning or end of its sentence, depending on what comes next:

✓ **If we are to compete with other companies in our region,** we must develop a core of knowledge about the state of the art in **effective industrial organizations. Such organizations provide** . . .

✓ **We** must develop a core of knowledge about the state of the art in effective industrial organizations **if we are to compete with other companies in our region. Increasing competition** . . .

An exception: When a prepositional phrase you can move is shorter than a long object, try putting the phrase between the verb and object:

> In a long sentence, put the newest and most important information that you want your reader to remember **at its end.**

✓ In a long sentence, put **at its end** the newest and most important information that you want your reader to remember.

Here's the point: Readers read most easily when you quickly get them to the subject of your main clause and then past that subject to its verb and object. Avoid long introductory phrases and clauses, long subjects, and interruptions between subjects and verbs and between verbs and objects.

Exercise 8.1

These sentences have long introductory phrases and clauses. Revise. Try to open your revised sentence with its point.

1. Since workfare has not yet been shown to be a successful alternative to welfare because evidence showing its ability to provide meaningful employment for welfare recipients is not yet available, those who argue that all the states should make a full-scale commitment to workfare are premature in their recommendations.

2. While grade inflation has been a subject of debate by teachers and administrators and even in newspapers, employers looking for people with high levels of technical and analytical skills have not had difficulty identifying desirable candidates.

3. Although one way to prevent foreign piracy of videos and CDs is for criminal justice systems of foreign countries to move cases faster through their systems and for stiffer penalties to be imposed, no improvement in the level of expertise of judges who hear these cases is expected any time in the immediate future.

4. Since school officials responsible for setting policy about school security have said that local principals may require students to pass through metal detectors before entering a school building, the need to educate parents and students about the seriousness of bringing onto school property anything that looks like a weapon must be made a part of the total package of school security.

5. If the music industry ignores the problem of how a rating system applied to offensive lyrics could be applied to music broadcast over FM and AM radio, then even if it were willing to discuss a system that could be used in the sale of music in retail stores, the likelihood of any significant improvement in its image with the public is nil.

These sentences have long subjects. Revise.

6. Explaining why Shakespeare decided to have Lady Macbeth die off stage rather than letting the audience see her die has to do with understanding the audience's reactions to Macbeth's death.

7. An agreement by the film industry and by television producers on limiting characters using cigarettes, even if carried out, would do little to discourage young people from smoking.

8. A student's right to have access to his or her own records, including medical records, academic reports, and confidential comments by advisers, will generally take precedence over an institution's desire to keep records private, except when limitations of those rights under specified circumstances are agreed to by students during registration.

These sentences are interrupted. First, eliminate wordiness, then correct the interruption.

9. The construction of the Interstate Highway System, owing to the fact that Congress, on the occasion when it originally voted funds for it, did not anticipate the rising cost of inflation, ran into serious financial problems.

10. Such prejudicial conduct or behavior, regardless of the reasons offered to justify it, is rarely not at least to some degree prejudicial to good order and discipline.

11. TV "reality" shows, because they have an appeal to our fascination with real-life conflict because of our voyeuristic impulses, are about the most popular shows that are regularly scheduled to appear on TV.

12. Insistence that there is no proof by scientific means of a causal link between tobacco consumption and various disease entities such as cardiac heart diseases and malignant growth, despite the fact that there is a strong statistical correlation between smoking behavior and such diseases, is no longer the officially stated position of cigarette companies.

13. The continued and unabated emission of carbon dioxide gas into the atmosphere, unless there is a marked reduction, will eventually result in serious changes in the climate of the world as we know it today.

Reshaping Sprawl

Once readers see the point of a sentence in an uninterrupted subject-verb-object clause, they can deal with longer, more complex chunks of information that follow. But they don't want to slog through sprawl like this:

> Of the many areas of science important to our future, few are more promising than genetic engineering, which is a new way of manipulating the elemental structural units of life itself, which are the genes and chromosomes that tell our cells how to reproduce to become the parts that constitute our bodies.

A sentence sprawls when after its verb and object, it tacks on a series of subordinate clauses of the same kind. It looks like this:

Of the many areas of science important to our future, *[opening phrase]*

few are more promising than genetic engineering, *[subject-verb core]*

which is a new way of manipulating the elemental structural units of life itself, *[tacked-on relative clause]*

which are the genes and chromosomes *[tacked-on relative clause]*

that tell our cells how to reproduce to become the parts *[tacked-on relative clause]*

that constitute our bodies. *[final tacked-on relative clause]*

QUICK TIP: If you are confused by a sprawling sentence when you read, focus on the relative pronouns *who, which,* and *that.* Pause a moment to figure out what each one refers to. Then reread the sentence, substituting nouns for the pronouns. That should unravel the sentence.

Diagnose this problem by having someone read your prose aloud. If that reader hesitates, stumbles over words, or runs out of breath before getting to the end of a sentence, so will your silent reader. You can revise in three ways:

1. **Cut.** Try reducing some of the relative clauses to phrases by deleting *who/that/which + is/was*, etc.:

   ✓ Of the many areas of science important to our future, few are more promising than genetic engineering, ~~which is~~ a new way of manipulating the elemental structural units of life itself, ~~which are~~ the genes and chromosomes that tell our cells how to reproduce to become the parts that constitute our bodies.

   Occasionally, you have to rewrite the remaining verb into an *-ing* form:

   The day is coming when we will all have numbers **that will identify** our financial transactions so that the IRS can monitor all activities **that involve** economic activity.

   ✓ The day is coming when we will all have numbers ~~that will~~ **identifying** our financial transactions so that the IRS can monitor all activities ~~that~~ **involving** economic activity.

2. **Turn subordinate clauses into independent sentences.**

   ✓ Many areas of science are important to our future, but few are more promising than genetic engineering. It is a new way of

manipulating the elemental structural units of life itself, the genes
and chromosomes that tell our cells how to reproduce to become
the parts that constitute our bodies.

If none of that works, you have to do some major restructuring.

3. **Change clauses to modifying phrases.** You can write a long
sentence but still avoid sprawl if you change relative clauses to
one of three kinds of APPOSITIVES: resumptive, summative, or
free. You have probably never heard of these terms before, but
they name stylistic devices you have read many times and
should know how to use.

> *Resumptive Modifiers* These two examples contrast a rela-
> tive clause and a resumptive modifier:

> > Since mature writers often use resumptive modifiers to extend
> > a line of thought, we need a word to name what I have not done
> > in this sentence, **which I could have ended at that comma
> > but extended to show you a relative clause attached to a
> > noun.**

> > ✓ Since mature writers often use resumptive modifiers to extend a
> > line of thought, we need a word to name what I am about to do in
> > this sentence, **a sentence that I could have ended at that
> > comma, but extended to show you how resumptive modifiers
> > work.**

The boldface resumptive modifier repeats a key word, *sentence*,
and rolls on.

To create a resumptive modifier, find a key noun just before
the tacked-on clause, pause after it with a comma, repeat the
noun, and continue with a restrictive relative clause beginning
with *that:*

> > Since mature writers often use resumptive modifiers to extend a
> > line of thought, we need a word to name what I am about to do in
> > **this sentence,**

> > > **a sentence that I could have ended at that comma, but ex-
> > > tended to show you how resumptive modifiers work.**

You can also resume with an adjective or verb. In that case,
you don't add a relative clause; you just repeat the adjective or
verb and continue:

> > ✓ It was American writers who found a voice that was both **true** and
> > **lyrical,**

> > > **true** to the rhythms of the working man's speech and **lyrical** in
> > > its celebration of his labor.

✓ All who value independence should **resist** the trivialization of government regulation,

> **resist** its obsession with administrative tidiness and compulsion to arrange things not for our convenience but for theirs.

Summative Modifiers Here are two sentences that contrast relative clauses and summative modifiers. Notice how the *which* in the first one feels "tacked on":

> Economic changes have reduced Russian population growth to less than zero, **which will have serious social implications.**

> ✓ Economic changes have reduced Russian population growth to less than zero, **a demographic event that will have serious social implications.**

To create a summative modifier, end a grammatically complete segment of a sentence with a comma, add a term that sums up the substance of the sentence so far, and continue with a restrictive relative clause beginning with *that*:

> Economic changes have reduced Russian population growth to less than zero,
>
> **a demographic event that will have serious social implications.**

Free Modifiers Like the other modifiers, a free modifier can appear at the end of a clause, but instead of repeating a key word or summing up what went before, it comments on the subject of the closest verb:

> ✓ Free modifiers resemble resumptive and summative modifiers, **letting you** [i.e., the free modifier lets you] **extend the line of a sentence while avoiding a train of ungainly phrases and clauses.**

Free modifiers usually begin with an *-ing* PRESENT PARTICIPLE, as those did, but they can also begin with a PAST PARTICIPLE verb, like this:

> ✓ Leonardo da Vinci was a man of powerful intellect,
>
> *driven* **by** [i.e., Leonardo was driven by] **an insatiable curiosity and** *haunted* **by a vision of artistic perfection.**

A free modifier can also begin with an adjective:

> ✓ In 1939, we began to assist the British against Germany,
>
> *aware* [i.e., we were aware] **that we faced another world war.**

We call these modifiers *free* because they can both begin and end a sentence:

- ✓ **Driven by an insatiable curiosity,** Leonardo da Vinci was . . .
- ✓ **Aware that we faced another world war,** in 1939 we began . . .

Here's the point: When you have to write a long sentence, don't just add one phrase or clause after another, willy-nilly. Particularly avoid tacking one relative clause onto another onto another. Try extending the line of a sentence with resumptive, summative, and free modifiers.

QUICK TIP: Some long introductory clauses can easily be converted into a main clause. The easiest is an *although*-clause. Drop the *although* and begin the following clause with *but* or *however:*

- ✓ **Although** some writers write well on their own, without the help of direct teaching or models of good prose, most benefit from instruction in the basics of writing graceful sentences.

- ✓ Some writers write well on their own, without the help of direct teaching or models of good prose, **but** most benefit from instruction in the basics of writing graceful sentences.

Another easy one is a *since*-clause. Drop the *since* and begin the next clause with *so, therefore, as a result,* or some other such connector.

- ✓ **Since** few writers write well on their own, without the help of direct teaching or models of good prose, most first-year college students would benefit from a course in composition.

- ✓ Few writers write well on their own, without the help of direct teaching or models of good prose, **so** most first-year college students would benefit from a course in composition.

4. **Coordinate.** Coordination is the foundation of a gracefully shaped sentence. It's harder to create good coordination than good modifiers, but when done well, it's more graceful. Compare these. My version is first; the original is second:

The aspiring artist may find that even a minor, unfinished work which was botched may be an instructive model for how things should be done, while for the amateur spectator, such works are the daily fare which may provide good, honest nourishment, which can lead to an appreciation of deeper pleasures that are also more refined.

✓ For the aspiring artist, the minor, the unfinished, or even the botched work, may be an instructive model for how things should—and should not—be done. For the amateur spectator, such works are the daily fare which provide good, honest nourishment—and which can lead to appreciation of more refined, or deeper pleasures.

—Eva Hoffman, "Minor Art Offers Special Pleasures"

My revision sprawls through a string of tacked-on clauses.

The aspiring artist may find that even a minor, unfinished work
  which was botched may be an instructive model for
    how things should be done,
      while for the amateur spectator, such works are the daily fare
        which may provide good, honest nourishment,
          which can lead to an appreciation of deeper pleasures
            that are also more refined.

Hoffman's original gets its shape from its multiple coordinations. Structurally, it looks like this:

For the aspiring artist, { the minor, the unfinished, or even the botched } work may be

an instructive model for how things { should and should not } be done.

For the amateur spectator, such works are

the daily fare {
which provide { good, honest } nourishment—
and
which can lead to appreciation of { more refined, or deeper } pleasures.
}

That second sentence in particular shows how elaborate coordination can get.

A General Design Principle: Short to Long   We should note a feature that distinguishes well-formed coordination. You can hear it if you read this next sentence aloud:

> We should devote a few final words to a matter that reaches beyond the techniques of research to the connections between those subjective values that reflect our deepest ethical choices and objective research.

That sentence seems to end too abruptly with *objective research*. Structurally, it looks like this:

$$
\ldots \text{between} \left\{ \begin{array}{c} \text{those subjective values that reflect our} \\ \text{deepest ethical choices} \\ \text{and} \\ \text{objective research.} \end{array} \right\}
$$

This next revision moves from shorter to longer by reversing the two coordinate elements and by adding a parallelism to the second one to make it longer still. Read this one aloud:

> ✓ We should devote a few final words to a matter that reaches beyond the techniques of research to the connections between objective research and those subjective values that reflect our deepest ethical choices and strongest intellectual commitments.

Structurally, it looks like this:

$$
✔ \ldots \text{between} \left\{ \begin{array}{c} \text{objective research} \\ \text{and} \\ \text{those subjective} \\ \text{values that reflect our} \end{array} \left\{ \begin{array}{c} \text{deepest ethical choices} \\ \text{and} \\ \text{strongest intellectual} \\ \text{commitments.} \end{array} \right\} \right\}
$$

A characteristic of especially elegant prose is how its writers elaborate all these devices for extending the line of a sentence, especially balanced coordination. I will discuss those devices and their elaboration in Lesson 9.

Here's the point: Coordination lets you extend the line of a sentence more gracefully than by tacking on one element to another. When you can coordinate, try to order the elements so that they go from shorter to longer, from simpler to more complex.

QUICK TIP: You can emphasize a coordination with CORRELATIVE CONJUNCTIONS: *both X and Y, not only X but Y, (n)either X (n)or Y.* Compare these:

✓ Great Britain is a good trading partner and a reliable ally in the war against terrorism.

✓ Great Britain is **both** a good trading partner **and** a reliable ally in the war against terrorism.

When you use one of these conjunctions, however, be sure to put the *and, but, or (n)or* before a word that is coordinate with what follows the *both, not only,* and *(n)either.* In the first sentence below, *not only* precedes the verb while the *but* precedes its subject:

When you punctuate carefully, you **not only** *help* readers understand a complex sentence more easily, **but** *you* enhance your own image as a good writer.

They should precede the same part of speech:

✓ When you punctuate carefully, you **not only** *help* readers understand a complex sentence more easily, **but** *enhance* your own image as a good writer.

Exercise 8.2

In these sentences, create resumptive, summative, and free modifiers. In the first five, start a resumptive modifier with the word in boldface. Then use the word in brackets to create another sentence with a summative modifier. For example:

Within ten years, we could meet our energy **needs** with solar power. [a possibility]

Resumptive:

✓ Within ten years, we could meet our energy **needs** with solar power, **needs** that will soar as our population grows.

Summative:

✓ Within ten years, we could meet our energy needs with solar power, **a possibility** that few anticipated ten years ago.

Free:

✓ Within ten years, we could meet our energy needs with solar power, **freeing** ourselves of dependence on foreign oil.

But before you begin adding modifiers, edit these sentences for redundancy, wordiness, nominalizations, and other problems.

1. Many different school systems are making a return back to traditional education in the **basics**. [a change]
2. Within the period of the last few years or so, automobile manufacturers have been trying to meet new and more stringent-type quality control **requirements**. [a challenge]
3. The reasons for the cause of aging are a **puzzle** that has perplexed humanity for millennia. [a mystery]
4. The majority of young people in the world of today cannot even begin to have an understanding of the **insecurity** that a large number of older people had experienced during the period of the Great Depression. [a failure]
5. The successful accomplishment of test-tube fertilization of embryos has raised many **issues** of an ethical nature that continue to trouble both scientists and laypeople. [an event]
6. Many who lived during the period of the Victorian era were appalled when Darwin put forth the suggestion that their ancestry might have included creatures related to apes.
7. In the period known to scholars and historians as the Renaissance, increases in affluence and stability in the area of political affairs had the consequence of allowing streams of thought of different kinds to merge and flow together.
8. The field of journalism has to an increasing degree placed its focus on the kind of news stories and events that at one time in our history were considered to be only gossip of a salacious and sexual nature.

Exercise 8.3

The best way to learn coordination is by imitating it. Try imitating any of the passages laid out above. For example, imitating the Eva Hoffman passage (p. 130), you might write this:

> For the serious student, the library sometimes provides a chance to be alone and to think through problems that may be too complex or too painful to think about in a noisy and crowded dormitory.

You can find other examples in famous speeches and dictionaries of quotations.

Troubleshooting Long Sentences

Even when you manage their internal structures, though, long sentences can still go wrong.

Faulty Grammatical Coordination   Ordinarily, we coordinate elements only of the same grammatical structure: clause and clause, prepositional phrase and prepositional phrase, and so on. When you coordinate different grammatical structures, readers may feel you have created an offensive lack of PARALLELISM. Careful writers avoid this:

<blockquote>
The committee recommends {

revising the curriculum to recognize trends in local employment

and

that the division be reorganized to reflect the new curriculum.

}
</blockquote>

They would correct that to this:

<blockquote>
✔ . . . recommends {

that the curriculum be revised to recognize . . .

and

that the division be reorganized to reflect. . . .

}
</blockquote>

Or to this:

$$
\checkmark \ldots \text{recommends} \left\{ \begin{array}{c} \textbf{revising the curriculum} \\ \text{to recognize} \ldots \\ \text{and} \\ \textbf{reorganizing the division} \\ \text{to reflect.} \ldots \end{array} \right\}
$$

However, some nonparallel coordinations do occur in well-written prose. Careful writers coordinate a noun phrase with a *how*-clause:

$$
\checkmark \text{We will attempt to delineate} \left\{ \begin{array}{c} \textbf{the problems} \text{ of education} \\ \text{in developing nations} \\ \text{and} \\ \textbf{how coordinated efforts} \\ \textbf{can address} \text{ them in} \\ \text{economical ways.} \end{array} \right\}
$$

They coordinate an adverb with a prepositional phrase:

$$
\checkmark \text{The proposal appears} \atop \text{to have been written} \left\{ \begin{array}{c} \textbf{quickly,} \\ \textbf{carefully,} \\ \text{and} \\ \textbf{with the help} \text{ of many.} \end{array} \right\}
$$

Careful readers do not blink at either.

Unclear Connections   Readers are bothered by a coordination so long that they lose track of its internal connections and pronoun references:

> Teachers should remember that students are vulnerable and uncertain about those everyday ego-bruising moments that adults ignore and that they do not understand that one day they will become as confident and as secure as the adults that bruise them.

We sense a flicker of hesitation about where to connect:

> . . . and that they do not understand that one day they . . .

To revise a sentence like that, shorten the first half of the coordination so that you can start the second half closer to the point where the coordination began:

> ✓ Teachers should remember that students are vulnerable to ego-bruising moments that adults ignore and that they do not understand that one day . . .

If you can't do that, repeat a word that reminds the reader where the coordination began (thereby creating a resumptive modifier):

> ✓ Teachers should try to remember that students are vulnerable to ego-bruising moments that adults ignore, **to remember** that they do not understand that . . .

Ambiguous Modifiers   Another problem with modifiers is that sometimes readers are unsure what they modify:

> Overtaxing oneself in physical activity too frequently results in injury.

What happens too frequently, overtaxing or injuries? We can make its meaning unambiguous by moving *too frequently:*

> ✓ Overtaxing oneself too frequently in physical activity results in injury.
> ✓ Overtaxing oneself in physical activity results too frequently in injury.

A modifier at the end of a clause can ambiguously modify either a neighboring or a more distant phrase:

> Scientists have learned that their observations are as subjective as those in any other field **in recent years.**

We can move the modifier to a less ambiguous position:

> ✓ **In recent years,** scientists have learned that . . .
> ✓ Scientists have learned that **in recent years** their . . .

A LAST PRINCIPLE

To keep a long sentence from sprawling, begin it so that readers can get through relatively short introductory phrases and clauses, then past a short subject to its verb. Following that verb, readers can make their way through subordinated and coordinated elements (usually arranged from shorter to longer). But every sentence has to end, ideally not with a whimper but at least a small thump, so you must also guide readers toward the emphasis you want them to hear. In Lesson 6, we looked into the matter of stress. In the next lesson, I discuss some of the ways that writers can end sentences in especially emphatic ways.

SUMMING UP

Here are the principles for giving sentences a coherent shape:

1. Open the sentence with its point in a short main clause stating the key claim that you want the sentence to make:

> A new sales initiative that has created a close integration between the garden and home products departments has made significant improvements to the customer services that Acme offers.

> ✓ Acme has significantly improved its customer services with a new sales initiative that closely integrates the garden and home products departments.

2. Get quickly to the subject, then to the verb and its object:

a. Avoid long introductory phrases and clauses. Revise them into their own independent clauses:

> Since most undergraduate students change their major fields of study at least once during their college careers, many more than once, **first-year students** who are not certain about the program of studies they want to pursue should not load up their schedules to meet requirements for a particular program.

> ✓ **Most undergraduate students** change their major fields of study at least once during their college careers, so **first-year students** should not load up their schedules with requirements for a particular program if they are not certain about the program of studies they want to pursue.

b. Avoid long subjects. Revise a long subject into an introductory subordinate clause:

> **A company that focuses on hiring the best personnel and then trains them not just for the work they are hired to do but for higher-level jobs** is likely to earn the loyalty of its employees.

> ✓ **When a company focuses on hiring the best personnel and then trains them not just for the work they are hired to do but for higher-level jobs later,** it is likely to earn the loyalty of its employees.

If the new introductory clause is long, shift it to the end of its sentence:

✓ A company is likely to earn the loyalty of its employees **when it focuses on hiring the best personnel . . .**

Or just break it out in a sentence of its own:

✓ **Some companies focus on hiring the best personnel and then train them not just for the work they are hired to do but for higher-level jobs later.** Such companies are likely to earn the loyalty of their employees.

c. Avoid interrupting subjects and verbs, and verbs and objects. Move the interrupting element to either the beginning or end of the sentence, depending on what the next sentence is about:

Some scientists, **because they write in a style that is impersonal and objective,** do not easily communicate with laypeople.

✓ **Because some scientists write in a style that is impersonal and objective,** they do *not easily communicate with laypeople. This lack of communication* damages . . .

✓ Some scientists do not easily communicate with laypeople *because they write in a style that is impersonal and objective. It is a kind of style filled with passives...*

3. After the main clause, avoid adding one subordinate clause to another to another to another . . .

a. Trim relative clauses and break the sentences into two:

Of the many areas of science **that** are important to our future, few are more promising than genetic engineering, **which** is a new way of manipulating the elemental structural units of life itself, **which** are the genes and chromosomes **that** tell our cells how to reproduce to become the parts **that** constitute our bodies.

✓ Many areas of science are important to our future, but few are more promising than genetic engineering. It is a new way of manipulating the elemental structural units of life itself, **which** are the genes and chromosomes **that** tell our cells how to reproduce to become the parts that constitute our bodies.

✓ Of the many areas of science ~~that are~~ important to our future, few are more promising than genetic engineering, ~~which is~~ a new way of manipulating the elemental structural units of life itself, ~~which are~~ the genes and chromosomes that tell our cells how to reproduce to become the parts ~~that~~ constituting our bodies.

b. Extend a sentence with resumptive, summative, or free modifiers:

✓ **Resumptive:**   When we discovered the earth was not the center of the universe, it changed our understanding of who we are, **an understanding changed again by Darwin, again by Freud, and again by Einstein.**

✓ **Summative:**   American productivity has risen to new heights, **an achievement that only a decade ago was considered an impossible dream.**

✓ **Free:**   Global warming will become a central political issue of the twenty-first century, **raising questions whose answers will affect the standard of living in every Western nation**.

c. Coordinate elements that are parallel both in grammar and in sense:

Besides the fact that no civilization has experienced such rapid alterations in their spiritual and mental lives, the material conditions of their daily existence have changed greatly too.

✓ No civilization has experienced such rapid alterations in their spiritual and mental lives and in the material conditions of daily existence.

4. End a sentence with the appropriate emphasis (review Lesson 6):

It is sometimes possible to represent a complex idea in simple sentences, but more often you cannot represent it in that kind of sentence.

✓ It is sometimes possible to represent a complex idea in simple sentences, but more often you cannot.

A last note: to write a long complex sentence that is also clear, you may need punctuation to help your reader through it. See Appendix I.

Lesson

9

Elegance

Anything is better than not to write clearly. There is nothing to be said against lucidity, and against simplicity only the possibility of dryness. This is a risk well worth taking when you reflect how much better it is to be bald than to wear a curly wig.
—Somerset Maugham

But clarity and brevity, though a good beginning, are only a beginning. By themselves, they may remain bare and bleak. When Calvin Coolidge, asked by his wife what the preacher had preached on, replied "Sin," and, asked what the preacher had said, replied "He was against it," he was brief enough. But one hardly envies Mrs. Coolidge.
—Frank L. Lucas

Read over your compositions, and wherever you meet with a passage which you think is particularly fine, strike it out.
—Samuel Johnson

In literature the ambition of the novice is to acquire the literary language; the struggle of the adept is to get rid of it.
—George Bernard Shaw

UNDERSTANDING ELEGANCE

Anyone who can write clearly, concisely, and coherently should rejoice to achieve so much. But while most of us prefer bald clarity to the density of institutional prose, others feel that relentless simplicity can be dry, even arid. It has the spartan virtue of unsalted meat and potatoes, but such fare is rarely memorable. A flash of elegance can not only fix a thought in our minds, but give us a flicker of pleasure every time we recall it.

Unfortunately, I can't tell you how to do that. In fact, I incline toward those who think that the most elegant elegance is disarming simplicity—and so when you think you have written something particularly fine, I second Samuel Johnson's advice: strike it out.

Nevertheless, there are a few devices that can shape a thought in ways that are both elegant and clear. Just knowing them, however, is about as useful as just knowing the ingredients in the bouillabaisse of a great cook, then thinking you can make it. Knowing ingredients and knowing how to use them are as different as reading cookbooks and cooking. Maybe elegant clarity is a gift. But even a gift has to be educated and exercised.

Balance and Symmetry

What most makes a sentence graceful is a balance and symmetry among its parts, one echoing another in sound, rhythm, structure, and meaning. A skilled writer can balance almost any parts of a sentence, but the most common balance is based on coordination.

Balanced Coordination   Here is a balanced passage and my revision of it. A tin ear can distinguish them:

> The national unity of a free people depends upon a sufficiently even balance of political power to make it impracticable for the administration to be arbitrary and for the opposition to be revolutionary and irreconcilable. Where that balance no longer exists, democracy perishes. For unless all the citizens of a state are forced by circumstances to compromise, unless they feel that they can affect policy but that no one can wholly dominate it, unless by habit and necessity they have to give and take, freedom cannot be maintained.
>
> —Walter Lippmann

The national unity of a free people depends upon a sufficiently even balance of political power to make it impracticable for an administration to be arbitrary against a revolutionary opposition that is irreconcilably opposed to it. Where that balance no longer exists, democracy perishes, because unless all the citizens of a state are habitually forced by necessary circumstances to compromise in a way that lets them affect policy with no one dominating it, freedom cannot be maintained.

My sentences lurch from one part to the next. In Lippmann's, we hear one clause and phrase echo another in word order, sound, and meaning, giving the whole passage an intricate architectural symmetry.

If we extend the idea of topic and stress from a whole sentence to its parts, we can see how he balances even short segments. Note how each significant word in one phrase echoes another in its corresponding one (I boldface topics of phrases and italicize stresses):

The national unity of a free people depends upon a sufficiently even balance of political power to make it impracticable.

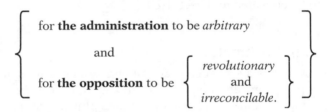

Lippmann balances the phrasal topics of *administration* and *opposition,* and closes by balancing the stressed sounds and meanings of *arbitrary, revolutionary,* and *irreconcilable.* He follows with a short concluding sentence whose stressed words are not coordinated, but still balanced (I use square brackets to indicate noncoordinated balance):

Where [**that balance** *no longer exists,* **democracy** *perishes.*]

Then he creates an especially intricate design, balancing many sounds and meanings:

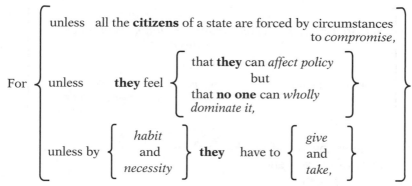

- He repeats *citizens* as the subject/topic of each clause: *all the citizens, they, they* (note the passive in the first one: *citizens are forced*; the active version would have unbalanced the coordination).
- He balances the sound and sense of *force* against *feel,* and the meaning of *affect policy* against the meaning of *dominate it.*
- In the last *unless*-clause, he balances the meaning of *habit* against *necessity,* and the stressed *give* against *take.*
- He balances the meanings of *compromise, affect, dominate,* and *give and take.*
- Then to balance the clauses of that short preceding sentence, *balance no longer exists—democracy perishes,* he concludes with an equally short clause, *freedom cannot be maintained,* whose meaning and structure echo the corresponding pair in the preceding sentence:

balance	no longer exists
democracy	perishes
freedom	cannot be maintained

For those who notice and care, it is an impressive construction.

Uncoordinated Balance   We can also balance structures that are not grammatically coordinate. In this example, the subject balances the object:

$$
\left[
\begin{array}{ll}
\textbf{Scientists} \text{ whose research} & \textit{creates revolutionary views of} \\
& \textit{the universe} \\
\text{invariably confuse} & \\
\textbf{those of us} \text{ who} & \textit{construct reality from our} \\
& \textit{common-sense experience of it.}
\end{array}
\right]
$$

Here, the PREDICATE of a relative clause in a subject balances the predicate of the sentence:

A government
$$
\left[
\begin{array}{l}
\text{that is unwilling to } \textit{listen } \text{ to } \text{ the} \\
\textit{moderate hopes} \text{ of } \textit{its citizenry} \\[4pt]
\text{must eventually } \textit{answer} \text{ to } \text{ the } \textit{harsh} \\
\textit{justice} \text{ of } \textit{its revolutionaries.}
\end{array}
\right]
$$

Here a direct object balances the object of a preposition:

Those of us concerned with our school systems will not sacrifice

$$
\left[
\begin{array}{lll}
\text{the } \textit{intellectual growth} \text{ of} & & \text{our } \textit{innocent children} \\
& \text{to} & \\
\text{the } \textit{social engineering} \text{ of} & & \textit{incompetent bureaucrats.}
\end{array}
\right]
$$

A more complicated balance:

Were I trading[1a]
$$
\left[
\begin{array}{c}
\text{scholarly principles}[2a] \\
\text{for} \\
\text{financial security,}[2b]
\end{array}
\right]
$$

I would not be writing[1b]
$$
\left[
\begin{array}{c}
\text{short books}[3a] \\
\text{on} \\
\text{minor subjects}[3b] \\
\text{for} \\
\text{small audiences.}[3c]
\end{array}
\right]
$$

In that sentence,

- a subordinate clause (1a), *Were I trading,* balances the main clause (1b), *I would not be writing;*
- the object of that subordinate clause (2a), *scholarly principles,* balances the object in the prepositional phrase (2b), *financial security.*
- the object in the main clause (3a), *short books,* balances objects in two prepositional phrases, (3b), *minor subjects,* and (3c), *small audiences* (with the balanced *short, minor,* and *small*).

Remember that you usually create the most rhythmical balance when the first element in a balance is shorter than the next ones (see p. 131).

These patterns even encourage you to think in ways that you otherwise might not. In that sense, they don't just frame your thinking; they generate it. Suppose you begin a sentence like this:

> In his earliest years, Picasso was a master draftsman of the traditional human form.

Now try this:

> In his earliest years, Picasso was **not only** a master draftsman of the traditional human form, **but also . . .**

Now you have to wonder what else he might have been. Or not have been.

I should remind you about another device that often appears in elegant prose, one described in Lesson 8—resumptive and summative modifiers (pp. 127–128):

> The British Empire brought its version of administrative bureaucratic order to societies around the globe, **an order that would endure in those lands long after Britons retreated to their own shores.**
>
> When the poem *Howl* first appeared, the "Beats" and other avant-gardes celebrated it as a revolutionary critique of the post-war American world, **a view not shared by most mainstream literary critics, who considered it incoherent rant.**

> *Here's the point:* The most striking feature of elegant prose is balanced sentence structures. You most easily balance one part of a sentence against another by coordinating them with *and, or, nor, but,* and *yet,* but you can also balance noncoordinated phrases and clauses. Used to excess, these patterns can seem merely clever, but used prudently, they can emphasize an important point or conclude a line of reasoning with a flourish that careful readers notice.

Climactic Emphasis

How you begin a sentence determines its clarity; how you end it determines its rhythm and grace.

Light and Heavy Words   When we get close to the end of a sentence, we expect words that deserve stress (pp. 85–86), so we may feel a sentence is anticlimactic if it ends on words of slight grammatical or semantic weight. At the end of a sentence, prepositions feel light—one reason we sometimes avoid leaving one there. The rhythm of a sentence should carry readers toward strength. Compare:

> Studies into intellectual differences among races is a project that only the most politically naive psychologist is willing to give support to.

> ✓ Studies into intellectual differences among races is a project that only the most politically naive scientist is willing to support.

Adjectives and adverbs are heavier than prepositions, but lighter than nouns, the heaviest of which are nominalizations. Readers have problems with nominalizations in the subject of a sentence, but at the end they provide a satisfyingly climactic thump, particularly when two of them are in coordinate balance. Consider this excerpt from Winston Churchill's "Finest Hour" speech. Churchill ended it with a parallelism climaxed by a balanced pair of nouns:

. . . until in God's good time,

the New World, with all its $\left\{ \begin{array}{c} \text{power} \\ \text{and} \\ \text{might} \end{array} \right\}$ steps forth to

$\left\{ \begin{array}{c} \text{the } \textbf{rescue} \\ \text{and} \\ \text{the } \textbf{liberation} \end{array} \right\}$ of the old.

He could have written more simply, and more banally:

> . . . until the New World rescues us.

Elegant Stress: Four Devices   Here are four ways to end a sentence with special emphasis.

1. *of* + **heavy word.** This seems unlikely, but it's true. Look at how Churchill ends his sentence: The light *of* (followed by a lighter *a* or *the*) quickens the rhythm of a sentence just before the stress of the climactic monosyllable, *old:*

   > . . . the rescue and the liberation of the **old.**

   We associate this pattern with self-conscious elegance, as in the first few sentences of Edward Gibbon's *History of the Decline and Fall of the Roman Empire* (contrast that title with *History of the Roman Empire's Decline and Fall*):

   > ✓ In the second century of the Christian era, the Empire of Rome comprehended **the fairest part *of* the earth,** AND **the most civilized portion *of* mankind.** The frontiers of that extensive monarchy were guarded **by ancient renown** AND **disciplined valour.** The gentle but powerful influence of laws and manners had gradually cemented **the union *of* the provinces.** Their peaceful inhabitants **enjoyed** AND **abused the advantages *of* wealth** AND **luxury.** The image of a free constitution was preserved with decent **reverence:** the Roman senate appeared to possess the sovereign authority, and devolved on the emperors all **the executive powers *of* government.**

   In contrast, this is flat:

   > In the second century AD, the Roman Empire comprehended **the earth's fairest, most civilized part.** Ancient renown and disciplined valour guarded **its extensive frontiers.** The gentle but powerful influence of laws and manners had gradually **unified the provinces.** Their peaceful inhabitants enjoyed and abused luxurious wealth while decently preserving what seemed to be **a free constitution.** Appearing to possess the sovereign authority, the Roman senate devolved on the emperors all **executive governmental powers.**

2. **Echoing salience.** At the end of a sentence, readers hear special emphasis when a stressed word or phrase balances the sound or meaning of an earlier one. (These examples are all from Peter Gay's *Style in History.*)

   > ✓ I have written these essays to anatomize this familiar yet really strange being, **style the centaur;** the book may be read as an extended critical commentary on Buffon's famous saying that **the style is the man.**

When we hear a stressed word echo an earlier one, these balances become even more emphatic:

✓ Apart from a few mechanical tricks of rhetoric, **manner** is indissolubly linked to **matter; style shapes,** and in turn is **shaped** by, **substance.**

✓ It seems frivolous, almost inappropriate, to be **stylish** about **style.**

Gay echoes both the sound and meaning of *manner* in *matter, style* in *substance, shapes* in *shaped by,* and *stylish* in *style.*

3. **Chiasmus.** This device (pronounced kye-AZZ-muss) is interesting perhaps only to those fascinated by the most arcane figures of style. The word *chiasmus* is from the Greek word for "crossing." It balances elements in two parts of a sentence, but the second part reverses the order of the elements in the first part. For example, this next sentence would be both coordinate and parallel, but it does not end with a chiasmus, because the elements in the two parts are in the same order (1A1B : 2A2B):

✔ A concise style can improve both
$$\left\{ \begin{array}{c} \textbf{our own}^{1A} \; thinking^{1B} \\ \text{and} \\ \textbf{our readers'}^{2A} \; understanding.^{2B} \end{array} \right\}$$

Were we seeking a special effect, we could reverse the order of elements in the second part to mirror those in the first. Now the pattern is not 1A1B : 2A2B, but rather 1A1B : 2B2A:

✔ A concise style can improve not only
$$\left\{ \begin{array}{c} \textbf{our own}^{1A} \; thinking^{1B} \\ \text{but} \\ \text{the } understanding^{2B} \textbf{ of our readers.}^{2A} \end{array} \right\}$$

The next example is more complex. The first two elements are parallel, but the last three mirror one another: AB CDE : AB EDC:

$$\left[\begin{array}{l} \text{You}^{A} \quad \text{reveal}^{B} \quad \textbf{your own}^{C} \; highest \; rhetorical^{D} \quad \text{\small SKILL}^{E} \\ \qquad\qquad \text{by the way} \\ \text{you}^{A} \quad \text{respect}^{B} \quad \text{\small THE BELIEFS}^{E} \; most \; deeply \; held^{D} \textbf{ by your reader.}^{C} \end{array} \right.$$

4. **Suspension.** Finally, you can wind up a sentence with a dramatic climax by ignoring advice offered in Lesson 8, where I advised you to open sentences with their point. Self-consciously elegant writers often begin a sentence with a series of parallel and coordinated phrases and clauses just so that they can delay and thereby heighten a sense of climax:

> If [journalists] held themselves as responsible for the rise of public cynicism as they hold "venal" politicians and the "selfish" public: if they considered that the license they have to criticize and defame comes with an implied responsibility to serve the public—if they did all or any of these things, they would make journalism more useful, public life stronger, and themselves far more worthy of esteem.
>
> —James Fallows. *Breaking the News*

Fallows opens that sentence (the last one in his book, by the way) with three *if*-clauses, then ends it with a triple coordination ending on its longest member, which itself ends with an *of* + nominalization. Keep in mind, however, that like all such devices, the impact of a long suspension is inversely proportional to its frequency of use: the less often you use it, the bigger its bang when you do.

Here's the point: An elegant sentence should end on strength. You can create that strength in five ways:

1. End with a strong word, or better, a pair of them.
2. End with a prepositional phrase introduced by *of*.
3. End with an echoing salience.
4. End with a chiasmus.
5. Build up to the end.

Extravagant Elegance

When writers combine all these elements in a single sentence, we know they are aiming at something special, as in this next passage:

> Far from being locked inside our own skins, inside the "dungeons" of ourselves, we are now able to recognize that our minds belong, quite naturally, to a collective "mind," a mind in which we share everything

that is mental, most obviously language itself, and that the old boundary of the skin is not boundary at all but a membrane connecting the
inner and outer experience of existence. Our intelligence, our wit, our
cleverness, our unique personalities—all are simultaneously "our
own" possessions and the world's.

—Joyce Carol Oates, "New Heaven and New Earth"

Here is the anatomy of that passage:

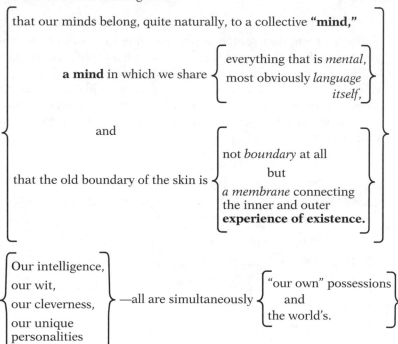

Far from being locked **inside** our own skins,

        inside the "dungeons" of ourselves,

we are now able to recognize

that our minds belong, quite naturally, to a collective **"mind,"**

a mind in which we share { everything that is *mental*,
most obviously *language itself*,

and

that the old boundary of the skin is { not *boundary* at all
but
a membrane connecting
the inner and outer
experience of existence.

Our intelligence,
our wit,
our cleverness,
our unique
personalities } —all are simultaneously { "our own" possessions
and
the world's.

In addition to all the coordination, note the two resumptive
modifiers:

Far from being locked **inside** our own skins,
        inside the "dungeons" of ourselves . . .
our minds belong . . . to a collective **"mind,"**
        a mind in which we share . . .

Note too the two nominalizations stressed at the end of the first sentence and the coordinate nominalizations at the end of the second:

> . . . the inner and outer experience of existence.
>
> . . . "our own" possessions and the world's.

But such patterns can be more elaborate yet. Here is the last sentence from Frederick Jackson Turner's The Frontier in American History:

> This then is the heritage of the pioneer experience—a passionate be-lief that a democracy was possible which should leave the individual a part to play in a free society and not make him a cog in a machine operated from above; which trusted in the common man, in his toler-ance, his ability to adjust differences with good humor, and to work out an American type from the contributions of all nations—a type for which he would fight against those who challenged it in arms, and for which in time of war he would make sacrifices, even the tem-porary sacrifice of his individual freedom and his life, lest that free dom be lost forever.

Note the following:

- the summative modifier in the opening segment: *a passionate belief that . . .*
- the increased length and weight of the second element in each coordination, even the coordinations inside coordinations
- the two resumptive modifiers beginning with *type* and *sacrifice*

That may be over the top, especially the quadruple chiasmus in the last sixteen words:

> **the temporary**[1] <u>sacrifice</u>[2] of his individual FREEDOM[3] **and** *his life*[4],
>
> *lest*[4]   that FREEDOM[3] be   <u>lost</u>[2]   **forever**[1].

The meaning of *temporary* balances *forever; sacrifice* balances *lost; freedom* echoes *freedom;* and the sound of *life* balances *lest* (not to mention the near rhyme of *lest* in *lost*). You just don't see that kind of sentence any more.

Here is the anatomy of that sentence:

This then is the heritage of the pioneer experience—
[summative modifier] → a passionate belief that a democracy was possible

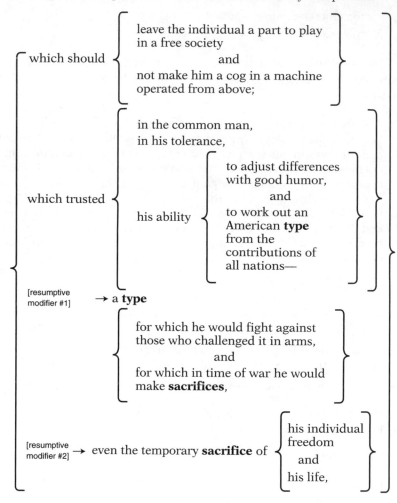

which should
- leave the individual a part to play in a free society

  and
- not make him a cog in a machine operated from above;

which trusted
- in the common man,
- in his tolerance,

  his ability
  - to adjust differences with good humor,

    and
  - to work out an American **type** from the contributions of all nations—

[resumptive modifier #1] → a **type**

- for which he would fight against those who challenged it in arms,

  and
- for which in time of war he would make **sacrifices**,

[resumptive modifier #2] → even the temporary **sacrifice** of
- his individual freedom

  and
- his life,

lest that freedom be lost forever.

Exercise 9.1

You develop a knack for balance by imitating models, not word for word, just their general pattern:

Survival in the wilderness requires the energy and wit to over-come the brute facts of an uncooperative Nature but rewards the person who acquires that power with the satisfaction of having done it once and with the confidence of being able to do it again.

Think of a subject close to that of the model to make your imitation easy—the academic life, then follow its outline:

Life as a college student offers a few years of intellectual excitement but imposes a sense of anxiety on those who look ahead and know that its end is in sight.

Use models you find here or in sermons, political speeches, and dictionaries of quotations. Try imitating the long sentences on pages 130, 141, 147, and 149.

Exercise 9.2

Here are some first halves of sentences to finish with balancing last halves. For example, given this:

Those who keep silent over the loss of small freedoms . . .

finish with something like this:

. . . will be silenced when they protest the loss of large ones.

1. Those who argue stridently over small matters . . .
2. While the strong are often afraid to admit weakness, the weak . . .
3. We should pay more attention to those politicians who tell us how to make what we have better than to those . . .
4. When parents raise children who scorn hard work, the adults those children become will . . .
5. Some teachers mistake neat papers that rehash old ideas for . . .

Exercise 9.3

These sentences end weakly. Edit them for clarity and concision, then revise them so that they end on more heavily stressed words, particularly with prepositional phrases beginning with *of.* For example:

Our interest in paranormal phenomena testifies to the fact that we have **empty spirits and shallow minds.**

✓ Our interest in paranormal phenomena testifies to **the emptiness of our spirits and the shallowness of our minds.**

In the first three, I boldface words you might nominalize.

1. If we invest our sweat in these projects, we must avoid appearing to work only because we are **interested** in ourselves.

2. The plan for political campaign was concocted by those who were not sensitive to what we **needed** most critically.

3. Throughout history, science has made progress because dedicated scientists have ignored a **hostile** public that is uninformed.

4. Not one tendency in our governmental system has brought about more changes in American daily life than federal governmental agencies that are very powerful.

5. The day is gone when school systems' boards of education have the expectation that local taxpayers will automatically go along with whatever extravagant things incompetent bureaucrats decide to do.

Nuances of Length and Rhythm

Most writers don't plan the length of their sentences, but that's not a problem, unless every sentence is shorter than fifteen words or so, or much longer. Artful writers, however, do use the length of a sentence for a purpose. Some write short sentences to strike a note of urgency:

> Toward noon Petrograd again became the field of military action; rifles and machine guns rang out everywhere. It was not easy to tell who was shooting or where. One thing was clear; the past and the future were exchanging shots. There was much casual firing; young boys were shooting off revolvers unexpectedly acquired. The arsenal was wrecked. . . . Shots rang out on both sides. But the board fence stood in the way, dividing the soldiers from the revolution. The attackers decided to break down the fence. They broke down part of it and set fire to the rest. About twenty barracks came into view. The bicyclists were concentrated in two or three of them. The empty barracks were set fire to at once.
>
> —Leon Trotsky, *The Russian Revolution,* trans. Max Eastman

Or terse certainty:

> The teacher or lecturer is a danger. He very seldom recognizes his nature or his position. The lecturer is a man who must talk for an hour. France may possibly have acquired the intellectual leadership of Europe when their academic period was cut down to 40 minutes. I also have lectured. The lecturer's first problem is to have enough words to fill 40 or 60 minutes. The professor is paid for his time, his results are almost impossible to estimate. . . . No teacher has ever failed from ignorance. That is empiric professional knowledge. Teachers fail because they cannot "handle the class." Real education must ultimately be limited to men who INSIST on knowing, the rest is mere sheep-herding.
>
> —Ezra Pound, *ABC of Reading*

Or passion. Here, D. H. Lawrence breaks what could have been a long paragraph into fragmented outbursts.

> Let us look at this American artist first. How did he ever get to America, to start with? Why isn't he a European still, like his father before him?
>
> Now listen to me, don't listen to him. He'll tell you the lie you expect. Which is partly your fault for expecting it.
>
> He didn't come in search of freedom of worship. England had more freedom of worship in the year 1700 than America had. Won by Englishmen who wanted freedom and so stopped at home and fought for it. And got it. Freedom of worship? Read the history of New England during the first century of its existence.
>
> Freedom anyhow? The land of the free! This the land of the free! Why, if I say anything that displeases them, the free mob will lynch me, and that's my freedom. Free? Why I have never been in any country where the individual has such an abject fear of his fellow countrymen. Because, as I say, they are free to lynch him the moment he shows he is not one of them. . . .
>
> All right then, what did they come for? For lots of reasons. Perhaps least of all in search of freedom of any sort: positive freedom, that is.
>
> —D. H. Lawrence, *Studies in Classic American Literature*

Self-conscious stylists also write extravagantly long sentences. Here is just a piece of one whose sinuous length seems to mirror the confused progress of a protest march:

> In any event, up at the front of this March, in the first line, back of that hollow square of monitors, Mailer and Lowell walked in this barrage of cameras, helicopters, TV cars, monitors, loudspeakers, and wavering buckling twisting line of notables, arms linked (line twisting so much that at times the movement was in file, one arm locked ahead, one behind, then the line would undulate about and the other arm would be ahead) speeding up a few steps, slowing down while a great happiness came back into the day as if finally one stood under some mythical arch in the great vault of history, helicopters buzzing about, chop-chop, and the sense of America divided on this day now liberated some undiscovered patriotism in Mailer so that he felt a sharp searing love for his country in this moment and on this day, crossing some divide in his own mind wider than the Potomac, a love so lacerated he felt as if a marriage were being torn and children lost—never does one love so much as then, obviously, then—and an odor of wood smoke, from where you knew not, was also in the air, a smoke of dignity and some calm heroism, not unlike the sense of freedom which also comes when a marriage is burst—Mailer knew for the first time why men in the front line of battle are almost always ready to die; there is a promise of some swift transit . . . [it goes on]
>
> —Norman Mailer, *The Armies of the Night*

We almost feel we are eavesdropping on Mailer's stream of thought. But of course, such a sentence is the product not of an overflow of feeling but of premeditated art.

- Mailer opens with short, staccato phrases to suggest confusion, but he controls them by coordination.
- He continues the sentence by coordinating free modifiers: *arms linked . . . (line twisting . . .) speeding up . . .*
- After several more free modifiers, he continues with a resumptive modifier: *a love so lacerated . . .*
- After another GRAMMATICAL SENTENCE, he adds another resumptive modifier: *a smoke of dignity and some calm heroism . . .*

Here's the point: Think about the length of your sentences only if they are all longer than thirty words or so or shorter than fifteen. Your sentences will vary naturally if you edit them in the ways you've seen here. But if the occasion allows, don't be reluctant to experiment.

Exercise 9.4

Combine Lawrence and Pound's short sentences into longer ones, like Mailer's. Break up Mailer's sentence into shorter ones in the style of Lawrence and Pound. How do they differ? Imitate the style of Lawrence, Pound, and Mailer. Then transform your Lawrence imitation into a Mailer imitation, and vice versa. Only by expressing the same thought in different styles can you see how different styles can seem to change a thought (a self-conscious chiasmus there).

Metaphor

Clarity, vigor, symmetry, rhythm—prose so graced is a great achievement. But it does not excite us to admire the reach of its imagination. This next passage displays all the devices we've seen, but it reaches beyond its grammar to reveal a truth about pleasure. It embeds a figure of speech in a comparison that is itself metaphorical (I boldface the metaphors):

> The secret of the enjoyment of pleasure is to know when to stop . . .
> We do this every time we listen to music. We do not **seize hold** of a

particular chord or phrase and shout at the orchestra to go on playing it for the rest of the evening; on the contrary, however much we
may like that particular moment of music, we know that its perpetu-
ation would interrupt and **kill** the movement of the melody. We
understand that the beauty of a symphony is less in these musical
moments than in the whole movement from beginning to end. If the
symphony tries to go on too long, if at a certain point the composer
exhausts his creative ability and tries to carry on just for the sake of
filling in the required **space** of time, then we begin to fidget in our
chairs, feeling that he has denied the natural rhythm, has **broken the
smooth curve from birth to death,** and that though a **pretense of
life** is being made, it is in fact a **living death**.

—Alan W. Watts, *The Meaning of Happiness*

Watts could have written this:

. . . however much we like that moment, we know that its perpetua-
tion would interrupt and spoil the movement of the melody. We begin
to fidget, feeling he has denied the natural rhythm, has interrupted
the regular movement from beginning to end, and that though he
makes a pretense of wholeness, it is in fact a repeated end.

Those sentences are clear, but lack the startling metaphor of birth
and its smooth curve into death.

Metaphor can vivify all kinds of prose. Social critics use it:

The schoolmaster is the person who takes the children off the parents' hands for a consideration. That is to say, he establishes a child
prison, engages a number of employee schoolmasters as turnkeys,
and covers up the essential cruelty and unnaturalness of the situation
by torturing the children if they do not learn, and calling this process,
which is within the capacity of any fool or blackguard, by the sacred
name of Teaching.

—George Bernard Shaw, *Sham Education*

So do historians:

This is what may be called the common-sense view of history. History
consists of a corpus of ascertained facts. The facts are available to the
historian in documents, inscriptions, and so on, like fish on the fish-
monger's slab. The historian collects them, takes them home, and
cooks and serves them in whatever style appeals to him. Acton, whose
culinary tastes were austere, wanted them served plain . . . Sir George
Clark, critical as he was of Acton's attitude, himself contrasts the
"hard core of facts" in history with the "surrounding pulp of dis-
putable interpretation"—forgetting perhaps that the pulpy part of the
fruit is more rewarding than the hard core.

—E. H. Carr, *What Is History?*

So do biologists:

> Some of you may have been thinking that, instead of delivering a scientific address, I have been indulging in a flight of fancy. It is a flight, but not of mere fancy, nor is it just an individual indulgence. It is my small personal attempt to share in the flight of the mind into new realms of our cosmic environment. We have evolved wings for such flights, in shape of the disciplined scientific imagination. Support for those wings is provided by the atmosphere of knowledge created by human science and learning: so far as this supporting atmosphere extends, so far can our wings take us in our exploration.
>
> —Julian Huxley, "New Bottles for Old Wine,"
> *Journal of the Royal Anthropological Institute*

And philosophers:

> Quine has long professed his skepticism about the possibility of making any sense of the refractory idioms of intentionality, so he needs opacity only to provide a quarantine barrier protecting the healthy, extensional part of a sentence from the infected part.
>
> —Daniel C. Dennett, "Beyond Belief"

And even physicists, when they lack terms for new ideas:

> Whereas the lepton pair has a positive rest mass when it is regarded as a single particle moving with a velocity equal to the vector sum of the motions of its two components, a photon always has zero rest mass. This difference can be glossed over, however, by treating the lepton pair as the offspring of the decay of a short-lived photonlike parent called a virtual photon.
>
> —Leon M. Lederman, "The Upsilon Particle," *Scientific American*

These metaphors serve different ends. Shaw and Carr use metaphor to make their language more intense. Dennett and Lederman use their comparisons simply to explain, and maybe to play a bit.

We have to be careful that a metaphor does not distort what we want to express, as do the metaphors in this passage:

> Societies give birth to new values through the osmotic flow of daily social interaction. Conflicts evolve when old values collide with new, a process that frequently spawns a new set of values that synthesize the conflict into a reconciliation of opposites.

The metaphor of birth suggests a traumatic event, but new values, it is claimed, emerge from osmotic flow, a process of invisibly small events. Conflicts do not "evolve"; they more often occur in an instant, as implied by the metaphor of collision. The spawning image echoes the metaphor of birth, but by this point the image is just silly. The writer might have expressed himself in literal language more exactly:

✓ As we interact in small ways, we gradually create new social values. When we behave according to an old value and someone else according to a new one, our values may conflict, but may create a third value that reconciles the conflict.

Aristotle wrote,

By far the greatest thing is to be a master of metaphor. It is the one thing that cannot be learned from others. It is a sign of genius, for a good metaphor implies an intuitive perception of similarity among dissimilars.

But when that perception is not quite right, a metaphor can seem just silly—Huxley comes close with his wings of inquiry flapping in an atmosphere of knowledge.

Metaphors can also embarrass us when their buried literal meanings unexpectedly revive, as in this student example:

The classic blitzkrieg relies on a tank-heavy offensive force, supported by ground-support aircraft, to destroy the defender's ability to fight by running amuck [sic] in his undefended rear, after penetrating his forward defenses.

We all write unfortunate metaphors like that, so when you do, don't think you're the only one who has. The only way to master them is to keep trying.

Here's the point: The risk in striving for elegance is that you fail spectacularly and never risk it again. I can only encourage you to accept with good humor those first failures that we all survive.

SUMMING UP

The qualities of elegance are too varied and subtle to capture in a summary. Nevertheless, elegant passages typically have three characteristics that may seem incompatible but are not:

- the simplicity of characters as subjects and actions as verbs
- the complexity of balanced syntax, meaning, sound, and rhythm
- the emphasis of artfully stressed endings

Walter Lippmann's passage illustrates all three:

> The national unity of a free people depends upon a sufficiently even balance of political power to make it impracticable for the administration to be arbitrary and for the opposition to be revolutionary and irreconcilable. Where that balance no longer exists, democracy perishes. For unless all the citizens of a state are forced by circumstances to compromise, unless they feel that they can affect policy but that no one can wholly dominate it, unless by habit and necessity they have to give and take, freedom cannot be maintained.

He uses only five nominalizations in eighty-eight words: *balance* twice, and *unity*, *necessity*, and *freedom* once each. Almost all subjects are short, naming his key characters, and most of his verbs express key actions. And he ends not just each sentence with the right stress, but every clause and even every phrase.

You won't acquire an elegant style just by reading this book. You must read those who write elegantly until their style runs along your muscles and nerves. Only then can you look at your own prose and know when it is elegant or just inflated. To make that distinction, I think the only reliable rule is *Less is more.* Of the many graces of style, the compression of a snail is still, I think, the first.

SUMMARY: PART 3

In addition to the principles we laid out in Part Two, we add these four:

1. Prune redundancy.
   - Delete words that mean little or nothing.
   - Delete words that repeat the meaning of other words.
   - Delete words implied by other words.
   - Replace a phrase with a word.
   - Change negatives to affirmatives.
2. Get the point of the sentence up front in a concise main clause.
3. Get to the verb in the main clause quickly.
   - Keep introductory clauses and phrases short.
   - Keep subjects short.
   - Don't interrupt the subject-verb connection.
4. Avoid extending the line of a sentence by attaching more than one subordinate clause to one of the same kind. Instead,
   - Coordinate phrases and clauses, balanced ones if you seek a special effect.
   - Use resumptive, summative, and free modifiers.
5. Try balancing parts of sentences against one another, especially their last few words.

PART FOUR

Clarity of Form

Well begun is half done.
—ANONYMOUS

The beginning is half of the whole.
—PLATO

10

Motivating Coherence

A problem well-put is half solved.
—John Dewey

Looking back, I think it was more difficult to see what the problems were than to solve them.
—Charles Darwin

The formulation of a problem is often more essential than its solution, which may be merely a matter of mathematical or experimental skill. To raise new questions, new possibilities, to regard old questions from a new angle, requires creative imagination and marks real advance in science.
—Albert Einstein

The uncreative mind can spot wrong answers, but it takes a creative mind to spot wrong questions.
—Antony Jay

Understanding Motives

If we are deeply interested in a topic, we will read anything about it we can get our hands on. We read even more attentively, however, when we read not just *about* an interesting topic, but about a *problem* that is important to us—from finding a good job to understanding the origins of life. When we are motivated to read attentively, not only do we read with greater understanding, but what we read seems more clearly written because we engage it so intently.

So from the moment you begin to plan a writing project, don't imagine your task as just writing *about* a topic, passing on information that happens to interest *you*. See yourself as posing a problem that *your readers* want to see solved.

The Importance of Introductions

Often, however, the problem you write about might not be one that your readers care about, or even know of. If so, you face a challenge: not only must you must overcome their inclination to ask *So what?*, but you get just one shot at answering it, in the introduction to your document. That's where you must motivate readers to see your problem as theirs.

For example, read this introduction (all these examples are much shorter than typical ones).

> When college students go out to relax on the weekend, many now "binge," downing several alcoholic drinks quickly until they are drunk or even pass out. It is a behavior that has been spreading through colleges and universities across the country, especially at large state universities. It once was done mostly by men, but now even women binge. It has drawn the attention of parents, college administrators, and researchers.

That introduction offers only a topic; it does not motivate us to care about it. Unless a reader is already interested in the issue, she may shrug and ask *So what? Who cares that college students drink a lot?*

Contrast that introduction with this one: it tells us why bingeing is not just a topic but a problem worth our attention:

> Alcohol has been a big part of college life for hundreds of years. From football weekends to fraternity parties, college students drink and often drink hard. But a new kind of drinking known as "binge" drinking is spreading through our colleges and universities. Bingers drink quickly not to be sociable but to get drunk or even to pass out. Bingeing is far from the harmless fun long associated with college life.

In the last six months, it has been cited in at least six deaths, many injuries, and considerable destruction of property. It crosses the line from fun to reckless behavior that kills and injures not just drinkers but those around them. We may not be able to stop bingeing entirely, but we must try to control its worst costs by educating students in how to manage its risks.

As short as that introduction is, it has three parts that appear in most introductions. Each part has a role in motivating a reader to read on. The parts are these:

Shared Context—Problem—Solution.

Alcohol has been a big part of college life . . . drink hard. shared context

But a new kind of drinking known as "binge" drinking is spreading . . . kills and injures not just drinkers but those around them. problem

We may not be able to stop bingeing entirely, but we must try to control its worst costs by educating students in how to manage its risks. solution

Part 1: Establishing a Shared Context   Not all pieces of writing open with a shared context, but most do. We see a shared context in the second introduction above:

Alcohol has been a big part of college life for hundreds of years. From football weekends to fraternity parties, college students drink and often drink hard. shared context But a new kind of drinking known as "binge" . . .

That shared context offers historical background, but it might have been a recent event, a common belief, or anything else that reminds readers of what they know, have experienced, or readily accept.

Event: A recent State U survey showed that 80% of first-year students engaged in underage drinking in their first month on campus, a fact that should surprise no one. shared context But what is worrisome is the spread among first-year students of a new kind of drinking known as "binge" . . .

Belief: Most students believe that college is a safe place to drink for those who live on or near campus. And for the most part they are right, shared context But for those students who get caught up in the new trend of "binge" drinking, . . .

These forms of shared context play a special role in motivating readers to read on: I wanted you to accept that context as a seemingly unproblematic base for thinking about binge drinking *just so that I could then challenge it.* I set you up so that I could say, in effect, *You may think you know the whole story,* **but** *you don't.* That *but* signals the coming qualification:

> . . . drink and often drink hard. _{shared context} **BUT a new kind of drinking known as "binge" drinking is spreading . . .**

In other words, college drinking seems unproblematic, *but it turns out not to be.* I wanted that small surprise to motivate you to go on reading.

No opening move is more common among experienced writers: open with a seeming truth, then qualify or even reject it. You can find countless examples of it in articles in newspapers, magazines, and especially professional journals. This opening context can be a sentence or two, as in these examples; in a journal, it can be paragraphs long, where it is called a *literature review*, a survey of what researchers have said that the writer will qualify or correct.

Not every piece of writing opens with this move; some jump to the second element of an introduction: the statement of a problem.

Part 2: Stating the Problem   If the writer opens with a shared context, she will typically introduce the problem with a *but* or *however:*

> Alcohol has been a big part of college life for hundreds of years. From football weekends to fraternity parties, college students drink and often drink hard. _{shared context} *But* **a kind of drinking known as "binge" drinking is spreading through our colleges and universities. Bingers drink quickly not to be sociable but to get drunk or even to pass out. Bingeing is far from the harmless fun long associated with college life. In the last six months, it has been cited in at least six deaths, many injuries, and considerable destruction of property. It crosses the line from fun to reckless behavior that kills and injures not just drinkers but those around them.** _{problem} We may not be able to . . .

The Two Parts of a Problem   Problems are more complicated than they seem. For readers to think that something is a problem, it must have two parts:

- The first part is some condition, situation, or recurring event: terrorism, rising tuition, binge drinking, anything that has the potential to cause trouble.

- The second part is the *intolerable consequence* of that condition, a *cost* that readers don't want to pay.

That cost is what motivates readers. They want to eliminate or at least ameliorate it, because it makes them unhappy: the cost of terrorism is injury and death; the cost of rising tuition is less money for other things or even a lost education. If rising tuition did not make parents and students unhappy, it would be no problem.

You can identify the cost of a problem if you imagine someone asking *So what?* after you state its condition. Answer *So what?* and you have found the cost:

> But a kind of drinking known as "binge" drinking is spreading through our colleges and universities. Bingers drink quickly not to be sociable but to get drunk or even to pass out. _{condition} *So what?* **Bingeing is far from the harmless fun long associated with college life. In the last six months, it has been cited in at least six deaths, many injuries, and considerable destruction of property. It crosses the line from fun to reckless behavior that kills and injures not just drinkers but those around them.** _{cost of the condition}

The condition part of the problem is binge drinking; the cost is death and injury. If bingeing had no cost, it would be no problem. Readers have to see the condition and cost *together* before they see the whole problem.

Two Kinds of Problems: Practical and Conceptual   Now it gets complicated, because there are two kinds of problems that motivate readers in different ways. You have to write about them differently.

- One kind of problem is common in the world of practical affairs, so we'll call it *practical*. Practical problems involve what we *do*. Binge drinking is a practical problem.

- The other is more commonly written about in the academic world; we'll call it *conceptual*. Conceptual problems involve what we *think*. That we don't know why students binge is a conceptual problem.

Practical Problems: What We Should Do   Binge drinking is an example of a practical problem for two reasons: First, it involves what students *do*. To solve it, someone must *act* differently. Second. it exacts palpable costs that make (or should make) readers unhappy. If we can't avoid a practical problem, we must *do* something in the world to change the condition, in order at least to ameliorate or at best to eliminate its costs.

We usually name a practical problem in a word or two: *cancer, unemployment, binge drinking*. But those terms name only its *condition*: they say nothing about costs. Most conditions sound like trouble, but *anything* can be the condition of a problem if its palpable costs make you unhappy. If winning the lottery made you suffer the loss of friends and family, it would be a practical problem.

You may think that the costs of a problem like bingeing are too obvious to state, but callous readers might ask, *So what if college students injure or kill themselves? What's that to me?* If so, you have to figure out how to make such readers see that those costs affect them. If you can't describe those costs so that they matter *to your readers*, they have no reason to care about what you've written.

Writers outside the academic world often address practical problems, but most writers inside it address conceptual ones.

Conceptual Problems: What We Should Think   A conceptual problem has the same two parts as a practical one, a condition and its costs. But beyond that, the two problems are very different.

- The condition of a conceptual problem is always *something that we do not know or understand.*

We can express the condition of a conceptual problem, what readers don't know, as a question: *How much does the universe weigh? Why does the hair on your head keep growing but the hair on your legs doesn't?*

- The cost of a practical problem is always the palpable unhappiness we feel from pain, suffering, and loss; the cost of a conceptual problem is the dissatisfaction we feel because we don't understand something important to us.

We can express the cost of a conceptual problem as something more important that readers don't know, as *another, larger question*:

> Cosmologists do not know how much the universe weighs. _{condition} *So what?* Well, if they knew, they might figure out something more important: Will time and space go on forever, or end, and if they do, when and how? _{cost/larger question}
>
> Biologists don't know why some hair keeps growing and other hair stops. _{condition} *So what?* If they knew, they might understand something more important: What turns growth on and off? _{cost/larger question}

That larger question may also involve something readers do not know how to do:

> Administrators do not know why students underestimate the risks of binge drinking. _{condition} *So what?* If they knew, they might figure out something more important: Would better information at orientation help students make safer decisions about drinking? _{cost/larger question}

I know that can sound baffling: the cost of one question is yet another question. It is why students new to academic writing find conceptual problems hard to grasp. Think of it like this: for a conceptual problem, you answer a small question so that your answer contributes to answering a larger, more important one. Readers are motivated because your small question inherits its importance from that larger one.

Here's the point: Like your readers, you will usually be more motivated by a large question, such as *Why do young people knowingly engage in dangerous behavior like binge drinking?*, than by a small one like *Why do bingers ignore known risks?* But you can't begin to answer a question as large as the one about dangerous behavior in three, five, or even a hundred pages. So you have to find a question you *can* answer. When you plan your paper, look for a question that is small enough to answer but is also connected to a question large enough for you *and your readers* to care about.

QUICK TIP: Some students think that they don't need a problem statement when their teacher assigns a specific topic, but they are wrong. If your assignment includes words like *discuss, explain,* or *analyze,* your job is to find a question behind that assignment. If your assignment states a question but not its significance, your job is to find a good answer to *So what?* Your paper will be both better written and better received if you begin it with a complete problem statement.

Framing a Conceptual Problem in Writing   There are countless ways to frame a conceptual problem. You can best learn them by reading lots of introductions. But for all of them, you must focus on two questions concerning what your readers don't know but should want to. The first question is the one your paper will answer. Be sure to state it not as a direct question but as an assertion that there is something we don't know or understand. To find the second, larger question, imagine readers responding to your small question with a question of their own, *So what?*

Shared context:

Colleges are reporting that binge drinking is increasing. We know its practical risks—death, injury, property damage. We also know that bingers ignore those risks, even after they have learned about them. shared context

Problem:

But we don't know what causes bingers to ignore the known risks: social influences, a personality attracted to risk, or a failure to understand the nature of the risks. condition/small question

[So what?]

If we can determine why bingers ignore known risks of their actions, we can better understand not only the causes of this dangerous behavior but also the nature of risk-taking behavior in general. cost/larger questions

Solution:

In this study, we analyzed . . . We found that . . . solution

All this can be hard to grasp if you're new to an academic field. We readily understand practical problems because the cost they make us pay is palpable. But those new to academic research don't see the costs of conceptual problems as readily: if you don't know what large questions are important to others in your field, you cannot find the small questions that might help answer them. (That's a practical problem that only time and experience solve.)

QUICK TIP: When you read an academic book or essay, look first for the implied question in its problem statement and then for its main claim, which answers that question. They will help focus your reading. If you don't find a question in the introduction, look for one in the conclusion. If that fails. find the main claim and ask yourself, *What question does this answer?* The more you understand *why* a writer is telling you something, the better you will understand what she writes.

Part 3: Stating the Solution   Practical and conceptual problems also differ in their solutions. We solve practical problems with action: readers (or someone) must *change what they do*. We solve conceptual problems with information: readers (or someone) must *change what they think*. Your answer to a small question then helps readers understand a larger one: *How much does the universe weigh? Well, it weighs* _____. *Now that we know that, we can answer a more important question: What is the fate of existence? The answer is that in 50 billion years or so, the universe will (or will not) exist.*

Practical Problems   To solve a practical problem, a solution must propose that the reader (or someone) *do* something to change a condition in the world:

> . . . behavior that crosses the line from fun to recklessness that kills and injures not just drinkers but those around them. _{problem} **We may not be able to stop bingeing entirely, but we must try to control its worst costs by educating students in how to manage its risks.** _{solution/point}

Conceptual Problems   To solve a conceptual problem, the solution must state something the writer wants readers to *understand* or *believe:*

> . . . we can better understand not only the causes of this dangerous behavior but also the nature of risk-taking behavior in general. _{problem} **This study reports on our analysis of the beliefs of 300 first-year college students. We found that students were more likely to binge if they knew more stories of other student's bingeing, so that they believed that bingeing is far more common than it actually is.** _{solution/point}

As Darwin and Einstein said, nothing is more difficult than finding a good question, because without one, you don't have an answer worth supporting.

Prelude

There is one more device that writers use in introductions. You may recall being told to "catch your readers' attention" by opening with a snappy quotation, fact, or anecdote. What catches attention best is a problem in need of a solution, but a catchy opening can vividly introduce concepts central to the problem you pose in the rest of your introduction. To name this device, we can use a musical term: *prelude*.

Here are three preludes that could establish key themes in a paper about binge drinking.

1. **A Quotation**
> "If you're old enough to fight for your country, you're old enough to drink to it."

2. A Startling Fact

A recent study reports that at most colleges three out of four students "binged" at least once in the previous thirty days, consuming more than five drinks at a sitting. Almost half binge once a week, and those who binge most are not just members of fraternities but their officers.

3. An Illustrative Anecdote

When Jim S., president of Omega Alpha, accepted a dare from his fraternity brothers to down a pint of whiskey in one long swallow, he didn't plan to become this year's eighth college fatality from alcohol poisoning.

We can combine all three:

It is often said that "if you're old enough to fight for your country, you're old enough to drink to it." quotation Tragically, Jim S., president of Omega Alpha, no longer has a chance to do either. When he accepted a dare from his fraternity brothers to down a pint of whiskey in one long swallow, he didn't expect to become this year's eighth college fatality from alcohol poisoning. anecdote According to a recent study, at most colleges, three out of four students have, like Jim, drunk five drinks at a sitting in the last thirty days. And those who drink the most are not just members of fraternities but—like Jim S. —officers. striking fact

Drinking, of course, has been a part of American college life since the first college opened . . . shared context But in recent years . . . problem

Writers in the natural and social sciences use preludes rarely. They are more common in the humanities and most common in writing for the general public.

Here, then, is a general plan for your introductions:

Prelude
Shared Context
Problem [Condition + Cost]
Solution / Main Point

Diagnosis and Revision

To diagnose how well your readers will be motivated by your introduction, do this:

1. **Determine whether you are posing a practical or conceptual problem.** Do you want readers to *do* something or just to *think* something?

2. **Draw a line after your introduction.** If you cannot quickly locate the end of your introduction, neither will your readers, who might then miss both your problem and its solution, the main point of your paper.

3. **Divide the introduction into its three parts: shared context + problem + claim.** If you cannot quickly make those divisions, your introduction is likely to seem unfocused.

4. **Is the first word of the first sentence after the shared context *but, however,* or some other word indicating that you will challenge that shared context?** If you don't explicitly signal the contrast between the shared context and the problem, readers may miss it.

5. **Divide the problem into two parts: condition and cost.**

   5a. **Is the condition the right kind for the problem?**

      • If you are addressing a practical problem, the condition can be whatever exacts a palpable cost.

      • If you are addressing a conceptual problem, the condition must be something not known or understood. This should be stated not as a direct question, *What causes bingeing?*, but as a statement of what we do not know: *But we do not know why bingers ignore known risks.*

   5b. **Does the cost appropriately answer *So what?***

      • If you are addressing a practical problem, the answer to *So what?* must state some palpable consequence of the condition that causes unhappiness.

      • If you are addressing a conceptual problem, the answer to *So what?* must state some more significant issue that is not known or understood.

6. **Underline your solution/claim.** It should be the main point of your paper and should, in the stress position at its end, state the key themes that the rest of your paper will develop (more on that in the next lesson).

CONCLUSIONS

A good introduction motivates your readers, introduces your key themes, and states your main point, the solution to your motivating problem. Get your introduction straight, and readers can read the rest more quickly and understand it better. A good conclusion, on the other hand, serves a different end: as the last thing your reader reads, it should bring together your point, its significance, and its implications for thinking further about your problem. Conclusions vary more than introductions, but in a pinch, you can map the parts of your introduction onto your conclusion. Just reverse their order:

1. **Open your conclusion by stating (or restating) the gist of your point, the main claim of your paper, the solution to your problem:**

   > Though we can come at the problem of bingeing from several directions, the most important is education, especially in the first week of a student's college life. But that means each university must devote time and resources to it.

2. **Explain its significance by answering *So what?* in a new way, if you can; if not, restate what you offered in the introduction, now as a benefit:**

   > If we do not start to control bingeing soon, many more students will die.

   > If we start to control bingeing now, we will save many lives.

3. **Suggest a further question or problem to be resolved, something still not known. Answer *Now what?*:**

   > Of course, even if we can control bingeing, the larger issue of risk-taking in general will remain a serious problem.

4. **End with an anecdote, quotation, or fact that echoes your prelude. We'll call this by another musical term, your *coda* (again, used most often in popular writing, rarely in the natural and social sciences):**

   > We should not underestimate how deeply entrenched bingeing is: We might have hoped that after Jim S.'s death from alcohol poisoning, his university would have taken steps to prevent more such tragedies. Sad to say, it reported another death from bingeing this month.

There are other ways to conclude, but this one works when nothing better comes to mind.

SUMMING UP

You motivate purposeful reading with an introduction that states a problem readers want to see solved.

For a practical problem the key is to state its costs so clearly that readers will ask not *So what?* but *What do we do?* Here is a plan for introducing a practical problem:

> Alcohol has been a part of college life for hundreds of years. From football weekends to fraternity parties, college students drink and often drink hard. $_{\text{shared context}}$

Open the introduction with *shared context*, a brief statement of what you will go on to qualify or even contradict.

> But a kind of drinking known as "binge" drinking is spreading through our colleges and universities. Bingers drink quickly not to be sociable but to get drunk or even to pass out. [*So what?*] $_{\text{condition}}$

Follow that with a statement of the condition of the problem. Introduce it with a *but, however, on the other hand*, etc. Imagine a *So what?* after it.

> Bingeing is far from harmless. In the last six months, it has been cited in six deaths, many injuries, and considerable destruction of property. It crosses the line from fun to reckless behavior that kills and injures not just drinkers but those around them. $_{\text{costs}}$

Answer that imagined *So what?* with a statement of the consequences of that condition, its costs *to your readers* that they do not want to pay.

> We may not be able to stop bingeing entirely, but we must try to control its worst costs by educating students in how to manage its risks. $_{\text{solution}}$

Conclude with a statement of the solution to the problem, an *action* that will eliminate or at least ameliorate the costs.

For conceptual problems, the key is to state a small question worth answering because it helps to answer a larger, more significant one. It seems unlikely that this question would help us understand anything important: *What color were Lincoln's socks when he delivered the Gettysburg Address?* But this one might: *How did Lincoln plan the Address?* If we knew that, we might learn about something more important: the nature of his creative process. Here is a plan for introducing conceptual problems:

Colleges are reporting that binge drinking is increasing. We know its practical risks. We also know that bingers ignore those risks, even after they have learned about them._{shared context}	Open the introduction with *shared context,* a brief statement of what you will go on to qualify or even contradict.
But we don't know what causes bingers to ignore the known risks: social influences, a personality attracted to risk, or a failure to understand the nature of the risks. [*So what?*]_{condition /} first, small question	Follow that with a statement of the condition of the problem. Introduce it with a *but, however, on the other hand,* etc. State something that is not known or well understood. Imagine a *So what?* after it.
If we can determine why bingers ignore known risks of their actions, we can better understand not only the causes of this dangerous behavior but also the nature of risk-taking behavior in general. cost/second, larger question	Answer that imagined *So what?* with the cost of the condition, a larger and more important issue that is not known or understood but that might be answered if we know the answer to the first question.
In this study, we analyzed the beliefs of 300 first-year college students to determine . . . We found that . . .] solution	Conclude your introduction with a statement of the solution to the problem, an answer to the first question that helps answer the second one, as well.

Lesson

11

Global Coherence

*One of the most difficult things [to write] is the first
paragraph. I have spent many months on a first paragraph,
and once I get it, the rest just comes out very easily. In the
first paragraph you solve most of the problems with your
book. The theme is defined, the style, the tone.*
—GABRIEL GARCÍA MÁRQUEZ

UNDERSTANDING COHERENCE

In the last lesson, I explained how you must create an introduction that does two things:

- It must motivate your readers by stating a problem that they care about.
- It must frame the rest of your document by stating the point and key concepts that you will develop in what follows.

In this lesson, I explain how that second point applies to all the parts of your document—its sections, subsections, and even paragraphs.

When we are interested in a subject, we can struggle through clotted sentences, if we must. That's why even bad writers get read if they motivate readers to make the effort to understand their gratuitous complexity. But regardless of our interest, we are just defeated by general incoherence. If we can't follow a line of thought, we are likely to give up. Like the terms *complex* and *unclear,* though, the terms *coherent* and *incoherent* don't refer to anything we see on the page. Coherence is an experience we create for ourselves as we make our own sense out of what we read.

That experience depends most on the knowledge we bring to our reading. We can make sense of almost anything, even incoherence, if we're motivated to read it and we already know a lot about its subject matter. But when we don't have prior knowledge to help us through a text, we depend on signals that we see on the page to help us integrate what we read with the knowledge we have. You help your readers do that by building those signals into your writing deliberately. This lesson explains how to do that.

Global Coherence

In Lessons 5 and 6, we looked at those features that help readers create "local" coherence in short passages, but readers need more than locally coherent passages to grasp the coherence of a whole document. To help them achieve that coherence, you can use a principle we have looked at for writing clear sentences: begin each major unit of a document—each section and subsection—with a short, easily grasped segment that states the point and introduces the rest, the part that is longer and more complex. Then in that part, expand on, develop, or explain what you stated as the point in the first part. (Paragraphs are a special case that we'll discuss later.)

To grasp the coherence of a substantial unit of discourse and therefore the coherence of the whole, readers must see four things:

1. **Your readers must know where one section stops and the next begins.** Use headings to identify the start of a new section. Create those headings out of the key concepts that you state in your point sentence (see (4) below).

2. **Readers must recognize a short segment that introduces each section and subsection.**

3. **At the end of that introductory segment, readers look for a sentence that states the *point* of the section, a statement that you expand on in the rest of that unit.** When readers see that point sentence at the end of a short, easily grasped opening segment, they read and understand what follows more easily.

4. **Toward the end of that point sentence, they must see words that express the concepts that you develop in the rest of that unit.** Readers use those repeated concepts to organize their understanding of the whole.

QUICK TIP: You can use these four elements of coherence to prepare yourself to read a conceptually difficult essay or chapter. First, highlight the question in the problem statement and the main claim that answers it (see pp. 167–172). Next, go through the four steps above for each section, highlighting its introduction, point, and key concepts. If you don't find them in the introduction to a section, look for them at the end of the section. Finally, read through just the parts that you highlighted. When you then begin reading in detail, you will have in mind an overview that will help you better understand and remember the rest.

In the limited space we have here, I can't illustrate these principles with entire documents, or even sections of them. I have to use paragraphs and ask you to analogize the structure of an illustrative paragraph to a whole section of a document.

For example, read this:

> 1a. Thirty sixth-grade students wrote essays that were analyzed to determine the effectiveness of eight weeks of training to distinguish fact from opinion. That ability is an important aspect of making sound arguments of any kind. In an essay written before instruction began, the writers failed almost completely to distinguish fact from opinion. In an essay written after four weeks of instruction, the students visibly attempted to distinguish fact from opinion, but did so inconsistently. In three more essays, they distinguished fact from opinion more consistently, but never achieved the predicted level of performance. In a final essay written six months after instruction ended, they did no better than they did in their pre-instruction essays. Their training had some effect on their writing during the instruction period, but it was inconsistent, and six months after instruction it had no measurable effect.

The first few sentences introduce the rest, but we don't see in them the key concepts that follow: *inconsistently, never achieved, no better, no measurable effect;* those terms are crucial to the *point* of the whole passage. Worse, not until we get to the end of the passage do we get to its point: training had no long-term effect. And so as we read it, that passage seems to ramble, until the end, when we can make some sense of it retrospectively. But that takes more effort than we should have to expend.

Compare this version:

1b. In this study, thirty sixth-grade students were taught to distinguish fact from opinion. They did so successfully during the instruction period, but the effect was inconsistent and less than predicted, and six months after instruction ended, the instruction had no measurable effect. In an essay written before instruction began, the writers failed almost completely to distinguish fact from opinion. In an essay written after four weeks of instruction, the students visibly attempted to distinguish fact from opinion, but did so inconsistently. In three more essays, they distinguished fact from opinion more consistently, but never achieved the predicted level of performance. In a final essay written six months after instruction ended, they did no better than they did in their pre-instruction essay. We thus conclude that short-term training to distinguish fact from opinion has no consistent or long-term effect.

In that passage, we quickly grasp that the first two sentences introduce what follows. And in the second sentence, we see two things: both the point of the passage and its key terms.

1b. In this study, thirty sixth-grade students were taught to distinguish fact from opinion. They did so successfully during the instruction period, but the **effect was inconsistent and less than predicted,** and six months after instruction ended, the instruction had **no measurable effect.** point of the passage

As a consequence, we feel the passage hangs together better and we read it with more understanding.

We can look at only short passages to illustrate these principles, but we can imagine how they apply to longer stretches of prose. Imagine two documents: in one, the point of each section and the whole appears at its *end* (as in (1a)) and what openings there are do not introduce the key terms that follow; in the other, each point appears in an *introductory* segment to every paragraph, section, and of the whole (as in (1b)). Which would be easier to read and understand? The second, of course.

Keep in mind this principle: put the point sentence at the *end* of the short opening segment; make it the *last* sentence that your reader reads before starting the longer, more complex segment that follows.

- In a very short passage, the introductory segment might be just a single sentence, so by default, it will be the last sentence readers read before they read what follows. If the passage has a *two*-sentence introduction (as did (1b)), be sure the point of the paragraph is the *second* sentence, still making it the last thing readers read before they read the rest.

- For longer sections, your introduction might be a paragraph or more. For a whole document, you might need several paragraphs. Even in those cases, put your point sentence at the end of that introductory segment, no matter how long it is. Make your point the last thing readers read before they begin reading the longer, more complex segments that follow.

Some inexperienced writers think that if they tip off their main point in their introduction, readers will be bored and not read on. Not true. If you ask an interesting question, readers will want to see how you support your answer.

Here's the point: To write a document that readers will think is coherent, open every section, subsection, and the whole with a short, easily grasped introductory segment. Put at the end of that opening segment a sentence that states both the point of the unit and the key concepts that follow. Point sentences constitute the outline of your document, its logical structure. If readers miss them, they may judge your writing to be incoherent.

Two More Requirements for Coherence

We can make sense of almost anything we read if we know its points. But to make full coherent sense of a passage, we must see two more things.

1. **Readers must see how everything in a section or whole is** *relevant* **to its point.** Consider this passage:

   We analyzed essays written by sixth-grade students to determine the effectiveness of training in distinguishing fact from opinion. In an essay written before training, the students failed almost completely to distinguish fact and opinion. These essays were also badly organized in several ways. In the first two essays after training began, the students attempted to distinguish fact from opinion, but did so inconsistently. They also produced fewer spelling and punctuation errors. In the essays four through seven, they distinguished fact from opinion more consistently, but in their final essay, written six months after completion of instruction, they did no better than they did in their first essay. Their last essay was significantly longer than their first one, however. Their training thus had some effect on their writing during the training period, but it was inconsistent and transient.

What are those sentences about spelling, organization, and length doing there? When readers can't see the relevance of sentences to a point, they are likely to judge what they read incoherent.

I am sorry to say that I can't give you a simple rule of relevance, because it's so abstract a quality. I can only list its most important kinds. Sentences are relevant to a point when they offer these:

- background or context
- points of sections and the whole
- reasons supporting a point
- evidence, facts, or data supporting a reason
- an explanation of reasoning or methods
- consideration of other points of view

2. **Readers must see how the parts of your document are ordered.** Readers want to see not just how everything they read is relevant to a point, but what principle is behind the order of its parts. We look for three kinds of order: chronological, coordinate, and logical.

- **Chronological**   This is the simplest order, from earlier to later (or vice versa), as a narrative or as cause and effect. Signal time with *first, then, finally;* signal cause and effect with *as a result, because of that,* and so on. The passage about the essay research was chronologically organized.

- **Coordinate**   Two or more sections are coordinate when they are like pillars equally supporting a common roof. *There are three reasons why . . .* Order those sections so that their sequence makes sense to your reader—by importance, complexity, and so on—then signal that order with words and phrases such as *first, second, . . .* or *also, another, more important, in addition,* and so on. That's how this section on order is organized.

- **Logical**   This is the most complex order: by example and generalization (or vice versa), premise and conclusion (or vice versa), or by assertion and contradiction. Signal logic with *for example, on the other hand, it follows that . . .*

On Paragraphs

It would be easy to say that all paragraphs should follow those principles:

- Begin with a short, easily grasped sentence or two that frame what follows.

- State the point of the paragraph (in traditional terms its *topic sentence*) in the last sentence of its introduction. If the introduction is just one sentence, it will be its point, by default.

- Toward the end of that point sentence, name the key themes that thread through what follows.

The problem is, not all paragraphs follow that tidy structure, and we get through most of the ones that don't just fine. In fact, in different kinds of writing, paragraphs follow different conventions: newspaper paragraphs are often just a sentence long; paragraphs in this book are a bit longer, but not as long as paragraphs in scholarly journals, which can run half a page or more. Second, even scholarly writers write two- or three-sentence paragraphs, some shorter, as transitions, conclusions, introductions, asides, special emphasis, and so on.

We can ignore short paragraphs that serve special functions, because we have no problem reading (or writing) them. But many substantial paragraphs of six or seven sentences or more seem to have no evident principle of design. Even so, we can see in most of them some kind of opening segment that frames the rest of the paragraph. It might not include its *point*—that may come later, usually at its end. But the first sentence or two do set up what follows, introducing its key terms. And that is usually enough to help us make sense of what follows.

For example, compare these two paragraphs:

2a. The team obtained exact sequences of fossils—new lines of antelopes, giraffes, and elephants developing out of old and appearing in younger strata, then dying out as they were replaced by others in still later strata. The most specific sequences they reconstructed were several lines of pigs that had been common at the site and had developed rapidly. The team produced family trees that dated types of pigs so accurately that when they found pigs next to fossils of questionable age, they could use the pigs to date the fossils. By mapping every fossil precisely, the team was able to recreate exactly how and when the animals in a whole ecosystem evolved.

2b. By precisely mapping every fossil they found, the team was able to recreate exactly how and when the animals in a whole ecosystem evolved. They charted new lines of antelopes, giraffes, and elephants developing out of old and appearing in younger strata, then dying out as they were replaced by others in still later strata. The most exact sequences they reconstructed were several lines of pigs that had been common at the site and had developed rapidly. The team produced family trees that dated types of pigs so accurately that when they found pigs next to fossils of questionable age, they could use the pigs to date the fossils.

Paragraph (2a) makes its point in the last sentence; paragraph (2b) in its first sentence. But in the context of an otherwise coherent text about fossil hunters and their work, we wouldn't have a big problem understanding (2a).

And that only emphasizes why it is so important to introduce the sections and subsections of your document clearly, accurately, and helpfully. If your readers begin a section knowing its point, they can manage their way through a few paragraphs that are less than perfect. But if they don't know what your paragraphs add up to, then no matter how well you write them individually, your readers may well feel that the section they constitute is incoherent.

DIAGNOSIS AND REVISION

To diagnose how easily your readers will see your points and the coherence of your document, do this:

1. Draw a line after the introduction to your whole document.
2. Divide the body of the document into its sections and subsections. (You might introduce them with headings constructed out of the key terms unique to those sections.)
3. Circle the introductory segment of each section.
4. Underline the point of every section.

Now look for the following:

1. Segments that introduce major sections should be separate paragraphs.
2. The *point* sentence for each unit should be at or near the end of each introductory segment.
3. Each point sentence should state at its end the key themes that thread through what follows.
4. When read in sequence, those point sentences along with the main point should coherently summarize your whole document.

If your readers might not see those features quickly, revise so that they will.

A BASIC PRINCIPLE OF CLARITY

Here is a basic principle of clarity that applies to individual sentences, to substantive paragraphs, to sections and subsections, and to wholes:

> Readers are more likely to judge as clear any unit of writing that opens with a short segment that they can easily grasp and that frames the longer and more complex segment that follows.

- In a simple sentence, that short, easily grasped segment is a subject/topic. Compare these two:

  > 1a. <u>Resistance in Nevada against its use as a waste disposal site</u> has been heated.

  > 1b. <u>Nevada</u> HAS heatedly RESISTED its use as a waste disposal site.

- In a complex sentence, that short, easily grasped segment is a main clause that expresses the *point* of its sentence. Compare these two:

  > 1a. Greater knowledge of pre-Columbian civilizations and the effect of European colonization destroying their societies by inflicting on them devastating diseases has led to a historical reassessment of Columbus' role in world history.

  > 1b. <u>Historians are reassessing Columbus' role in world history</u>, because they know more about pre-Columbian civilizations and how European colonization destroyed their societies by inflicting on them devastating diseases.

The point of sentence (1a) is buried at its end. In (1b), the opening clause states the *main point* of the sentence, its most important claim: *Historians are reassessing Columbus' role* . . . That claim is then supported by the longer and more complex clause that follows.

- In a paragraph, that short, easily grasped unit is an introductory sentence or two that both expresses the point of the paragraph and introduces its key concepts. Compare these two paragraphs:

  > 3a. Thirty sixth-grade students wrote essays that were analyzed to determine the effectiveness of eight weeks of training to distinguish fact from opinion. That ability is an important aspect of making sound arguments of any kind. In an essay written before instruction began, the writers failed almost completely to distinguish fact from opinion. In an essay written after four weeks of instruction, the students visibly attempted to distinguish fact from opinion, but did so inconsistently. In three more essays, they distinguished fact from opinion more consistently, but never achieved the predicted level.

In a final essay written six months after instruction ended, they did no better than they did in their pre-instruction essay. Their training had some effect on their writing during the instruction period, but it was inconsistent, and six months after instruction it had no measurable effect.

3b. In this study, thirty sixth-grade students were taught to distinguish fact from opinion. They did so **successfully** during the instruction period, but the effect was **inconsistent** and **less than predicted**, and six months after instruction ended, the instruction had **no measurable effect.** <small>opening segment/point</small> In an essay written before instruction began, the writers failed almost completely to distinguish fact from opinion. In an essay written after four weeks of instruction, the students visibly attempted to distinguish fact from opinion, but did so inconsistently. In three more essays, they distinguished fact from opinion more consistently, but never achieved the predicted level. In a final essay written six months after instruction ended, they did no better than they did in their pre-instruction essay. We thus conclude that short-term training to distinguish fact from opinion has no consistent or long term effect.

Paragraph (3a) has no clearly distinguished opening unit, and it does not announce the key themes of the paragraph. Paragraph (3b) has a clearly marked opening unit that states the point, and it clearly announces the key themes of the paragraph.

○ In a section or subsection, that short easily grasped unit may be just a paragraph; in longer units, it will be proportionally longer. Even so, at its end it expresses the point of its unit and introduces the key concepts that follow. There is not enough space here to illustrate how that principle applies to a passage several paragraphs long, but it is easy to imagine.

○ In a whole document, that introductory unit might be one or more paragraphs long, perhaps even a few pages. Even so, it should be substantially shorter than the rest, and in a sentence at its end, it states the point of the whole document and introduces its key concepts.

QUICK TIP: Budget your time for both drafting and revision so that you spend most of it on beginnings: the introduction to the whole, then the introductions to major sections, then introductions to subsections, and long paragraphs, then the beginnings of sentences. Get beginnings straight and the rest is likely to take care of itself.

The Costs and Benefits of Cookie-Cutter Writing

Some writers fear that patterns like these will inhibit their creativity and bore their readers. That's a reasonable concern, if you are writing a literary essay that explores your own thoughts as you have them, for readers who have the time and patience to follow the twists and turns of your thinking. If you are writing that kind of essay for that kind of reader, go to it. Don't tie yourself to what I've said here.

On most occasions, however, most of us read less for aesthetic pleasures than for an end more practical—to understand what we need to know. Writers help us do that when they locate point sentences where we expect them and when their sentences follow the principles we've looked at over the course of these eleven lessons.

Such writing may seem cut and dried—when *you* write it, because you will be so conscious of the forms you followed. But it earns the gratitude of readers who have too little time to read, understand, and remember everything they must and who will, in any event, focus more on understanding the substance of your writing than on critiquing its form.

Summing Up

Plan your paragraphs, sections, and the whole on this model:

<u>Researchers</u> have made strides in the **early and accurate diagnosis** of *Alzheimer's*, [But <u>those</u> **diagnoses** have raised A NEW HUMAN PROBLEAM about **informing** *those at risk* before they show any *symptoms of it*.] _{point}	Open each unit with a relatively short segment introducing it.
	End that segment with a sentence stating the point of that unit.
	Toward the end of that point sentence, use key themes that the rest of the unit develops.

Not too long ago, when <u>physicians</u> examined an older patient who seemed *out of touch with reality,* <u>they</u> had to **guess** whether that person had *Alzheimer's* or was *only senile.* In the past few years, however, <u>they</u> have been able to use **new and more reliable tests** focusing on genetic clues. But in **the accuracy of these new tests** lies the RISK OF ANOTHER KIND OF HUMAN TRAGEDY: <u>Physicians</u> may be able to **predict** *Alzheimer's* long before its overt appearance, but such an **early diagnosis** could PSYCHOLOGICALLY DEVASTATE AN APPARENTLY HEALTHY PERSON.

In the longer segment that follows, use consistent topics (underlined).

Repeat key terms introduced toward the end of the opening segment (boldfaced, italicized, and capitalized).

Make every sentence follow the old-new principle.

Order sentences, paragraphs, and sections in a way that readers understand.

Make all sentences relevant to the point of the unit that they constitute.

PART FIVE

Ethics

Ethics is in origin the art of recommending to others the sacrifices required for cooperation with oneself.
—BERTRAND RUSSELL

Lesson

12

The Ethics of Style

There is no artifice as good and desirable as simplicity.
—ST. FRANCIS DE SALES

Affected simplicity is refined imposture.
—LA ROCHEFOUCAULD

Everything should be made as simple as possible, but not simpler.
—ALBERT EINSTEIN

Simplicity is not a given. It is an achievement, a human invention,
a discovery, a beloved belief.
—WILLIAM GASS

Style is the ultimate morality of mind.
—ALFRED NORTH WHITEHEAD

BEYOND POLISH

It is easy to think that style is just the polish that makes a sentence go down more smoothly, but more than appeal is at stake in choosing subjects and verbs in these two sentences:

1a. **Shiites, Sunnis, and Kurds** DISTRUST one another because **they** HAVE ENGAGED in generations of cultural conflict.

1b. **Generations of cultural conflict** HAVE CAUSED distrust among Shiites, Sunnis, and Kurds.

Which sentence more accurately reflects what causes the distrust among the three—their deliberate actions, as in (1a), or, as in (1b), the circumstances of their history? Such a choice of subjects and verbs even implies a philosophy of human action: do we freely choose our actions, or do circumstances cause them? Later, we'll look at the way this issue plays itself out in our own Declaration of Independence.

Our choice of what character to tell a story about—people or their circumstances—involves more than ease of reading, even more than a philosophy of action, because every such choice also has an ethical dimension.

The Ethical Responsibilities of Writers and Readers

In the last eleven lessons, I have emphasized the responsibility we owe readers to be clear. But if we are responsible readers, we also have a responsibility toward writers to read them hard enough to understand the necessary complexity of ideas that can't be expressed in Dick-and-Jane sentences. It would be impossible, for example, for an engineer to revise this into language clear to everyone:

> The drag force on a particle of diameter d moving with speed u relative to a fluid of density p and viscosity μ is usually modeled by F = $0.5C_D u^2 A$, where A is the cross-sectional area of the particle at right angles to the motion.

Most of us do work hard to understand—at least until we decide that a writer apparently failed to work equally hard to help us understand, or, worse, deliberately made our reading more difficult than it has to be. Once we decide that a writer was careless or lazy or self-indulgent—well, our days are too few to spend them on those indifferent to our needs.

But our response to gratuitous complexity only re-emphasizes how responsible we are for our own writing, for it seems axiomatic that if we don't want others to impose carelessly complex writing on us, then we ought not impose it on others. If we are socially responsible writers, we should make our ideas no simpler than they deserve, but no more difficult than they have to be.

Responsible writers follow a rule whose more general theme you probably recognize:

> Write to others as you would have others write to you.

Few of us violate that principle deliberately. It's just that we are all so inclined to think that our own writing is clear: If our readers struggle to understand it, the problem must be not the flawed expression of our deep thoughts but their shallow reading.

But that's a mistake, because if you underestimate your readers' real needs, you risk losing more than their attention. You risk losing your reputation, what writers since Aristotle have called your *ethos*—the character that readers infer from your writing: Does it make them think you are accessible or difficult? amiably candid or impersonally aloof? trustworthy or deceitful?

Over time, the ethos you project in individual pieces of writing hardens into your reputation. So it's not just altruistically generous to go an extra step to help readers understand. It's pragmatically smart, because we tend to trust most a writer with a reputation for being thoughtful, reliable, and considerate of her readers' needs.

But there is more at stake here than even reputation. What is at stake is the ethical foundations of a literate society.

An Ethic of Style

We write ethically when as a matter of principle, we would trade places with our intended readers and experience the consequences they do after they read our writing. Unfortunately, it's not quite that simple. How, for example, do we judge those who write opaquely without knowing they do; or those who knowingly write that way and defend it?

Unintended Obscurity   Those who write in ways that seem dense and convoluted rarely think they do, much less intend to. For example, I do not believe that the writers of this next passage *intended* to write it as unclearly as they did:

> A major condition affecting adult reliance on early communicative patterns is the extent to which the communication has been planned prior to its delivery. Adult speech behaviour takes on many of the characteristics of child language, where the communication is spontaneous and relatively unpredictable.
>
> —E. Ochs and B. Schieffelin, *Planned and Unplanned Discourse*

That means (I think):

> When we speak spontaneously, we rely on patterns of child language.

The authors might object that I have oversimplified their meaning, but those eleven words express what I remember from their forty-four, and what really counts, after all, is not what we understand *as* we read, but how well we remember it the next day.

The ethical issue here is not those writers' willful indifference, but their innocent ignorance. In that case, when writers don't know better, we readers have the duty to meet another term of the reader-writer contract: we must not just read carefully, but when given the opportunity, respond candidly and helpfully. I know many of you think that right now you do not have the standing to do that. But one day, you will.

Intended Misdirection   The ethics of writing are clearer when writers knowingly use language in their own self-interest rather than yours.

Example #1: Who Erred?   For example, a few years ago, the Sears Company was accused of overcharging for automobile repairs. It responded with an ad saying,

> With over two million automotive customers serviced last year in California alone, mistakes may have occurred. However, Sears wants you to know that we would never intentionally violate the trust customers have shown in our company for 105 years.

In the first sentence, the writer avoided mentioning Sears as the party responsible for mistakes. He could have used a PASSIVE verb:

> . . . mistakes **may have been made.**

But that would have encouraged us to wonder *By whom?* Instead, the writer found a verb that moved Sears off stage by saying mistakes just "occurred," seemingly on their own.

In the second sentence of that ad, though, the writer focused on *Sears,* the responsible agent, because he wanted to emphasize its good intentions.

> **Sears** . . . would never intentionally violate . . .

If we revise the first sentence to focus on Sears and the second to hide it, we get a different effect:

> When we serviced over two million automotive customers last year in California, we made mistakes. However, you should know that no intentional violation of 105 years of trust occurred.

That's a small point of stylistic manipulation, self-interested but innocent of any malign motives. This next one is more significant.

Example #2: Who Pays?   Consider this letter from a natural gas utility telling me and hundreds of thousands of other customers that it was raising our rates. (The topic/subject in every clause, main or subordinate, is boldfaced.)

> **The Illinois Commerce Commission** has authorized a restructuring of our rates together with an increase in Service Charge revenues effective with service rendered on and after November 12, 1990. **This** is the first increase in rates for Peoples Gas in over six years. **The restructuring of rates** is consistent with the policy of the Public Utilities Act that **rates for service to various classes of utility customers** be based upon the cost of providing that service. **The new rates** move revenues from every class of customer closer to the cost actually incurred to provide gas service.

That notice is a model of misdirection: after the first sentence, the writer never begins a sentence with a human character, least of all the character whose interests are most at stake—me, the reader. He (or perhaps she) mentions me only twice, in the third person, never as a topic/agent/subject:

> . . . for service to various classes of utility **customers**
>
> . . . move revenues from every class of **customer**

The writer mentions the company only once, in the third person, and not as a responsible topic/agent/subject:

> . . . increase in rates for **Peoples Gas**

Had the company wanted to make clear who the real "doer" was and who was being done to, the notice would have read more like this:

> According to the Illinois Commerce Commission, **we** can now make **you** pay more for your gas service after November 12, 1990. **We** have not made **you** pay more in over six years, but under the Public Utilities Act, now **we** can.

If the writer *intended* to deflect responsibility, then we can reasonably charge him with breaching the First Rule of Ethical Writing, for surely, he would not want that same kind of writing directed to him, systematically hiding who is doing what in a matter close to his interests.

Example #3: Who Dies?   Finally, here is a passage that raises an even greater ethical issue, one involving life and death. Some time ago, the Government Accounting Office investigated why more than half the car owners who got recall letters did not get their cars fixed. The GAO found that car owners could not understand the letters or were not sufficiently alarmed by them to bring their cars back to the dealer for service.

I received the following. It shows how writers can meet a legal obligation while evading an ethical one (I number the sentences):

> [1]A defect which involves the possible failure of a frame support plate may exist on your vehicle. [2]This plate (front suspension pivot bar support plate) connects a portion of the front suspension to the vehicle frame, and [3]its failure could affect vehicle directional control, particularly during heavy brake application. [4]In addition, your vehicle may require adjustment service to the hood secondary catch system. [5]The secondary catch may be misaligned so that the hood may not be adequately restrained to prevent hood fly-up in the event the primary latch is inadvertently left unengaged. [6]Sudden hood fly-up beyond the secondary catch while driving could impair driver visibility. [7]In certain circumstances, occurrence of either of the above conditions could result in vehicle crash without prior warning.

(When asked my make of car, I dodge the question.)

First, look at the subject/topics of the sentences:

[1]a defect	[2]this plate	[3]its failure
[4]your vehicle	[5]the secondary catch	
[6]sudden hood fly-up	[7]occurrence of either condition	

The main character/topic of that story is not me, the driver, but my car and its parts. In fact, the writers ignored me almost entirely (I am in *your vehicle* twice and *driver* once), and omitted all references to themselves. In sum, it says,

> There is a car that might have defective parts. Its plate could fail and its hood fly up. If they do, it could crash without warning.

The writers—probably a committee of lawyers—also nominalized verbs and made others passive when they referred to actions that might alarm me (n = nominalization, p = passive):

Failure$_n$	vehicle directional control$_n$	heavy brake application$_n$
be misaligned$_p$	not restrained$_p$	hood fly-up$_n$
left unengaged$_p$	driver visibility$_n$	warning$_n$

If the writers intended to deflect my fear and maybe my anger, then they violated their ethical duty to write to me as they would have me write to them, for surely they would not swap places with a reader deliberately lulled into ignoring a condition that threatened his life.

Of course, being candid has its costs. I would be naive to claim that everyone is free to write as he or she pleases, especially when a writer's job depends on protecting an employer's self-interest. Maybe the writers of that letter felt coerced into writing it as they did. But that doesn't mitigate the consequences. When we knowingly write in ways that we would not want others to write to us, we abrade the trust that sustains a civil society.

We should not, of course, confuse unethical indirectness with the human impulse to soften bad news. When a supervisor says *I'm afraid our new funding didn't come through*, we know it means 'You have no job.' But that indirectness is motivated not by dishonesty, but by kindness.

In short, our choice of subjects is crucial not only when we want to be clear, but also when we want to be honest or deceptive.

Exercise 12.1

Revise the gas rate notice, using *you* as a topic/agent/subject. Then revise again, using *we*. For example:

> As the Illinois Commerce Commission has authorized, **you** will have to pay us higher service charges after November 12, 1990/**we** can charge you more after November 12 . . .

Would the company resist sending either revision? Why? Was the original "good" writing? What do you mean by *good*?

Exercise 12.2

Revise the recall letter, making *you* the subject of as many verbs and naming as many actions in verbs as you can. One of the sentences will read,

> If **you** BRAKE hard and the plate FAILS, **you** could . . .

Would the company be reluctant to send out that version? Is the original letter "good" writing? Which of the following, if either, is closer to the "truth"? Is that even the right question?

> If the plate fails, you could crash.
>
> If the plate fails, your car could crash.

Rationalizing Opacity

Necessary Complexity   A more complicated ethical issue is how we should respond to those who know they write in a complex style, but claim they must, because they are breaking new intellectual ground. Are they right, or is that self-serving rationalization? This is a vexing question, not just because we can settle it only case-by-case, but because we may not be able to settle some cases at all, at least not to everyone's satisfaction.

Here, for example, is a sentence from a leading figure in contemporary literary theory:

> If, for a while, the ruse of desire is calculable for the uses of discipline soon the repetition of guilt, justification, pseudo-scientific theories, superstition, spurious authorities and classifications can be seen as the desperate effort to "normalize" *formally* the disturbance of a discourse of splitting that violates the rational, enlightened claims of its enunciatory modality.
>
> —Homi K. Babba

Does that sentence express a thought so complex, so nuanced that its substance can be expressed only as written? Or is it babble? How do we decide whether in fact his nuances are, at least for ordinarily competent readers, just not accessible, given the time most of us have for figuring them out?

We owe readers an ethical duty to write precise and nuanced prose, but we ought not assume that they owe us an indefinite amount of their time to unpack it. If we choose to write in ways that we know will make readers struggle—well, it's a free country. In the marketplace of ideas, truth is the prime value, but not the only one. Another is what it costs us to find it.

In the final analysis, I can suggest only that when writers claim their prose style must be difficult because their ideas are new, they are, as a matter of simple fact, more often wrong than right. The philosopher of language Ludwig Wittgenstein said,

> Whatever can be thought can be thought clearly; whatever can be written can be written clearly.

I'd add a nuance:

> Whatever can be written can usually be written *more* clearly, with just a bit more effort.

Salutary Complexity/Subversive Clarity   There are two more defenses of complexity: one claims that complexity is good for us, the other that clarity is bad.

As to the first claim, some argue that the harder we have to work to understand what we read, the more deeply we think and the better we understand. Everyone should be happy to know that no evidence supports so foolish a claim, and substantial evidence contradicts it.

As to the second claim, some argue that "clarity" is a device wielded by those in power to mislead us about who really controls our lives. By speaking in deceptively simple ways, they say, those who control the facts dumb them down, rendering us unable to understand the full complexity of our political and social circumstances:

> The call to write curriculum in a language that is touted as clear and accessible is evidence of a moral and political vision that increasingly collapses under the weight of its own anti-intellectualism. . . . [T]hose who make a call for clear writing synonymous with an attack on critical educators have missed the role that the "language of clarity" plays in a dominant culture that cleverly and powerfully uses "clear" and "simplistic" language to systematically undermine and prevent the conditions from arising for a public culture to engage in rudimentary forms of complex and critical thinking.
>
> —Stanley Aronowitz, *Postmodern Education*

The writer makes one good point: language is deeply implicated in politics, ideology, and control. In our earliest history, the educated elite used writing itself to exclude the illiterate, then Latin and French to exclude those who knew only English. More recently, those in authority have relied on a vocabulary thick with Latinate nominalizations and on a Standard English that requires those Outs aspiring to join the Ins to submit to a decade-long education, during which time they are expected to acquire not only the language of the Ins, but their values, as well.

Moreover, clarity is not a natural virtue, corrupted by fallen academics, bureaucrats, and others jealous to preserve their authority. Clarity is a value that is created by society and that society must work hard to maintain, for writing clearly is not just hard, it is almost an unnatural act. It has to be learned, sometimes painfully (as this book demonstrates).

So is clarity an ideological value? Well of course it is. How could it be otherwise? But those who attack clarity as a conspiracy to oversimplify complicated social issues are as wrong as those who attack science because some use it for malign ends: neither science nor clarity is a threat; we are threatened by those who use clarity (or science) to deceive us. It is not clarity that subverts, but the unethical use of it. We must simply insist that, in principle, those who manage our affairs have a duty to tell us the truth as clearly as they can. They probably won't, but that just shifts the burden to us to call them out on it.

With every sentence we write we have to choose, and the ethical quality of our choices depends on the motives behind them. Only by knowing motives can we know whether a writer of clear or complex prose would willingly be the object of such writing, to be influenced (or manipulated) in the same way, with the same result.

That seems simple enough. But it's not.

An Extended Analysis

It is easy to abuse writers who seem to manipulate us through their language for their own, self-interested ends. It is more difficult to think about these matters when we are manipulated by those whom we would never charge with deceit. But it is just such cases that force us to think the hardest about matters of style and ethics.

The most celebrated texts in our history are the Declaration of Independence, the Constitution, and Abraham Lincoln's Gettysburg Address and Second Inaugural Address. In previous editions, I discussed how Lincoln artfully manipulated the language of his Gettysburg Address and Second Inaugural Address. Here I examine how Thomas Jefferson managed his prose style in the Declaration of Independence to influence how we judge the logic of his argument.

The Declaration is celebrated for its logic. After a discussion of human rights and their origin, Jefferson laid out a simple syllogism:

Major premise:	When a long train of abuses by a government evinces a design to reduce a people under despotism, they must throw off such government.
Minor premise:	These colonies have been abused by a tyrant who evinces such a design.
Conclusion:	We therefore declare that these colonies are free and independent states.

Jefferson's argument is as straightforward as the language expressing it is artful.

Jefferson begins with a preamble that explains why the colonists decided to justify their declaration, based on the surprising idea that revolutionaries must have, and declare, good reasons:

> When, in the course of human events, it becomes necessary for one people to dissolve the political bonds which have connected them with another, and to assume among the powers of the earth, the separate and equal station to which the laws of nature and of nature's God entitle them, a decent respect to the opinions of mankind requires that they should declare the causes which impel them to the separation.

He then organizes the Declaration into three parts. In the first, he offers his major premise, a philosophical justification for a people to throw off a tyranny and replace it with a government of their own:

> We hold these truths to be self-evident, that all men are created equal, that they are endowed by their Creator with certain unalienable rights, that among these are life, liberty and the pursuit of happiness. That to secure these rights, governments are instituted among men, deriving their just powers from the consent of the governed. That whenever any form of government becomes destructive to these ends, it is the right of the people to alter or to abolish it, and to institute new government, laying its foundation on such principles and organizing its powers in such form, as to them shall seem most likely to effect their safety and happiness. Prudence, indeed, will dictate that governments long established should not be changed for light and transient causes; and accordingly all experience hath shown that mankind are more disposed to suffer, while evils are sufferable, than to right themselves by abolishing the forms to which they are accustomed. But when a long train of abuses and usurpations, pursuing invariably the same object evinces a design to reduce them under absolute despotism, it is their right, it is their duty, to throw off such government, and to provide new guards for their future security. Such has been the patient sufferance of these colonies; and such is now the necessity which constrains them to alter their former systems of government. The history of the present King of Great Britain is a history of repeated injuries and usurpations, all having in direct object the establishment of an absolute tyranny over these states.

Part 2 of the Declaration begins with the words *To prove this, let Facts be submitted to a candid world*. Those facts constitute a list of King George's offenses against the colonies, evidence supporting Jefferson's minor premise that the king intended to establish "an absolute Tyranny over these States":

> He has refused his assent to laws, the most wholesome and necessary for the public good.
>
> He has forbidden his governors to pass laws of immediate and pressing importance, unless suspended in their operation till his assent should be obtained; and when so suspended, he has utterly neglected to attend to them.
>
> He has refused to pass other laws for the accommodation of large districts of people, unless those people would relinquish the right of representation in the legislature, a right inestimable to them and formidable to tyrants only.
>
> He has called together legislative bodies at places unusual, uncomfortable, and distant . . .

Part 3 opens by reviewing the colonists' attempts to avoid separation:

> In every stage of these oppressions we have petitioned for redress in the most humble terms: Our repeated petitions have been answered only by repeated injury. A prince, whose character is thus marked by every act which may define a tyrant, is unfit to be the ruler of a free people.
>
> Nor have we been wanting in attention to our British brethren. We have warned them from time to time of attempts by their legislature to extend an unwarrantable jurisdiction over us. We have reminded them of the circumstances of our emigration and settlement here. We have appealed to their native justice and magnanimity, and we have conjured them by the ties of our common kindred to disavow these usurpations, which, would inevitably interrupt our connections and correspondence. We must, therefore, acquiesce in the necessity, which denounces our separation, and hold them, as we hold the rest of mankind, enemies in war, in peace friends.

Part 3 ends with the declaration of independence:

> We, therefore, the representatives of the United States of America, in General Congress, assembled, appealing to the Supreme Judge of the world for the rectitude of our intentions, do, in the name, and by the authority of the good people of these colonies, solemnly publish and declare, that these united colonies are, and of right ought to be free and independent states; that they are absolved from all allegiance to the British Crown, and that all political connection between them and the state of Great Britain, is and ought to be totally dissolved; and that as free and independent states, they have full power to levy war, conclude peace, contract alliances, establish commerce, and to do all other acts and things which independent states may of right do. And for the support of this declaration, with a firm reliance on the protection of divine providence, we mutually pledge to each other our lives, our fortunes and our sacred honor.

Jefferson's argument is a model of cool logic, but as logical as it is, he artfully managed his language in its tacit support.

Parts 2 and 3 reflect the principles of clarity explained in Lessons 3–7. In part 2, Jefferson made *He* (King George) the short, concrete topic/subject/agent of all the actions named.

He *has refused . . .*
He *has forbidden . . .*
He *has refused . . .*
He *has called together . . .*

He could have written this:

His assent to laws, the most wholesome and necessary for the public good, *has not been forthcoming* . . .

His governors *have failed* to pass laws of immediate and pressing importance . . .

Legislative bodies *have had to meet* at places unusual, uncomfortable, and distant from the depository of their public Records . . .

Or he could have consistently focused on the colonists:

We *have been deprived* of Laws, the most wholesome and necessary . . .

We *lack* Laws of immediate and pressing importance . . .

We *have had to meet* at places usual, uncomfortable . . .

In other words, Jefferson was not forced by the nature of things to make King George the active agent of every oppressive action. But that choice supported his argument that the king was a willfully abusive tyrant. That choice of subject seems so natural, however, that we don't notice that it was a *choice*.

In part 3, Jefferson also wrote in a style that reflects our principles of clarity: he again matched the characters in his story to the subject/topics of his sentences. But here he switched characters to the colonists, named *we*:

Nor *have* **we** *been wanting* in attentions to our British brethren.

We *have warned* them from time to time . . .

We *have reminded* them of the circumstances of our emigration . . .

We *have appealed* to their native justice and magnanimity . . .

. . . **we** *have conjured* them by the ties of our common kindred . . .

They too *have been deaf* to the voice of justice and of consanguinity.

We *must*, therefore, *acquiesce* in the necessity . . .

We . . . *do* . . . solemnly *publish and declare* . . .

. . . **we** mutually *pledge* to each other our Lives . . .

With the one exception of *They too have been deaf*, all the subject/topics are *we*.

And again, Jefferson was not forced by the nature of things to do that. He could have written this:

Our British brethren *have heard* our requests . . .

They *have received* our warnings . . .

They *know* the circumstances of our emigration . . .

They *have ignored* our pleas . . .

But he chose to assign agency to the colonists to focus on their attempts to negotiate, then on their declaring independence.

Again, his choices were not inevitable, but they seem natural, even unremarkable: *King George did all those bad things, so we must declare our independence.* What more is there to say about the style of parts 2 and 3, other than that Jefferson made the obviously right choices?

Far more interesting are Jefferson's choices in part 1, the words we have committed to our national memory. In that part, he chose a quite different style. In fact, in part 1, he wrote only two sentences that make a person the subject of an active verb:

> . . . **they** [the colonists] *should declare* the causes . . .
>
> **We** *hold* these truths to be self-evident . . .

There are four other subject-verb sequences that have short, concrete subjects, but they are all in the passive voice:

> . . . **all men** *are created* equal . . .
>
> . . . **they** *are endowed* by their Creator with certain unalienable Rights . . .
>
> . . . **governments** *are instituted* among **Men** . . .
>
> . . . **governments long established** *should* not *be changed* for light and transient causes . . .

The last two passives explicitly obscure the agency of people in general and the colonists in particular.

In the rest of part 1, Jefferson chose a style that is *even more* impersonal, making abstractions the topic/subject/agents of almost every important verb. In fact, most of his sentences would yield to the kind of revisions we described in Lessons 2–6:

> When in the course of human events, **it** *becomes necessary* for one people to dissolve the political bands which have connected them with another . . .
>
> When in the course of human events, **we** *decide* **we** *must dissolve* the political bands which have . . .
>
> . . . **a decent respect to the opinions of mankind** *requires* that they should declare **the causes** which *impel* them to the separation.
>
> If **we** decently *respect* the opinions of mankind, **we** *should declare* why **we** *have decided to separate.*
>
> . . . **it** *is the right* of the people to alter or to abolish it, and to institute new Government . . .
>
> **We** *may alter or abolish* it, and *institute* new government . . .

Prudence, indeed, *will dictate* that governments long established should not be changed for light and transient causes . . .

If **we** *are prudent*, **we** *will not change* governments long established for light and transient causes.

. . . **all experience** *hath shewn*, that **mankind** *are more disposed* to suffer, while evils are sufferable . . .

We *know* from experience that **we** *choose* to suffer, while **we** *can suffer* evils . . .

. . . **a long train of abuses and usurpations** . . . *evinces* a design to reduce them under absolute Despotism.

We *can see* a design in a long train of abuses and usurpations pursuing invariably the same Object—to reduce us under absolute Despotism.

Necessity . . . *constrains* them to alter their former Systems of government.

We now *must alter* our former Systems of government.

Instead of writing as clearly and directly as he did in parts 2 and 3, why in part 1 did Jefferson *choose* to write in a style so indirect and impersonal? One ready answer is that he wanted to lay down a philosophical basis not for our revolution in particular, but for justified revolution in general, a profoundly destabilizing idea in Western political philosophy and one that needed more justification than the colonists' mere desire to throw off a government they disliked.

But what is most striking about the style of part 1 is not just its impersonal generality, but how relentlessly Jefferson uses that style to strip the colonists of any free will of their own and to invest agency in higher forces that coerce the colonists to act:

- **respect** for opinion *requires* that [the colonists] explain their action
- **causes** *impel* [the colonists] to separate
- **prudence** *dictates* that [the colonists] not change government lightly
- **experience** has *shown* [the colonists]
- **necessity** *constrains* [the colonists]

Jefferson echoes that coercive power again in part 3: the colonists must *acquiesce* to the *necessity* that demands their separation.

Even when abstractions do not explicitly coerce the colonists, Jefferson implies that they are not free agents:

- It [is] *necessary* to sever bonds.
- Mankind *are disposed* to suffer.
- It is their *duty* to throw off a tyrant.

In this light, even *We hold these truths to be self-evident* is a claim that implies the colonists did not discover those truths, but rather, those truths revealed themselves to the colonists.

In short, Jefferson manipulated his language three times, twice in ways that seem transparent, unremarkable, so predictable that we don't even notice the choice: in part 2, he made King George a freely acting agent of his actions by making him the subject/topic of every sentence; in part 3, Jefferson made the colonists the agents of their own actions.

But to make the first part of his argument work, Jefferson had to make the colonists seem to be the coerced objects of higher powers. Since the only higher power named in the Declaration is a Creator, nature's God, that Creator is impliedly the coercive power that "constrains them to alter their former systems of government."

The Declaration of Independence is a majestic document for reasons beyond its grammar and style. The same words that brought our nation into existence laid down the fundamental values that justify the self-governance of all people everywhere.

But we ought not ignore Jefferson's rhetorical powers, and in particular, the genius of his style. He created a relentlessly logical argument justifying our independence, but he also manipulated, managed, massaged—call it what you will—his language to support his logic in ways not apparent to a casual reading.

If his end did not justify his means, we might argue that Jefferson was being marginally deceptive here, using language instead of logic to establish the colonists' lack of freedom to do other than what they wanted. It is, finally, an ethical issue. Do we trust a writer who seeks to manage our responses not just explicitly with a logical argument but implicitly through his prose style? We would say *No* about the writer of that automobile recall letter, because it was almost certainly *intended* to deceive us. We are, however, likely to say *Yes* about Jefferson, but only if we agree that his intended end justified his means, a principle that we ordinarily reject on ethical grounds.

SUMMING UP

How, finally, do we decide what counts as "good" writing? Is it clear, graceful, and candid, even if it fails to achieve its end? Or is it writing that does a job, regardless of its integrity and means? We have a problem so long as *good* can mean either ethically sound or pragmatically successful.

We resolve that dilemma by our First Principle of Ethical Writing:

> We are ethical writers when we would willingly put ourselves in the place of our readers and experience what they do as they read what we've written.

That puts the burden on us to imagine our readers and their feelings.

If you are even moderately advanced in your academic or professional career, you've experienced the consequences of unclear writing, especially when it's your own. If you are in your early years of college, though, you may wonder whether all this talk about clarity, ethics, and ethos is just so much finger wagging. At the moment, you may be happy to find enough words to fill three pages, much less worry how clear they are. And you may be reading textbooks that have been heavily edited to make them clear to first-year students who know little or nothing about their content. So you may not yet have experienced much carelessly dense writing. But it's only a matter of time before you will.

Others wonder why they should struggle to learn to write clearly when bad writing seems so common and seems to have no cost. What experienced readers know, and you eventually will, is that clear and graceful writers are so few that when we find them, we are desperately grateful. They do not go unrewarded.

I also know that for many writers crafting a good sentence or paragraph gives them pleasure enough. It is an ethical satisfaction some of us find not just in writing, but in everything we do: we find joy in doing good work, no matter the job. It is a view expressed by the philosopher Alfred North Whitehead, with both clarity and grace (my emphasis in the last sentence):

> Finally, there should grow the most austere of all mental qualities; I mean the sense for style. It is an aesthetic sense, based on admiration for the direct attainment of a foreseen end, simply and without waste. Style in art, style in literature, style in science, style in logic, style in practical execution have fundamentally the same aesthetic qualities, namely, attainment and restraint. The love of a subject in itself and for itself, where it is not the sleepy pleasure of pacing a mental quarter-deck, is the love of style as manifested in that study. Here we are brought back to the position from which we started, the utility of education. Style, in its finest sense, is the last acquirement of the educated mind; it is also the most useful. It pervades the whole being. The administrator with a sense for style hates waste; the engineer with a sense for style economizes his material; the artisan with a sense for style prefers good work. *Style is the ultimate morality of mind.*
>
> —Alfred North Whitehead, *The Aims of Education and Other Essays*

Appendix I
Punctuation

*I know there are some Persons who affect to despise it, and treat this
whole Subject with the utmost Contempt, as a Trifle far below their
Notice, and a Formality unworthy of their Regard: They do not hold
it difficult, but despicable; and neglect it, as being above it. Yet many
learned Men have been highly sensible to its Use; and some
ingenious and elegant Writers have condescended to point their
Works with Care; and very eminent Scholars have not disdained to
teach the Method of doing it with Propriety.*
—James Burrow

*In music, the punctuation is absolutely strict; the bars
and rests are absolutely defined. But our prose cannot be quite
strict, because we have to relate it to the audience. In other
words we are continually changing the score.*
—Sir Ralph Richardson

*There are some punctuations that are interesting
and there are some that are not.*
—Gertrude Stein

UNDERSTANDING PUNCTUATION

Most writers think that punctuation must obey the same kind of rules that govern grammar, and so managing commas and semicolons is about as interesting as making verbs agree with subjects. In fact, you have more choices in how to punctuate than you might think, and if you choose thoughtfully, you can help readers not only understand a complex sentence more easily but create nuances of emphasis that they will notice. It takes more than a few commas to turn a monotone into the Hallelujah Chorus, but a little care can produce gratifying results.

I will address punctuation as a functional problem: How do we punctuate the end of a sentence, then its beginning, and finally its middle? But first, we have to distinguish different kinds of sentences.

Simple, Compound, and Complex Sentences

Sentences have traditionally been called *simple, compound,* and *complex*. If a sentence has just one INDEPENDENT CLAUSE, it is *simple:*

> SIMPLE: The greatest English dictionary is the *Oxford English Dictionary*

If it has two or more independent clauses, it is *compound:*

> COMPOUND: [There are many good dictionaries][1],
>   [but the greatest is the *Oxford English Dictionary*][2].

If it has an independent clause and one or more subordinate clauses, it is *complex.*

> COMPLEX: [While there are many good dictionaries] subordinate clause
>   [the greatest is the *Oxford English Dictionary*]. independent clause

(*Compound-complex* is self-explanatory.)

But those terms are potentially misleading, because they suggest that a grammatically simple sentence should *seem* simpler than one that is grammatically complex. But that's not always true. For example, most readers think that of the next two sentences, the grammatically simple one *feels* more complex than the grammatically complex one:

> GRAMMATICALLY SIMPLE: Our review of the test led to our modification
>   of it as a result of complaints by teachers.

GRAMMATICALLY COMPLEX: After we reviewed the test, we modified it because teachers complained.

Those two terms do not reliably indicate how we are likely to respond to such sentences. We need a more useful set of terms.

Punctuated and Grammatical Sentences

We can make more useful distinctions between what we will call *punctuated* sentences and *grammatical* sentences:

- A punctuated sentence begins with a capital letter and ends with a period or question/exclamation mark. It might be one word or a hundred.

- A grammatical sentence is a subject and verb in a main clause along with everything else depending on that clause.

We distinguish these two kinds of sentences because readers can respond to them very differently: the one you are now reading, for example, is one long punctuated sentence, but it is not as hard to read as many shorter sentences that consist of many subordinate clauses; I have chosen to punctuate as one long sentence what I might have punctuated as a series of shorter ones: that colon, those semicolons, and the comma before that *but* could have been periods, for example—and that dash could have been a period too.

Here is that long sentence you just read repunctuated with virtually no change in its grammar, creating seven punctuated sentences:

> We must distinguish these two kinds of punctuated sentences because readers respond to them very differently. The one you are now reading, for example, is a short punctuated sentence, consisting of just one subject and one verb plus what depends on them. But this paragraph is not as hard to read as many shorter sentences that consist of many subordinate clauses. I have chosen to punctuate as separate sentences what I could have punctuated as one long one. The period before that *but*, for example, could have been a comma. The last two periods could have been semicolons. And that period could have been a dash.

Though I changed little but the punctuation, those seven grammatical sentences, now punctuated as seven punctuated sentences, feel different from those same grammatical sentences in a single punctuated sentence. In short, we can create different stylistic effects simply by the way we punctuate: punctuation is not governed by rules, but by choices.

PUNCTUATING THE ENDS OF SENTENCES

Above all other rules of punctuation, a writer must know how to punctuate the end of a grammatical sentence. You have a lot of choices in how to do that, but signal it you must, because readers have to know where one grammatical sentence stops and the next begins. The punctuation of this one does not help us do that:

> In 1967, Congress passed civil rights laws that remedied problems of registration and voting this had political consequences throughout the South.

When you write that kind of sentence you create a *fused* or *run-on sentence,* an error you cannot afford to make, because it signals a writer who does not understand the basics of writing.

You can *choose* to separate pairs of grammatical sentences in ten ways. Three are common.

Three Common Forms of End Punctuation

1. **Period (or Question/Exclamation Mark) Alone** The simplest, least noticeable way to signal the end of a grammatical sentence is with a period:

   ✓ In 1967, Congress passed civil rights laws that remedied problems of registration and **voting. This** had political consequences throughout the South.

   But if you create too many short punctuated sentences, your readers may feel your prose is choppy or simplistic (as on p. 43). Experienced writers revise a series of very short grammatical sentences into subordinate clauses or phrases, turning two or more grammatical sentences into one:

   ✓ **When Congress passed civil rights laws to remedy problems of registration and voting in 1967, they** had political consequences throughout the South.

   ✓ The civil rights laws **that Congress passed in 1967 to remedy problems of registration and voting** had political consequences throughout the South.

   Be cautious, though: combine too many short grammatical sentences into one long one, and you create a sentence that sprawls.

2. **Semicolon Alone** A semicolon is like a soft period; whatever is on either side of it should be a grammatical sentence (with an exception we'll discuss on p. 227). Use a semicolon instead

of a period only when the first grammatical sentence has less than fifteen or so words, and the content of the second grammatical sentence is closely linked to the first:

> In 1967, Congress passed civil rights laws that remedied problems of registration and **voting; those** laws had political consequences throughout the South.

A special problem with semicolons and *however* In one context, even well-educated writers often incorrectly end one grammatical sentence with a comma and begin the next grammatical sentence with *however*.

> Taxpayers have supported public education, **however,** they now object because taxes have risen so steeply.

Those sentences must be separated by a semicolon (but keep the comma after *however*):

> ✓ Taxpayers have supported public education; **however,** they now object because taxes have risen so steeply.

Many writers avoid semicolons because they find them mildly intimidating. So learning their use might be worth your time, if you want to be judged a sophisticated writer. Once every couple of pages is probably about right.

3. **Comma + Coordinating Conjunction** Readers also are ready to recognize the end of a grammatical sentence when they see a comma followed by two signals:

   - a coordinating conjunction: and, *but, yet, for, so, or, nor*
   - another subject and verb

     > ✓ In the 1950s religion was viewed as a bulwark against **communism, so it was** not long after that that atheism was felt to threaten national security.

     > ✓ American intellectuals have often followed **Europeans, but our culture has proven** inhospitable to their brand of socialism.

Choose a period if the two grammatical sentences are long and have their own internal punctuation.

When readers begin a coordinated series of three or more grammatical sentences, they accept just a comma between them, but only if they are short and have no internal punctuation:

> ✓ Baseball satisfies our admiration for **precision, basketball** speaks to our love of speed and **grace, and** football appeals to our lust for violence.

If any of the grammatical sentences has internal punctuation, separate them with semicolons:

✓ Baseball, the oldest indigenous American sport and essentially a rural one, satisfies our admiration for **precision; basketball,** our newest sport and now more urban than rural, speaks to our love of speed and **grace; and** football, a sport both rural and urban, appeals to our lust for violence.

An exception: Omit the comma between a coordinated pair of short grammatical sentences if you introduce them with a modifier that applies to both of them:

✓ Once the upheaval after the collapse of the Soviet Union had settled down, the economies of its former satellites had begun to **rebound but Russia's** had yet to hit bottom.

Too many grammatical sentences joined with *and* and *so* feel simplistic, so avoid more than one or two a page.

QUICK TIP: When you begin a grammatical sentence with *but*, you either can put a comma at the end of the previous sentence or begin a new punctuated sentence by putting a period there and capitalizing *but*. Use a period + *But* if what follows is important and you intend to go on discussing it:

✓ The immediate consequence of higher gas prices was some curtailment of **driving. But the long term** effect changed the car buying habits of Americans, perhaps permanently, a change that the Big Three car manufacturers could not ignore. They . . .

Use a comma + *but* if what follows only qualifies what preceded.

✓ The immediate consequence of higher gas prices was some curtailment of **driving, but that did not** last long. The long-term effect was changes in the car buying habits of Americans, a change that the Big Three car manufacturers could not ignore. They . . .

Four Less Common Forms of End Punctuation

Some readers have reservations about these next four ways of signaling the end of a grammatical sentence, but careful writers everywhere use them.

4. **Period** + **Coordinating Conjunction** Some readers think it's wrong to begin a punctuated sentence with a coordinating conjunction such as *and* or *but* (review p. 15). But they are wrong; this is entirely correct:

> ✓ Education cannot guarantee a **democracy. And** when it is available to only a few, it becomes a tool of social repression.

Use this pattern no more than once or twice a page, especially with *and*.

5. **Semicolon** + **Coordinating Conjunction** Writers occasionally end one grammatical sentence with a semicolon and begin the next with a coordinating conjunction:

> ✓ In the 1950s religion was viewed as a bulwark against **communism; so** soon thereafter atheism was felt to threaten national security.

Use a comma instead of a semicolon if the two grammatical sentences are short. But readers are grateful for a semicolon if the two grammatical sentences are long with their own internal commas:

> ✓ Problem solving, one of the most active areas of psychology, has made great strides in the last decade, particularly in understanding the problem-solving strategies of experts; **so** it is no surprise that educators have followed that research with interest.

But then readers would probably prefer a period there even more.

6. **Conjunction Alone** Some writers signal a close link between short grammatical sentences with a coordinating conjunction alone, omitting the comma:

> ✓ Oscar Wilde violated a fundamental law of British **society and** we all know what happened to him.

But a warning: though writers of the best prose do this, some teachers consider it an error.

7. **Comma Alone** Though readers rarely expect to see just a comma separate two grammatical sentences, they can manage if the sentences are short and closely linked in meaning, such as cause-effect, first-second, *if-then*, etc.

> Act in haste, repent at leisure.

Be sure, though, that neither has internal commas; not this:

> Women, who have always been underpaid, no longer accept that discriminatory treatment, they are now doing something about it.

A semicolon would be clearer:

> ✓ Women, who have always been underpaid, no longer accept that discriminatory treatment; they are now doing something about it.

But the same warning: though writers of the best prose separate short grammatical sentences with just a comma, many teachers disapprove, because a comma alone is traditionally condemned as a "comma splice," in their view, a grave error. So be sure of your readers before you experiment.

Three Special Cases: Colon, Dash, Parentheses

These last three ways of signaling the end of a grammatical sentence are a bit self-conscious, but might be interesting to those who want to distinguish themselves from most other writers.

8. **Colon**   Discerning readers are likely to think you are a bit sophisticated if you end a sentence with an appropriate colon: they take it as shorthand for *to illustrate, for example, that is, therefore*:

> ✓ Dance is not widely **supported: no** company operates at a profit, and there are few outside major cities.

A colon can also signal more obviously than a comma or semicolon that you are balancing the structure, sound, and meaning of one clause against another:

> ✓ Civil disobedience is the public conscience of a democracy: mass enthusiasm is the public consensus of a tyranny.

If you follow the colon with a grammatical sentence, capitalize the first word or not, depending on how much you want to emphasize what follows (note: some handbooks claim that the first word after a colon should not be capitalized).

QUICK TIP: Avoid a colon if it breaks a clause into two pieces, neither of which is a grammatically complete sentence. Avoid this:

> **Genetic counseling requires: a knowledge** of statistical genetics, an awareness of choices open to parents, and the psychological competence to deal with emotional trauma.

Instead, put the colon only after a whole subject-verb-OBJECT structure:

> ✓ **Genetic counseling requires the following: a** knowledge of statistical genetics, an awareness of choices open to parents, and the psychological competence to deal with emotional trauma.

9. **Dash**   You can also signal balance more informally with a dash—it suggests a casual afterthought:

   ✓ Stonehenge is a **wonder—only** a genius could have conceived it.

   Contrast that with a more formal colon: it makes a difference.

10. **Parentheses**   You can insert a short grammatical sentence inside another one with parentheses, if what you put in the parentheses is like a short afterthought. Do not put a period after the sentence inside the parenthesis; put a single period outside:

    ✓ Stonehenge is a **wonder** (**only** a genius could have conceived it).

Here's the point: You can end a grammatical sentence in ten ways. Three are conventional and common:

1. Period	I win. You lose.
2. Semicolon	I win; you lose.
3. Comma + coordinating conjunction	I win, and you lose.

Four are a bit debatable, but good writers use them, especially the first:

4. Period + coordinating conjunction	I win. And you lose.
5. Semicolon + coordinating conjunction	I win; and you lose.
6. Coordinating conjunction alone	I win and you lose.
7. Comma alone	I win, you lose.

Three are for writers who want to be a bit stylish in their punctuation:

8. Colon	I win: you lose.
9. Dash	I win—you lose.
10. Parentheses	I win (you lose).

Though some ways of punctuating the end of a sentence are flat-out wrong, you can choose from among many that are right, and each has a different effect. If you look again at the short sentences on pp. 154–155 and Mailer's long sentence on p. 155, you can see those choices in contrast. Those writers could have chosen otherwise and thereby created a different stylistic effect.

Intended Sentence Fragments

Most readers will think you've made a serious error if you inadvertently punctuate a fragment of a grammatical sentence as a complete one. Among the most common sentence fragments is a subordinate dependent clause detached from its main clause, especially one beginning with *because*:

> You cannot break a complex sentence into two shorter ones merely by replacing commas with periods. **Because if you do, you will be considered at least careless, at worst uneducated.**

Another common fragment begins with *which*:

> Most fragments occur when you write a sentence that goes on so long and becomes so complicated that you start to feel that you are losing control over it and so need to drop in a period to start another sentence. **Which is why you must understand how to write a long but clearly constructed sentence that readers can follow easily**.

Traditionally, a punctuated sentence that fails to include an independent main clause is wrong. At least in theory.

In fact, experienced writers often write fragments deliberately, as I just did. When intended, those fragments typically have two characteristics:

- They are relatively short, fewer than ten or so words.
- They are intended to reflect a mind at work, as if the writer were speaking to you, finishing a sentence, then immediately expanding and qualifying it. Almost as an afterthought, often ironically.

A good example of a passage with several fragments is the one by D.H. Lawrence in Lesson 9 (fragments are boldfaced):

> Now listen to me, don't listen to [the American colonist]. He'll tell you the lie you expect. **Which is partly your fault for expecting it.**
> He didn't come in search of freedom of worship. England had more freedom of worship in the year 1700 than America had. **Won by Englishmen who wanted freedom and so stopped at home and**

fought for it. And got it. Freedom of worship? Read the history of New England during the first century of its existence.

Freedom anyhow? The land of the free! This the land of the free! Why, if I say anything that displeases them, the free mob will lynch me, and that's my freedom. **Free?** Why I have never been in any country where the individual has such an abject fear of his fellow countrymen. **Because, as I say, they are free to lynch him the moment he shows he is not one of them . . .**

You should know, however, that writers rarely use sentence fragments in academic prose. They are considered a bit too casual. If you decide to experiment, be sure that your audience can see that you know what you're doing.

PUNCTUATING BEGINNINGS

You have no issues in punctuating the beginning of a sentence when you begin directly with its subject, as I did this one. However, as with this one, when a sentence forces a reader to plow through several introductory words, phrases, and clauses, especially when they have their own internal punctuation and readers might be confused by it all (as you may be right now), forget trying to punctuate it right: revise it.

There are a few rules that your readers expect you to follow, but more often you have to rely on judgment.

Five Reliable Rules

1. **Always separate an introductory element from the subject of a sentence with a comma if a reader might misunderstand the structure of the sentence, as in this one:**

   When a lawyer concludes her argument has to be easily remembered by a jury.

   Do this:

   ✓ When a lawyer **concludes, her** argument has to be easily remembered by a jury.

2. **Never end an introductory clause or phrase with a semicolon, no matter how it long is.** Readers take semicolons to signal the end of a grammatical sentence (but see p. 227). Never this:

   Although the Administration knew that Iraq's invasion of Kuwait threatened American interests in Saudi **Arabia; it** did not immediately prepare a military response.

Always use a comma there:

✓ Although the Administration knew that Iraq's invasion of Kuwait threatened American interests in Saudi **Arabia,** it did not immediately prepare a military response.

3. **Never put a comma right after a subordinating conjunction if the next element of the clause is its subject.** Never this:

   Although, the art of punctuation is simple, it is rarely mastered.

4. **Avoid putting a comma after the coordinating conjunctions *and, but, yet, for, so, or,* and *nor* if the next element is the subject.** Do not do this:

   But, we cannot know whether life on other planets exists.

   Some writers who punctuate heavily put a comma after a coordinating or subordinating conjunction if an introductory word or phrase follows:

   ✓ **Yet, during this period, prices** continued to rise.
   ✓ **Although, during this period, prices** continued to rise, interest rates did not.

   Punctuation that heavy retards a reader a bit, but it's your choice. These are also correct and for the reader, perhaps a bit brisker:

   ✓ Yet during this **period, prices** continued to rise.
   ✓ Yet during this **period prices** continued to rise.

5. **Put a comma after an introductory word or phrase if it comments on the whole of the following sentence or connects one sentence to another.** These include elements such as *fortunately, allegedly,* etc. and connecting adverbs like *however, nevertheless, otherwise,* etc. Readers hear a pause after such words.

   ✓ **Fortunately, we** proved our point.

   But avoid starting many sentences with an introductory element and a comma. When we read a series of such sentences, the whole passage feels hesitant.

   Three Exceptions: We typically omit a comma after *now, thus,* and *hence:*

   ✓ **Now it** is clear that many will not support this position.
   ✓ **Thus the** only alternative is to choose some other action.

Two Reliable Principles

1. **Readers usually need no punctuation between a short introductory phrase and the subject:**

   ✓ **Once again we** find similar responses to such stimuli.

   ✓ **In 1945 few** realized how the war had transformed us.

   It is not wrong to put a comma there, but it slows readers just as you may want them to be picking up speed.

2. **Readers usually need a comma between a long (four or five words or more) introductory phrase or clause and the subject:**

   ✓ When a lawyer begins her opening statement with a dry recital of the law and how it must be applied to the case before the **court, the** jury is likely to nod off.

Here's the point: These are strong rules of punctuation. Observe them.

1. Always separate an introductory element from the subject if a reader might misunderstand the structure of the sentence.

2. Never end an introductory clause or phrase with a semicolon.

3. Do not put a comma after a subordinating conjunction if the next element of the clause is its subject.

4. Do not put a comma after a coordinating conjunction if the next element of the clause is its subject.

5. Put a comma after a short introductory word or phrase if it comments on the whole of the following sentence or if it connects one sentence to another.

These are reliable principles:

1. Put a comma after a short introductory phrase or not, as you choose.

2. Readers need a comma after a long introductory phrase or clause.

PUNCTUATING MIDDLES

This is where explanations get messy, because to punctuate inside a grammatical sentence—more specifically, inside a clause—you have to consider not only the grammar of that clause, but the nuances of rhythm, meaning, and the emphasis that you want readers to hear in their mind's ear. There are, however, a few reliable rules.

Subject—Verb, Verb—Object

Do not put a comma between a subject and its verb, no matter how long the subject (nor between the verb and its object). Do not do this:

> A sentence that consists of many complex subordinate clauses and long phrases that all precede a **verb, may** seem to some students to demand a comma somewhere.

If you keep subjects short, you won't feel that you need a comma.

Occasionally, you cannot avoid a long subject, especially if it consists of a list of items with internal punctuation, like this:

> **The president, the vice president, the secretaries of the departments, senators, members of the House of Representatives, and Supreme Court justices take** an oath that pledges them to uphold the Constitution.

You can help readers sort it out with a summative subject:

- Insert a colon or a dash at the end of the list of subjects.
- Add a one-word subject that summarizes the preceding list:

  ✓ The president, the vice president, the secretaries of the departments, senators, members of the House of Representatives, and Supreme Court justices: **all** take an oath that pledges them to uphold the Constitution.

Choose a dash or a colon depending on how formal you want to seem.

Interruptions

When you interrupt a subject-verb or verb-object, you make it harder for readers to make the basic grammatical connections that create a sentence. So in general, avoid such interruptions, except for reasons of emphasis or nuance (see p. 123).

If you must interrupt a subject and verb or verb and object with more than a few words, always put paired commas around the interruption.

✓ A sentence, **if it includes subordinate clauses,** may seem to need commas.

Generally speaking, do not use a comma when you tack on a subordinate clause at the end of an independent clause, if that clause is necessary to understand the meaning of the sentence (this is analogous to a restrictive relative clause):

✓ No one should violate the law just because it seems unjust.

If the clause is not necessary, separate it from the main clause with a comma.

✓ No one should violate the law, because in the long run, it will do more harm than good.

This distinction can be tricky at times.

You may locate ADVERBIAL PHRASES before, after, or in the middle of a clause, depending on the emphasis you want readers to hear. If in the middle, put a comma before and after. Compare the different emphases in these:

✓ **In recent years** modern poetry has become more relevant to the average reader.

✓ Modern poetry **has, in recent years, become** more relevant to the average reader.

✓ Modern poetry has **become, in recent years, more** relevant to the average reader.

✓ Modern poetry has become more relevant to the average reader **in recent years.**

Loose Commentary

"Loose commentary" differs from an interruption, because you can usually move an interruption elsewhere in a sentence. But loose commentary modifies what it stands next to, so it usually cannot be moved. It still needs to be set off with paired commas, parentheses, or dashes, unless it comes at the end of a sentence; in that case, replace the second comma or dash with a period.

It is difficult to explain exactly what counts as loose commentary because it depends on both grammar and meaning. One familiar distinction is between restrictive clauses and nonrestrictive clauses (see pp. 16–17), including APPOSITIVES.

We use no commas with restrictive modifiers, modifiers that uniquely identify the noun they modify:

✓ The house **that I live in** is 100 years old.

But we always set off nonrestrictive modifiers with *paired* commas (unless the modifier ends the sentence):

✓ We had to reconstruct the **larynx, which is the source of voice,** with cartilage from the shoulder.

An appositive is just a truncated nonrestrictive clause:

✓ We had to rebuild the **larynx, ~~which is~~ the source of voice,** with cartilage from the shoulder.

You can achieve a more casual effect with a dash or parenthesis:

✓ We had to rebuild the **larynx—the source of voice—with** cartilage from the shoulder.

✓ We had to rebuild the **larynx (the source of voice) with** cartilage from the shoulder.

A dash is useful when the loose commentary has internal commas. Readers are confused by the long subject in this sentence:

The nations of Central Europe, Poland, Hungary, Romania, Bulgaria, the Czech Republic, Slovakia, Bosnia, Serbia have for centuries been in the middle of an East-West tug-of-war.

They can understand that kind of structure more easily when they can see that loose modifier set off with dashes or parentheses:

✓ The nations of Central **Europe—Poland, Hungary, Romania, Bulgaria, the Czech Republic, Slovakia, Bosnia, Serbia—have** for centuries been in the middle of an East-West tug-of-war.

Use parentheses when you want readers to hear your comment as a *sotto voce* aside:

✓ The brain **(at least that part that controls non-primitive functions)** may comprise several little brains operating simultaneously.

Or use it as an explanatory footnote inside a sentence:

✓ Lamarck **(1744–1829)** was a pre-Darwinian evolutionist.

✓ The poetry of the *fin de siècle* **(end of the century)** was characterized by a world-weariness and fashionable despair.

When loose commentary is at the end of a sentence, use a comma to separate it from the first part of the sentence. Be certain, however, that the meaning of the comment is not crucial to the meaning of the sentence. If it is, do not use a comma. Contrast these:

✓ I wandered through **Europe, seeking a place** where I could write undisturbed.

✓ I spent my **time seeking a place** where I could write undisturbed.

✓ Offices will be closed July **2–6, as announced in the daily bulletin.**

✓ When closing offices, secure all safes **as prescribed in the manual.**

✓ Historians have studied social changes, **at least in this country.**

✓ These records must be kept **at least until the IRS reviews them.**

Here's the point: These are reliable rules of internal punctuation. Observe them.

1. Do not interrupt a subject and verb or verb and object with any punctuation, unless absolutely necessary for clarity.

2. Inside a clause, always set off long interruptions with *paired* marks of punctuation—commas, parentheses, or dashes. Never use semicolons.

3. Put a comma at the end of an independent clause before a tacked-on subordinate clause when that clause is not essential to the meaning of the sentence.

PUNCTUATING COORDINATED ELEMENTS

Punctuating Two Coordinated Elements

Generally speaking, do not put a comma between just two coordinated elements. Compare these:

As computers have become **sophisticated, and** powerful they have taken over more **clerical, and** bookkeeping tasks.

✓ As computers have become **sophisticated and** powerful they have taken over more **clerical and** bookkeeping tasks.

Four Exceptions

1. **For a dramatic contrast, put a comma after the first coordinate element to emphasize the second (keep the second short):**

   ✓ The ocean is nature's most glorious **creation, and** its most destructive.

   To emphasize a contrast, use a comma before a *but* (keep the second part short):

   ✓ Organ transplants are becoming more **common, but** not less expensive.

2. **If you want your readers to feel the cumulative power of a coordinated pair (or more), drop the *and* and leave just a comma.** Compare these:

   ✓ Lincoln never had a formal **education and** never owned a large library.
   ✓ Lincoln never had a formal **education, never** owned a large library.
   ✓ The lesson of the pioneers was to ignore conditions that seemed difficult or even **overwhelming and** to get on with the business of subduing a hostile environment.
   ✓ The lesson of the pioneers was to ignore conditions that seemed difficult or even **overwhelming, to** get on with the business of subduing a hostile environment.

3. **Put a comma between long coordinated pairs only if you think your readers need a chance to breathe or to sort out the grammar.** Compare:

   It is in the graveyard that Hamlet finally realizes that the inevitable end of life is the **grave and clay and that the** end of all pretentiousness and all plotting and counter-plotting, regardless of one's station in life, must be dust.

   A comma after *clay* signals a natural pause:

   ✓ It is in the graveyard that Hamlet finally realizes that the inevitable end of all life is the **grave and clay, and that the** end of all pretentiousness and all plotting and counter-plotting, regardless of one's station in life, must be dust.

   More important, the comma after *clay* sorts out the structure of a potentially confusing *grave and clay and that regardless*.

In this next sentence, the first half of a coordination is long, so a reader might have a problem connecting the second half to its origin:

> Conrad's *Heart of Darkness* brilliantly dramatizes those primitive impulses that lie deep in each of us and stir only in our darkest **dreams but asserts** the need for the values that control those impulses.

A comma after *dreams* would clearly mark the end of one coordinate member and the beginning of the next:

> ✓ Conrad's *Heart of Darkness* brilliantly dramatizes those primitive impulses that lie deep in each of us and stir only in our darkest **dreams, but asserts** the need for the values that control those impulses.

On the other hand, if you can make sense out of a complicated sentence like that only with punctuation, you need to revise the sentence.

4. **If a sentence begins with a phrase or subordinate clause modifying two following clauses that are independent and coordinated, put a comma after the introductory phrase or clause but do not put a comma between the two coordinated independent clauses:**

> ✓ After the Soviet Union collapsed, Russia's economy declined for several years **[no comma here]** but the economies of former satellites to the west began to expand.

Punctuating Three or More Coordinated Elements

Finally, there is the matter of punctuating a series of three or more coordinated elements. Writers disagree on this one. A few omit it, but most insist a comma must always precede the last one:

> ✓ His wit, his **charm and his loyalty** made him our friend.
> ✓ His wit, his **charm, and his loyalty** made him our friend.

Both are correct, but be consistent.

If any of the items in the series has its own internal commas, use semicolons to show how readers should group the coordinated items:

> ✓ In mystery novels, the principal action ought to be economical, organic, and **logical; fascinating,** yet not **exotic; clear,** but complicated enough to hold the reader's interest.

> ***Here's the point:*** Use commas to separate items in a series if the items have no internal punctuation. Use semicolons to set off items in a series only if they do.

APOSTROPHES

There are few options with apostrophes, only rules, and they are Real Rules (review pp. 13–14). Those who violate them are objects of abuse by those who police such matters.

Contractions

Use an apostrophe in all contracted words:

don't   we'll   she'd   I'm   it's

Writers in the academic world often avoid contractions in their professional writing, because they don't want to seem too casual. I've used them in his book, because I wanted to avoid a formal tone. Check with your instructor before you experiment.

Plurals

Except for two cases, *never use an apostrophe to form a plural*. Never this: *bus's, fence's, horse's*. That error invites withering abuse.

   Use an apostrophe to form plurals in only two contexts: (1) with all lower case single letters and (2) with the single capital letters *A, I,* and U (the added *s* would seem to spell the words *As, Is,* and *Us*):

   Dot your i's and cross your t's   many A's and I's

However, when a word is unambiguously all numbers or multiple capital letters, add just *s*, with no apostrophe:

The ABCs	the 1950s	767s
CDs	URLs	45s

Possessives

With a few exceptions, form the possessive of a singular common or proper noun by adding an apostrophe + *s*.

   FDR's third term   the U.S.'s history   a 747's wingspan

The exceptions include singular nouns that already end in *s* or with the sound of *s*. For these, add the apostrophe only:

politics' importance   the United States' role

Descartes' *Discourse on Method*   Sophocles' plays

the audience' attention   for appearance' sake

(Some handbooks give different advice on this issue, recommending ' + *s* in all cases. Whatever you choose, be consistent.)

For plural common and proper nouns that end in *s*, form the possessive by adding an apostrophe only.

workers' votes   the Smiths' house

Form the possessive of a singular compound noun by adding an apostrophe and *s* to the last word:

the attorney general's decision   his sister-in-law's business

SUMMING UP

Rather than summarize this detailed material, I offer just four bits of advice:

- Always signal the end of a grammatical sentence.
- Always observe the five reliable rules on pp. 219–220.
- Always set off long interrupting elements with commas.
- Never put a single comma between a subject and its verb or between a verb and its object.

Beyond that, use your judgment: punctuate in ways that help your readers see the connections and separations that they have to see to make sense of your sentences. That means you must put yourself in the place of your reader, not easy to do, but something you must learn. On the other hand, write a clearly structured sentence in the first place, and your punctuation will take care of itself.

Exercise A.1

These passages lack their original punctuation. Slash marks indicate grammatical sentences. Punctuate them three times, once using the least punctuation possible, a second time using as much varied punctuation as you can, and then a third time as you think best. You might also analyze these passages for features of elegance, especially how their sentences begin and end. You can even improve them some.

1. Scientists and philosophers of science tend to speak as if "scientific language" were intrinsically precise as if those who use it must understand one another's meaning even if they disagree / but in fact scientific language is not as different from ordinary language as is commonly believed / it too is subject to imprecision and ambiguity and hence to imperfect understanding / moreover new theories or arguments are rarely if ever constructed by way of clear-cut steps of induction deduction and verification or falsification / neither are they defended rejected or accepted in so straightforward a manner / in practice scientists combine the rules of scientific methodology with a generous admixture of intuition aesthetics and philosophical commitment / the importance of what are sometimes called extra-rational or extra-logical components of thought in the *discovery* of a new principle or law is generally acknowledged / . . . but the role of these extra-logical components in persuasion and acceptance in making an argument convincing is less frequently discussed partly because they are less visible / the ways in which the credibility or effectiveness of an argument depends on the realm of common experiences or extensive practice in communicating those experiences in a common language are hard to see precisely because such commonalities are taken for granted / only when we step out of such a "consensual domain" when we can stand out on the periphery of a community with a common language do we begin to become aware of the unarticulated premises mutual understandings and assumed practices of the group / even in those subjects that lend themselves most readily to quantification discourse depends heavily on conventions and interpretation, conventions that are acquired over years of practice and participation in a community.

   —Evelyn Fox Keller, A Feeling for the Organism:
   The Life and Work of Barbara McClintock

2. In fact of course the notion of universal knowledge has always been an illusion / but it is an illusion fostered by the monistic view of the world in which a few great central truths determine in all its wonderful and amazing proliferation everything else that is true / we are not today tempted to search for these keys that unlock the whole of human knowledge and of man's experience / we know that we are ignorant / we are well taught it / and the more surely and deeply we know our own job the better able we are to appreciate the full measure of our pervasive ignorance / we know that these are inherent limits compounded no doubt and exaggerated by that sloth and that complacency without which we would not be men at all / but

knowledge rests on knowledge / what is new is meaningful because it departs slightly from what was known before / this is a world of frontiers where even the liveliest of actors or observers will be absent most of the time from most of them / perhaps this sense was not so sharp in the village that village which we have learned a little about but probably do not understand too well the village of slow change and isolation and fixed culture which evokes our nostalgia even if not our full comprehension / perhaps in the villages men were not so lonely / perhaps they found in each other a fixed community a fixed and only slowly growing store of knowledge of a single world / even that we may doubt / for there seem to be always in the culture of such times and places vast domains of mystery if not unknowable then imperfectly known endless and open.

—J. Robert Oppenheimer, "The Sciences
and Man's Community," from Science
and the Common Understanding

Appendix II

Using Sources

*Everything of importance has been said before
by somebody who did not discover it.*
—Alfred North Whitehead

*There is not less wit nor less invention in applying
rightly a thought one finds in a book, than in being
the first author of that thought.*
—Pierre Bayle

Using Sources Properly

Few writers can get by on their own thoughts alone, and a researcher never can. We all write better when our thinking is enriched by what we learn from others. But there are rules for using the words and ideas of others: some that readers use to judge your ethos, how trustworthy you seem; and others that you ignore to your peril. Mistakes here can damage your credibility, your grade, and even your reputation for honesty. You have some choices, but not many. Your challenge is to learn and follow a plan that helps you use sources properly and without costly errors, but also without having to reduplicate and re-reduplicate your efforts.

Although there are rules for quotations and other uses of sources, I will as always emphasize your readers and the choices you make with them in mind: not what you must do to follow the rules, but you what can do to assure readers that you have dealt with your sources accurately and fairly.

AVOIDING THE APPEARANCE OF PLAGIARISM

I begin with those matters where mistakes are most costly. Of all the ethical transgressions that a writer can commit, few are worse than plagiarism: lying and other forms of deception are worse, but not far behind is the theft of another person's words and ideas.

The plagiarist steals more than words. He or she also steals the respect and recognition that a source deserves for her work. And the student plagiarist steals not only words and ideas, but the recognition due his colleagues by making their work seem worse in comparison to his own. When such theft becomes common, the community grows suspicious, then distrustful, then cynical—*So who cares? Everyone does it.* Teachers then have to be concerned less with teaching and learning, and more with detecting dishonesty. Those who plagiarize betray not just a duty owed a source, but the ethical fabric of their entire community.

Honest students who never intend to plagiarize might think they have no reason to fear being charged with doing so. But we read words, not minds. You invite at least the appearance of dishonesty if you don't know or, worse, don't take care to avoid what might make teachers suspect it.

Three Principles

To avoid that risk, you must understand and follow the principles that every teacher expects every writer to observe. The overriding principle is this: Avoid anything that might lead an informed reader to think that you are taking credit for words or ideas not your own. This principle applies to sources of *any* kind: print, online, recorded, or oral. Some students think that if something is freely circulated online, they are free to treat it as their own. They are wrong: cite everything you borrow.

In particular, follow these rules:

1. **When you quote the exact words of a source, cite the source (including page numbers) and put those words in quotation marks or in a block quotation (see pp. 236–237).**

2. **When you paraphrase a source, cite the source (including page numbers). Do not use quotation marks, but you must**

> **recast it entirely in your own words in a new sentence structure.**

3. **When you use an idea or method you found in a source, cite the source. If the entire source concerns the idea or method, do not add page numbers.**

If you follow those three rules, you will never be suspected of trying to pass off someone else's words and ideas as your own.

Take Good Notes

To use and cite source material correctly, you must start by taking good notes. Since the work can be tedious, set up a system to get things right the first time so that you don't have check and recheck, again and again.

1. **Record bibliographical information the first time you touch a source.** Do this early, not when you are rushing to meet a deadline.

   For books, record
   - ❑ author(s)
   - ❑ title (and subtitle)
   - ❑ title of series (if any)
   - ❑ edition or volume (if any)
   - ❑ city and publisher
   - ❑ year published
   - ❑ pages for chapter (if any)

   For articles, record
   - ❑ author(s)
   - ❑ title (and subtitle)
   - ❑ journal, magazine, etc.
   - ❑ volume and issue number
   - ❑ online database (if any)
   - ❑ date published
   - ❑ pages for article

   Online sources are less predictable. In addition to the above information, record at least the URL and the access date, and any other information that might help you identify the source for readers.

2. **Record quotations exactly.** Copy quotations *exactly* as they appear in the original, down to every comma and semicolon. If the quotation is long, photocopy or download it.

3. **Mark quotations and paraphrases unambiguously as the words of others.** This is crucial: take notes so that weeks or months later you *cannot possibly* think that words and ideas from a source are your own. Whether you take notes longhand or on a computer, *always* highlight, underline, or use a different font to distinguish direct quotations. Then use another way to distinguish paraphrases and summaries. Prominent scholars have been humiliated by accusations of plagiarism because,

they claimed, they did not clearly mark words they copied or paraphrased, then "forgot" they were not their own.

4. **Don't paraphrase too closely.**   When you paraphrase a source in your notes, don't just replace words in the source with synonyms. That is also considered plagiarism, even if you cite the source. For example, the first paraphrase below is plagiarism because it tracks its sentence structure almost word for word. The second paraphrase is fair use.

> **Original:**   The drama is the most social of literary forms, since it stands in so direct a relationship to its audience.
>
> **Plagiarized:** The theater is a very social genre because it relates so directly with its viewers.
>
> **Fair use:**   Levin claims that we experience the theater as the most social form of literature because we see it taking place before us.

Weaving Quotations into Your Text

You use quotations best when you integrate them so fully that they seem made for your text. Readers become suspicious when they see bare quotations dropped into your paper with no effort to connect them to your own points: Is it you or your source that's doing all the thinking? So prepare readers for each quotation by stating *before you use it* how the quotation fits into the mesh of *your* argument. Then weave the quotation into your text, so that the fit is as seamless as possible.

Four or Fewer Lines

Drop in the Quotation   An acceptable but artless way to insert a quotation into your text is simply to drop it in, introducing it with something like

> *Smith says, states, claims,* etc.   *As Smith says, asserts, suggests,* etc. *According to Smith, In Smith's view,* etc.

The verb indicates your attitude toward the quotation, so choose carefully:

> says *vs.* asserts *vs.* claims *vs.* suggests *vs.* thinks *vs.* wants to believe

Put a comma after the introductory phrase and capitalize the first letter of the quotation only if it was capitalized in the quotation:

> Williams said, "An acceptable but artless way to insert a quotation into your text is simply to drop it in."

If you introduce the quotation with *stated **that**, claimed **that**, said **that***, etc., do not use a comma and do not capitalize the first letter:

> He went on to say that "if you introduce the quotation with *stated that, claimed that, said that*, etc., do not use a comma."

Weave in the Quotation   A more graceful way to use a quotation is to weave it into the structure of your own sentence (doing that also helps you incorporate it into your own thinking):

> In *The Argument Culture*, Deborah Tannen treats the male-female polarity "more like ends of a continuum than a discrete dualism," because the men and women we know display "a vast range of behaviors, personalities, and habits."

To make the quotation fit your sentence, you can modify its grammar, even add a word or two, so long as you follow these principles:

- Don't change its meaning.
- Indicate added or changed words with square brackets.
- Signal deletions with three spaced dots, called *ellipses*.

This sentence quotes the original intact:

> Although it is clear that we have long thought of argument as verbal combat, Deborah Tannen suggests that there is something new in the way we argue: "The increasingly adversarial spirit of our contemporary lives is fundamentally related to a phenomenon that has been much remarked upon in recent years: the breakdown of a sense of community."

This version both shortens and modifies the quotation to fit the grammar of the writer's sentence:

> Although it is clear that we have long thought of argument as verbal combat, Deborah Tannen suggests that our "increasingly adversarial spirit . . . is fundamentally related " to new social developments in "the breakdown of a sense of community."

If you delete a whole sentence or more, use four ellipses.

You can italicize, boldface, or underline words in a quotation to emphasize them, but if you do, always add *my emphasis* or *emphasis mine* in square brackets:

> Lipson recommends that when you paraphrase that you "write it down *in your own words* [my emphasis] . . . and then compare your sentence with the author's original."

Five Lines or More

If you quote five lines or more, put the quotation into a block quotation (with no quotation marks around it). Indent the same number of spaces as you indent a paragraph; if the quotation begins with a paragraph indentation, indent the first line again:

> Lipson offers this advice about paraphrase:
>> So, what's the best technique for rephrasing a quote? Set aside the other author's text and try to think of the point *you* want to get across. Write it down in your own words (with a citation) and then compare your sentence to the author's original. If they contain several identical words or merely substitute a couple of synonyms, rewrite yours.

As in that example, introduce most block quotations with words that announce it, followed by a period or colon. But you can also let the quotation complete the grammar of your introductory sentence. In that case, punctuate the end of your sentence as if you were running the block quotation into your text:

> A good way to avoid paraphrasing too closely is to
>> think of the point *you* want to get across. Write it down in your own words (with a citation) and then compare your sentence to the author's original. If they contain several . . .

Never begin a quotation in your running text and complete it in a block quotation, like this:

> A good way to avoid paraphrasing too closely is to "think of the point" *you* want to get across. Write it down in your own words (with a citation) and then compare your sentence to the author's original. If they . . .

Five Words or Less

If you repeat just a few words from a source, you may have to treat them as quotations. If they are words that anyone might use, treat them as your own. But if they are strikingly original or especially important, put them in quotation marks and cite their source. For example, read this passage from Jared Diamond's *Guns, Germs, and Steel*:

> Because technology begets more technology, the importance of an invention's diffusion potentially exceeds the importance of the original invention. Technology's history exemplifies what is termed an autocatalytic process: that is, one that speeds up at a rate that increases with time, because the process catalyzes itself (301).

Phrases such as *the importance of the original invention*, are so ordinary that they require neither a citation nor quotation marks. But two phrases do, because they are so striking: *technology begets more technology* and *autocatalytic process:*

> The power of technology goes beyond individual inventions because technology "begets more technology." It is, as Diamond puts it, an "autocatalytic process."

Once you cite those words, you can use them again without quotation marks or citation:

> As one invention begets another one and that one still another, the process becomes a self-sustaining catalysis that spreads exponentially across all national boundaries.

Punctuating Quotations

Here are three principles for using punctuation with quotation marks:

1. **If the quotation ends in a period, comma, semicolon, or colon, replace it with the punctuation you need in your own sentence.**

   - If your punctuation is a period or comma, put it *before* a final quotation mark:

     President Nixon said, "I am not a crook."

     Falwell claimed, "This is the end," but he was wrong.

   - If your punctuation is a question mark, colon, or semicolon, put it *after* the final quotation mark:

     My first bit of advice is "Quit complaining"; my second is "Get moving."

     The Old West served up plenty of "rough justice": lynchings and other forms of casual punishment were not uncommon.

     How many law professors believe in "natural law"?

     Was it Freud who famously asked, "What do women want"?

2. **If the quotation ends with a question mark or exclamation point and your punctuation is a period or comma, drop your punctuation and put the question mark *before* the quotation mark:**

   Freud famously asked, "What do women want?"

3. **If you use quotation marks inside a quotation, put your comma or period before both of the marks:**

> She said "I have no idea how to interpret 'Ode to a Nightingale.'"

Cite Sources Appropriately

Your last task is to cite your sources fully, accurately, and appropriately. No one will accuse you of plagiarism for a misplaced comma, but some will conclude that if you cannot get these little matters right, you can't be trusted on the big ones. There are many styles of citations, so find out which one your reader expects. Three are most common:

- Chicago style, from the *University of Chicago Manual of Style*, common in the humanities and some social sciences
- MLA style, from the Modern Language Association, common in literary studies
- APA style, from the American Psychological Association, common in the social sciences

You can find a guide to citations in the reference section of almost any bookstore.

Summing Up

To use sources accurately, fairly, and effectively, follow three principles:

1. Give credit to a source whenever you use its words or ideas.

    - Whenever you use the exact words of a source, cite the source and page numbers and put the words in quotations marks or a block quote.
    - Whenever you paraphrase a source, cite the source and page numbers.
    - Whenever you rely on the ideas or methods of a source, cite the source.

2. Make each quotation fit seamlessly into your text.

    - Before you use it, indicate how each quotation relates to your ideas.

- Whenever possible, don't just drop in a quotation, weave it in.
  - ° Run in quotations of four lines or less.
  - ° Set of as a block quotations of five lines or more.
  - ° Quote distinctive words or phrases the first time you use them.
3. Use a standard citation style; three are most common:
   - Chicago style, common in the humanities and some social sciences
   - MLA style, common in literary study
   - APA style. common in the social sciences

When you use material from a source, you create a chain of thinking that passes from you to your sources, from them to their sources, and on to their sources, and on, and on. That chain of thinking must also be a chain of trust: You can trust your sources (and through them, their sources) if they show you that they have taken care not only with their own ideas but with what they borrowed from others. If, in turn, you want your readers to trust you, you have to show them that you too have taken care. These principles help you do that.

GLOSSARY

Grammar is the ground of all.
—WILLIAM LANGLAND

Most of the grounds of the world's troubles are matters of grammar.
—MONTAIGNE

*There is a satisfactory boniness about grammar which the flesh of
sheer vocabulary requires before it can become vertebrate and walk
the earth. But to study it for its own sake, without relating it to
function, is utter madness.*
—ANTHONY BURGESS

*Thou hast most traitorously corrupted the youth of the realm in
erecting a grammar school. . . . It will be proved to thy face, that
thou hast men about thee that usually talk of a noun and a verb,
and such abominable words as no Christian ear can endure to hear.*
—WILLIAM SHAKESPEARE, 2 HENRY VI, 4.7

What follows is no tight theory of grammar, just definitions useful for the terms in this book. Where the text discusses something at length, I refer you to those pages. If you want to do a quick review to get started, read the entries on SUBJECT, SIMPLE SUBJECT, WHOLE SUBJECT, and VERB.

Action: Prototypically, action is expressed by a verb: *move, hate, think, discover.* But actions also appear in NOMINALIZATIONS: *movement, hatred, thought, discovery.* Actions are also implied in some adjectives: *advisable, resultant, explanatory,* etc.

Active: See p. 53.

Adjectival Clause: Adjectival clauses modify nouns. Also called RELATIVE clauses, they usually begin with a relative pronoun: *which, that, whom, whose, who*. There are two kinds: RESTRICTIVE and NONRESTRICTIVE. See pp. 16–17.

Restrictive   The book **that** *I read* was good.

Nonrestrictive   My car, **which** *you saw*, is gone.

Adjective: A word you can put *very* in front of: *very old, very interesting*. There are exceptions: *major, additional*, etc. Since this is also a test for ADVERBS, distinguish adjectives from adverbs by putting them between *the* and a noun: *The* **occupational** *hazard, the* **major** *reason*, etc. Some nouns also appear there—*the* **chemical** *hazard*.

Adjective Phrase: An ADJECTIVE and what attaches to it: *so* **full** *that it burst*.

Adverb: Adverbs modify all parts of speech except NOUNS:

Adjectives   **extremely** large, **rather** old

Verbs   **frequently** spoke, **often** slept

Adverbs   **very** carefully, **somewhat** rudely

Articles   **precisely** the man I meant, **just** the thing I need

Sentences   **Fortunately,** we were on time.

Adverb Phrase: An adverb and what attaches to it: *as* **soon** *as I could*.

Adverbial Clause: This is a kind of SUBORDINATE CLAUSE. It modifies a VERB or ADJECTIVE, indicating time, cause, condition, etc. It usually begins with a SUBORDINATING CONJUNCTION such as *because, when, if, since, while, unless*:

If you leave, I will stop.   **Because he left**, I did too.

Agent: Prototypically, agents are flesh-and-blood sources of an ACTION, but for our purposes, an agent is the *seeming* source of any action, an entity without which the action could not occur: ***She*** *criticized the program in this report*. Often, we can make the means by which we do something a seeming agent: ***This report*** *criticizes the program*. Do not confuse agents with SUBJECTS. Agents prototypically are subjects, but an agent can be in a grammatical OBJECT: *I underwent an interrogation by* ***the police***.

Appositive: A noun phrase that is left after deleting **which** and **be:** *My dog, ~~which is~~ **a dalmatian**, ran away.*

Article: They are easier to list than to define: *a, an, the, this, these, that, those.*

Character: See pp. 29–30.

Clause: A clause has two defining characteristics:

1. It has a sequence of at least one SUBJECT + VERB.
2. The verb must agree with the subject in number and can be made past or present.

By this definition, these are clauses:

> She left   that they leave   if she left   why he is leaving

These next are not, because the verbs cannot be made past tense nor do they agree in number with the putative subject:

> for them to **go**   her **having gone**

Comma Splice: You create a comma splice when you join two independent clauses with only a comma:

> Oil-producing countries depend too much on oil revenues, they should develop their educational and industrial resources, as well. See p. 216.

Complement: Whatever completes a VERB:

> I am **home.**   You seem **tired.**   She helped **me.**

Compound Noun: See p. 62.

Conjunction: Usually defined as a word that links words, PHRASES, or CLAUSES. They are easier to illustrate than define (the first two are also categorized as SUBORDINATING conjunctions):

adverbial conjunctions	because, although, when, since
relative conjunctions	who, whom, whose, which, that
sentence conjunctions	thus, however, therefore, nevertheless
coordinating conjunctions	and, but, yet, for, so, or, nor
correlative conjunctions	both X and Y, not only X but Y, (n)either X (n)or Y, X as well as Y

Coordination: Coordination joins two grammatical units of the same order with *and, or, nor, but, yet*:

same part of speech	you **and** I, red **and** black, run **or** jump
phrases	in the house **but** not in the basement
clauses	when I leave **or** when you arrive

Dangling Modifier: See p. 58.

Dependent Clause: Any CLAUSE that cannot be punctuated as a MAIN CLAUSE, one beginning with a capital letter and ending with a period or question mark. It usually begins with a subordinating conjunction such as *because, if, when, which, that:*

| why he left | because he left | which he left |

Direct Object: The NOUN that follows a TRANSITIVE VERB and can be made the SUBJECT of a PASSIVE verb:

I found **the money.** → **The money** was found by me.

Finite Verb: A verb that can be made past or present. These are finite verbs because we can change their tense from past to present and vice versa:

She **wants** to leave. → She **wanted** to leave.

These are not finite verbs because we cannot change the INFINITIVE to a past tense:

She wants to **leave.** → She wanted to **left.**

Fragment: A PHRASE or DEPENDENT CLAUSE that begins with a capital letter and ends with a period, question mark, or exclamation mark:

| Because I left. | Though I am here! | What you did? |

These are complete sentences:

| He left because I did. | Though I am here, she is not! | I know what we did. |

Free Modifier: See pp. 128–129.

Gerund: A NOMINALIZATION created by adding *-ing* to a VERB:

When she **left** we were happy. → Her **leaving** made us happy.

Goal: That toward which the ACTION of a VERB is directed. In most cases, goals are DIRECT OBJECTS:

I see **you.**   I broke **the dish.**   I built **a house.**

But in some cases, the literal goal of an action can be the SUBJECT of an ACTIVE VERB:

I underwent an interrogation.   **She** received a warm welcome.

Grammatical Sentence: See p. 211.

Hedge: See pp. 109–110.

Independent Clause: A CLAUSE that that can be punctuated as a grammatical sentence.

Infinitive: A VERB that cannot be made past or present. It often is preceded by the word to: *He decided to **stay**.* But sometimes not: *We helped him **repair** the door.*

Intensifier: See pp. 110–111.

Intransitive Verb: A verb that does not take an OBJECT and so cannot be made PASSIVE. These are not TRANSITIVE verbs:

He **exists.**   They **left** town.   She **became** a doctor.

Linking Verb: A VERB with a COMPLEMENT that refers to its SUBJECT.

He **is** my brother.   They **became** teachers.   She **seems** reliable.

Main Clause: A main or independent clause has at least a SUBJECT and VERB (imperatives are the exception) and can be punctuated as an independent sentence:

I left.   Why did you leave?   We are leaving.

A SUBORDINATE or DEPENDENT CLAUSE cannot be punctuated as an independent sentence. These are incorrectly punctuated:

Because she left.   That they left.   Whom you spoke to.

Main Subject: SUBJECT of the MAIN CLAUSE.

Metadiscourse: See pp. 57–58.

Nominalization: See pp. 32–33.

Nonrestrictive Clause: See pp. 16–17.

Noun: A word that fits this frame: *The* [   ] *is good.* Some are concrete: *dog, rock, car;* others abstract: *ambition, space, speed.* The nouns that most concern us are NOMINALIZATION, nouns derived from VERBS or ADJECTIVES: *act* → *action*, *wide* → *width*.

Noun Clause: A noun clause functions like a noun, as the SUBJECT or OBJECT of a VERB: *That you are here* proves *that you love me*.

Object: There are three kinds:

1. DIRECT object: the NOUN following a TRANSITIVE VERB:

    I *read* **the book.**   We *followed* **the car.**

2. PREPOSITIONAL object: the noun following a preposition:

    in **the house**   *by* **the walk**   *across* **the street**   *with* **fervor**

3. INDIRECT object: the noun between a VERB and its direct object:

    I *gave* **him** a tip.

Parallel: Sequences of COORDINATED words, PHRASES, or CLAUSES are parallel when they are of the same grammatical structure. This is parallel:

  I decided to work hard and do a good job.

This is not:

  I decided to work hard and that I should do a good job.

Passive: See p. 53.

Past Participle: Usually the same form as the past tense *-ed: jumped, worked*. Irregular VERBS have irregular forms: *seen, broken, swum*, etc. It follows forms of *be* and *have*: *I have* GONE. *I am* FOUND. It also serves as a modifier: FOUND *money*.

Personal Pronoun: Easier to list than define: *I, me, we, us, my, mine; our, ours; you, your, yours; he, him, his, her; she, her, hers; they, them, their, theirs*.

Phrase: A group of words constituting a unit but not including a SUBJECT and a FINITE VERB: *the dog, too old, was leaving, in the house, ready to work*.

Possessive: *my, your, his, her, its, their* or a NOUN ending with *-'s* or *-s'*: the **dog's** tail.

Predicate: Whatever follows the whole SUBJECT, beginning with the VERB PHRASE, including the COMPLEMENT and what attaches to it:

  He [left yesterday to buy a hat]. _{predicate}

Preposition: Easier to list than to define: *in, on, up, over, of, at, by, etc*.

Prepositional Phrase: The preposition plus its OBJECT: *in + the house*.

Present Participle: The *-ing* form of a VERB: *running, thinking*.

Progressive: The PRESENT PARTICIPLE form of the VERB: *Running streams are beautiful*.

Punctuated Sentence: See p. 211.

Relative Clause: See pp. 16–17.

Relative Pronoun: *who, whom, which, whose, that* when used in a relative clause.

Restrictive Clause: See pp. 16–17.

Resumptive Modifier: See pp. 127–128.

Run-on Sentence: A PUNCTUATED SENTENCE consisting of two or more GRAMMATICAL SENTENCES not separated by either a COORDINAT-ING CONJUNCTION or any mark of punctuation this entry illustrates a run-on sentence.

Simple Subject: The simple subject is the smallest unit inside the WHOLE SUBJECT that determines whether a VERB is singular or plural:

[The [books] simple subject that are required reading] whole subject **are** listed.

The simple subject should be as close to its verb as you can get it.

If **a book** is required reading, **it** is listed.

Stress: See pp. 85–86.

Subject: The subject is what the VERB agrees with in number:

Two men *are* at the door.   **One man** *is* at the door.

Distinguish the WHOLE SUBJECT from its SIMPLE SUBJECT.

Subjunctive: A form of the VERB used to talk about events that are contrary to fact:

If he **were** President . . .

Subordinate Clause: A clause that usually begins with a SUBORDI-NATING CONJUNCTION such as *if, when, unless,* or *which, that, who*.

There are three kinds of subordinate clauses: NOUN, ADVERBIAL, and ADJECTIVAL.

Subordinating Conjunction: *because, if, when, since, unless, which, who, that, whose,* etc.

Summative Modifier: See p. 128.

Thematic Thread: A sequence of THEMES running through a passage.

Theme: See pp. 92–93.

Topic: See pp. 72–75.

Topic String: The sequence of TOPICS through a series of sentences.

Transitive Verb: A VERB with a DIRECT OBJECT. The direct object prototypically "receives" an ACTION. The prototypical direct object can be made the SUBJECT of a PASSIVE verb:

> We **read** the book. → The book **was read** by us.

By this definition, *resemble, become,* and *stand* (as in *He stands six feet tall*) are not transitive.

Verb: The word that must agree with the SUBJECT in number and that can be inflected for past or present:

> The book **is** ready.   The books **were** returned.

Whole Subject: You can identify a whole subject once you identify its VERB: Put a *who* or a *what* in front of the verb and turn the sentence into a question. The fullest answer to the question is the whole subject:

> The ability of the city to manage education is an accepted fact.
>
> Question: **What** is an accepted fact?
>
> Answer (and whole subject): the ability of the city to manage education

Distinguish the whole subject from the SIMPLE SUBJECT:

> The **ability** of the city to manage education **is** an accepted fact.

SUGGESTED ANSWERS

You will almost certainly come up with answers different from these, many much better. Don't worry whether yours is word-for-word like mine; focus only on the general principle of the lesson and exercise.

EXERCISE 3.4

1a. Verbs: *argue, elevate*. No nominalizations.

1b. Verbs: *has been*. Nominalizations: *speculation, improving, achievement*.

3a. Verbs: *identified, failed, develop, immunize*. Nominalizations: *risk*.

3b. Verbs: *met*. Nominalizations: *attempts, defining, employment, failure*.

5a. Verbs: *resulted in*. Nominalizations: *loss, share, disappearance*.

5b. Verbs: *discover, use, teach*. Nominalizations: *instruction*.

7a. Verbs: *fail, realize, are unprepared, protect, adjust*. Nominalizations: *life*.

7b. Verbs: *have, are*. Nominalizations: *understanding, increases, resistance, costs, education*.

EXERCISE 3.5

1b. Some educators have speculated whether the family improves educational achievement (helps students achieve more).

3b. Economists have attempted but failed to define full employment.

5a. When domestic automakers lost market share to the Japanese, hundreds of thousands of jobs disappeared.

7b. Colleges understand that they can no longer increase tuition yearly because parents are strongly resisting the soaring cost of higher education.

Exercise 3.6

1. Lincoln hoped to preserve the Union without war, but when the South attacked Fort Sumter, war became inevitable.
3. Business executives predicted that the economy would quickly revive.
5. Because the health care industry cannot control costs, the public may decide that Congress must act.
7. Several candidates attempted to explain why more voters voted in this year's elections.
9. The business sector did not independently study why the trade surplus suddenly increased.
11. The CIA is uncertain whether North Korea intends to cease missile testing.
13. If the data contradict each other, you must explain why.
15. They performed the play enthusiastically, but did not stage it intelligently.

Exercise 3.7

There are many plausible alternatives here, depending on the characters we invent.

1. Although we use models to teach prose style, students do not write more clearly or directly.
3. If members depart from established procedures, the Board may terminate their membership.
5. To implement a new curriculum successfully, faculty must cooperate with students to set goals that they can achieve within a reasonable time.

Exercise 4.1

1. In recent years, historians have reassessed the place of Columbus in Western history because they have interpreted the discovery of America in new ways.
3. To write more coherently, trace the transitions in a book or well-written article.
5. Networks are aware that they must revise their programming because viewers are watching network TV less and rental DVDs and cable more.

Exercise 4.2

1. Those on welfare become independent when they learn skills valued by the marketplace. [I like the passive here in order to stress "marketplace."]

3. In this article, I argue that the United States fought the Vietnam War to extend its influence in Southeast Asia and did not end it until North Vietnam made it clear that it could be defeated only if the United States used atomic weapons.

5. Bierce presents the first section of . . . dispassionately. In the first sentence, he describes . . . but he takes all emotion away from them . . . In paragraph 2, he describes . . . but betrays no feeling because he uses neutral and unemotional language. He presents this entire . . . even though he fills it with details. [Some will object here that the repeated use of "Bierce/he" is monotonous. Two points: first, most of us never notice when subjects are repeated, and second, we can make more changes: "Even though this section is devoid of emotion, it has many details." Again, the question is *not* which is the correct revision, but how we think about it and decide what we like best. That means going beyond simply repeating the rule, "write in the active voice."]

EXERCISE 4.3

1. We believe that students binge because they do not understand the risks of alcohol.

3. We suggest that Russia's economy has improved because it has exported more crude oil for hard currency.

5. In Section IV, I argue that the indigenous culture overcultivated the land and thereby exhausted it as a food-producing area.

7. To evaluate how the flow rate changed, the current flow rate was compared to the original rate on the basis of figures collected by Jordan in his study of diversion patterns of slow-growth swamps. [This sentence technically has a dangling modifier, but it is so common that no reader of technical prose would balk. That last clump of nominalizations is acceptable, because it is a technical term.]

EXERCISE 4.4

1. We analyzed your figures to determine their accuracy. We will announce the results when we think it appropriate.

3. When the author treats the conspiracy theories, he abandons his impassioned narrative style and adopts a cautious one, but when he picks up the narrative line again, he invests his prose with the same vigor and force.

5. For many years, courts enforced federal regulations concerning the use of wiretaps. Only recently has the Department of Justice loosened restrictions on the circumstances that warrant it.

7. We wrote these directives as simply as possible to communicate effectively with employees who do not read well.

EXERCISE 4.6

1. The committee on standards for plant safety discussed recent announcements about regulating air quality.

3. The goal of this article is to describe how readers comprehend text and produce protocols about recall.

5. This paper investigates how computers process information in games that simulate human cognition.

7. The Social Security program guarantees a potential package of benefits based on what individuals contribute to the program over their lifetime.

EXERCISE 5.1

1. When the president assumed office, he had two aims—the recovery of . . . He succeeded in the first as testified to by the drop in . . . But he had less success with the second, as indicated by our increased involvement . . . Nevertheless, the American voter was pleased by vast increases in the military . . .

EXERCISE 5.2

1. Except for those areas covered with ice or scorched by continual heat, the earth is covered by vegetation. Plants grow most richly in fertilized plains and river valleys, but they also grow at the edge of perpetual snow in high mountains. Dense vegetation grows in the ocean and around its edges as well as in and around lakes and swamps. Plants grow in the cracks of busy city sidewalks as well as on seemingly barren cliffs. Vegetation will cover the earth long after we have been swallowed up by evolutionary history.

3. In his paper on children's thinking, Jones (1985) stressed the importance of language skills in the ability of children to solve problems. He reported that when children improved their language skills, they improved their ability to solve nonverbal problems. Jones thinks that they performed better because they used previously acquired language habits to articulate the problems and activate knowledge learned through language. We might therefore explore whether children could learn to solve problems better if they practiced how to formulate them.

EXERCISE 5.3

1. Though modern mass communication offers many advantages, it also poses many threats. If it were controlled by a powerful minority, it could manipulate public opinion through biased reporting. And

while it provides us with a knowledge of public affairs through its national coverage, it may accentuate divisiveness and factionalism by connecting otherwise isolated, local conflicts into a single larger conflict when it shows us conflicts about the same issues occurring in different places. It will always be true that human nature produces differences of opinion, but the media may reinforce the threat of faction and division when it publishes uninformed opinion in national coverage. According to some, media can suppress faction through education when it communicates the true nature of conflicts, but history has shown that the media give as much coverage to people who encourage conflict as to people who try to remove it.

3. When Truman considered the Oppenheimer committee's recommendation to stop the hydrogen bomb project, he had to consider many issues. Russia and China had just proclaimed a Sino-Soviet bloc, so one issue he had to face was the Cold War. He was also losing support for his foreign policy among Republican leaders in Congress, and when the Russians tested their first atom bomb, the public demanded that he respond strongly. It was inevitable that Truman would conclude he could not let the public think he had allowed Russia to be first in developing the most powerful weapon yet. In retrospect, according to some historians, Truman should have risked taking the Oppenheimer recommendation, but he had to face political issues that were too powerful to ignore.

EXERCISE 6.1

1. [One can imagine different rationales for different stresses.] In my opinion, at least, the Republic is most threatened by the President's tendency to rewrite the Constitution.

3. In large American universities the opportunities for faculty to work with individual students are limited.

5. College students commonly complain about teachers who assign a long term paper and then give them a grade but no comments.

EXERCISE 6.2

1. During the reign of Queen Elizabeth, the story of King Lear and his daughters was so popular that by the time she died, readers could find it in at least a dozen books. Most of these stories, however, did not develop their characters and were simple narratives with an obvious moral. Several versions of this story must have been available to Shakespeare when he began work on *Lear*, perhaps his greatest tragedy. But while he based his characters on these stock figures of legend, he turned them into credible human beings with complex motives.

3. Because the most important event in Thucydides' *History* is Athens' catastrophic Sicilian Invasion, Thucydides devotes three-quarters of his book to setting it up. We can see this anticipation especially in how he describes the step-by-step decline in Athenian society so that he could create the inevitability that we associate with the tragic drama.

5. Revenues changed as follows during July 1–August 31: Ohio and Kentucky, up 73 percent from $32,934 to $56,792; Indiana and Illinois, up 10 percent from $153,281 to $168,651; Wisconsin and Minnesota, down 5 percent from $200,102 to $190,580. [The important thing here is to get the sequence of items in a regular order. I could imagine an argument insisting that the percentage be at the end of sentence.]

EXERCISE 6.3

The second sentence best introduces the themes of turmoil and disputed succession to the throne, because it is that sentence that announces those themes in its stress.

EXERCISE 7.1

1. Critics must use complex and abstract terms to analyze literary texts meaningfully.

3. Graduate students face an uncertain future at best in finding good teaching jobs.

5. Most patients who go to a public clinic do not expect special treatment, because their health problems are minor and can be easily treated.

7. We can reduce the federal deficit only if we reduce federal spending.

9. A person may be rejected from a cost-sharing educational program only if that person receives a full hearing into why she was rejected. *Or*: An agency may reject a person from . . . only when that agency provides a full hearing into why it rejected her.

11. If we pay taxes, the government can pay its debts.

13. Catholics and Protestants will reconcile only when they agree on the Pope's authority.

EXERCISE 7.3

1. Recent research has applied schemata theory to the pedagogy of solving mathematical problems. [Sounds dull to me, but who knows?]

3. Because of their methodological differences, American and British historians have interpreted what caused the War of 1812 in radically different ways. [Sounds significant.]

5. Egyptian and Greek thought influenced scientific thinking. [Sounds banal to me.]

7. Birth order relates to academic success. [Seems significant.]

EXERCISE 7.4

1. On the other hand, some TV programming will always appeal to our most prurient interests.

3. One principle governs how to preserve the wilderness from exploitation.

5. Schools transmit more social values than do families.

EXERCISE 8.1

1. Proponents of workfare have not yet shown it is a successful alternative to welfare because they have not shown evidence that it can provide meaningful and regular employment for welfare recipients. Therefore, it is premature to recommend that all the states should fully commit themselves to it.

3. We could prevent foreign piracy of videos and CDs if the justice systems of foreign countries moved cases faster through their courts and imposed stiffer penalties. But we can not expect any immediate improvement in the level of expertise of judges who hear these cases.

5. The music industry has ignored the problem of how to apply a rating system to offensive lyrics broadcast over FM and AM radio. Until it does, stations are unlikely to improve their public image, even if they were willing to discuss such a system.

7. Young people will not be discouraged from smoking just because the film and TV industries agree not to show characters smoking.

9. When Congress funded the Interstate Highway System, it did not anticipate inflation, and so the system has run into financial problems.

11. "Reality" shows are the most popular shows on TV because they appeal to our voyeuristic impulses.

13. If carbon monoxide continues to be emitted, world climate will change.

EXERCISE 8.2

1. Many school systems are returning to the basics, basics that have been the foundation of education for centuries./ . . . a change that is long overdue . . . /trying to stem an ever rising drop-out rate.

3. For millennia, why we age has been a puzzle, a puzzle that only now can be answer with any certainty./ . . . a mystery that we can answer

either biologically or spiritually./ . . . hoping that one day we might stop our inevitable decline into infirmity and death.

5. Both scientists and laypeople have been troubled by the ethical issues of test-tube fertilization, issues that require the most delicate balancing between religion and medical hope./ . . . an event that has changed the way we think about what it means to be human./ . . . finding in them inevitable conflicts between self-interest and religious values.

7. In the Renaissance, greater affluence and political stability allowed streams of thought to merge, streams that originated in ancient Greece, in the Middle East, and in Europe itself./ . . . a historical development that both undermined the dominance of religious authority over knowledge and laid the groundwork for everything that we know about the world./ . . . bringing together knowledge and modes of thought that resulted in a new vision of humankind's potential.

EXERCISE 9.2

1. Those who argue stridently over small matters are unlikely to think clearly about large ones.

3. We should pay more attention to those politicians who tell us how to make what we have better than to those who tell us how to get what we don't have.

5. Some teachers mistake neat papers that rehash old ideas for great thoughts wrapped in impressive packaging.

EXERCISE 9.3

1. If we invest our sweat in these projects, we must avoid appearing to be working only for our own self-interest.

3. Throughout history, science has progressed because dedicated scientists have ignored the hostility of an uninformed public.

5. Boards of education can no longer expect that taxpayers will support the extravagancies of incompetent bureaucrats.

EXERCISE 12.1

As the Illinois Commerce Commission has authorized, **you** will have to pay . . . **You** have not had to pay . . . , but **you** will now pay rates that have been restructured consistent with the policy of The Public Utilities Act that lets us base what **you** pay on what it costs to provide you with service.

As the Illinois Commerce Commission has authorized, **we** are charging you . . . **We** have not raised rates . . . but **we** are restructuring the rates now . . . so that **we** can charge you for what **we** pay to provide you with service.

EXERCISE 12.2

Your car may have a defective part that connects the suspension to the frame. If you brake hard and the plate fails, you won't be able to steer. We may also have to adjust the secondary latch on your hood because we may have misaligned it. If you don't latch the primary latch, the secondary latch might not hold the hood down. If the hood flies up while you are driving, you won't be able to see. If either of these things occurs, you could crash.

EXERCISE A.3

Here are the two passages, first with the least punctuation I can imagine, and then with much more.

1. Scientists and philosophers . . . precise, as if those . . . disagree. But in fact scientific language . . . believed. It too is subject to . . . understanding. Moreover, new theories or arguments are rarely if ever constructed by way of clear-cut steps of induction, . . . falsification. Neither are they defended, rejected or accepted in so straightforward a manner. In practice scientists combine . . . of intuition, aesthetics commitment. The importance . . . generally acknowledged. . . . But the role of . . . less visible. The ways in . . . common experiences, on extensive practice . . . taken for granted. Only when we step out of such a "consensual domain," when we can stand out . . . the unarticulated premises, mutual understandings and assumed practices of the group. Even in those subjects . . . to quantification, discourse depends heavily on conventions and interpretation, conventions that are acquired over years of practice and participation in a community.

   Scientists and philosophers of science . . . were intrinsically precise, as if those who use it . . . meaning, even if they disagree. But, in fact, scientific language . . . commonly believed: it, too, is subject to imprecision and ambiguity, and hence to imperfect understanding. Moreover, new theories, or arguments, are rarely, if ever, constructed by way of clear-cut steps of induction, deduction, and verification or falsification; neither are they defended, rejected, or accepted in so straightforward a manner. In practice, scientists combine the rules of scientific methodology with a generous admixture of intuition, aesthetics, and philosophical commitment. The importance of what are, sometimes, called extra-rational, or extra-logical components of . . . law is generally acknowledged. . . . But the role of these extra-logical . . . frequently discussed, partly because they are less visible. The ways in which the credibility, or effectiveness, of an argument depends on the realm of common experiences, on extensive practice . . . a common language, are hard to see precisely, because such commonalities are taken for granted. Only when we step out of such a "consensual domain," when we can stand . . . language, do we begin to become aware of the unarticulated premises, mutual understandings, and assumed practices of the group. Even in those subjects . . . quantification, discourse depends heavily on conventions and interpretation, conventions that . . . participation in a community.

2. In fact of course, the notion of . . . been an illusion. But it is an illusion fostered . . . else that is true. We are not today . . . man's experience. We know that we are ignorant. We are well taught it. And the more surely and deeply we know our own job, the better able . . . pervasive ignorance. We know . . . men at all. But knowledge rests on knowledge. What is new is . . . known before. This is a world . . . from most of them. Perhaps this sense was not so sharp in the village, that village which . . . not understand too well, the village of slow change . . . full comprehension. Perhaps in the villages men were not so lonely. Perhaps they found in each other a fixed community, a fixed and . . . single world. Even that we may doubt. For there seem . . ., endless and open.

In fact, of course, the notion of universal knowledge . . . illusion, but it is an illusion . . . view of the world, in which a few great, central truths determine, in all its wonderful and amazing proliferation, everything else that is true. We are not, today, tempted to search . . . and of man's experience: we know that we are ignorant; we are well taught it; and the more surely and deeply we know our own job, the better able . . . pervasive ignorance. We know that these are inherent limits, compounded, no doubt, and exaggerated by . . . men at all. But knowledge rests on knowledge: what is new is meaningful, because it departs, slightly, from what was known before. This is a world of frontiers, where even the liveliest . . . of the time, from most of them. Perhaps, this sense was not so sharp in the village, that village which we have learned a little about, but probably do not understand too well—the village of slow change, and isolation, and fixed culture, which evokes our nostalgia, even if not our full comprehension. Perhaps in the villages men were not so lonely; perhaps they found in each other a fixed community, a fixed and . . . single world. Even that we may doubt, for there seem . . . and places, vast domains of mystery, if not unknowable, then imperfectly known—endless and open.

ACKNOWLEDGMENTS

INDEX